KU-208-606

THE
OPEN-AIR NATURE BOOK

THE HEDGE   THE POND   THE WOOD
THE MEADOW   THE STREAM
THE COMMON

THE HEDGE I KNOW

THE
HEDGE I KNOW

EDITED BY

W. PERCIVAL WESTELL, D.Sc., F.L.S.
& HENRY E. TURNER

General Secretary of the School
Nature Study Union

WITH

13 COLOURED

& MANY BLACK AND WHITE
ILLUSTRATIONS

LONDON
J. M. DENT & SONS LTD.

CONTENTS

There is a majesty and mystery in Nature, take her as you will. The essence of poetry comes breathing to a mind that feels from every province of her empire.—CARLYLE.

LIST OF ILLUSTRATIONS

COLOURED PLATES AND HALF-TONES

ILLUSTRATIONS IN THE TEXT

9

THE "COUNTRY" I KNOW

WHAT does the country mean to you? Does it suggest a shady walk beneath the leafy trees, wherein the birds build their wondrous nests and sing their magic songs? Does it call to mind a ramble along some silvery stream whose ever-running waters shelter the slippery silent fish? Or does it mean a wild and lonely common, where one may roam with freedom among the stately Bracken and the golden Gorse?

To others, perhaps, the word " Country " recalls a vision of a green grassy meadow, rich with Daisies and Buttercups ; or, maybe, a glorious lane wending its way between steep hedges, all aglow with colour and life.

But although each may have a favourite spot, yet if we would understand Nature better, we must seek her in all her phases, and learn from her in all her moods. Spring will summon her from her long wintry sleep; Summer will clothe her in all the colours of the rainbow; Autumn will herald the season of seed and harvest; Winter, eager to repay her for the loss of leaf and blossom, will softly spread over her a mantle of white, fleecy snow, and bid Jack Frost prepare a glittering crown to adorn her brow.

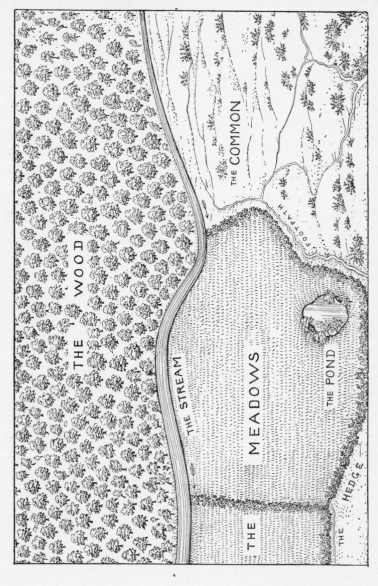

PLAN SHOWING HEDGE, POND, WOOD, MEADOW, STREAM, AND COMMON.

THE HEDGE I KNOW

I.

WE are told that many hundreds of years ago, when our forefathers buried their dead comrade, they placed by his side the wild fruits, nuts, and seeds that he used to eat when alive. They then noticed that more fruit and seeds of the same kind grew from the earth, which had been dug to make the grave, and they thought that these were their dead comrade's thanks for the food that had been given.

It took a very long time, however, for our ancestors to learn how important it was to dig the earth and sow the seed, but at last agriculture commenced in real earnest, and thus it was we came to possess our hedgerows, which were found necessary for dividing the land and separating the fields. To such an extent has this been carried out, that the green meadows of England and her hedgerows have become quite a feature of the landscape; they are now to be numbered among the glories of our country, and are perhaps unsurpassed in any other land.

The hedge, however, should be for us something more than a pretty picture of green leaf and coloured blossom, for within its leafy bowers and beneath its shady branches dwells a throng of wonderful and busy creatures, whose every act is full of interest, and whose daily life affords constant instruction and delight to those who patiently watch and wait.

If you look at a hedge, does it not convey to you an idea of " climbing," or of things that are searching for light and air? Carefully examine it, and you will probably be struck with the great struggle for existence that is going on, for this phase of Nature can better be seen, perhaps, in this situation than in any other.

Select a square yard of ground almost anywhere along the country-side, and a most interesting series of observations may be carried out. The Thistles, for instance, when they first come above ground in the early Spring, appear in the form of a dense rosette of leaves, and thus prevent any other plant from growing anywhere in their immediate vicinity.

Other plants, which bear the Thistles company in this respect, are the Common Daisy and the too-often despised Dandelion. Both of these form a stubborn rosette, and refuse to make way for any other form of vegetation. Eventually, however, taller growing plants make their appearance, and almost choke the Dandelions out of existence.

There is a wealth of interest and information to be derived from a study of this battle of the plants, and the young scholar would be amply repaid for interesting himself in this matter. Many plants, that are there, seem to be fighting one against the other. Some appear to steal a march, as it were, over their fellows; others take advantage of the presence of some neighbouring tree or shrub, either to climb, or grasp it, for support.

Since it is interesting to notice how and why these plants climb, let us set out the various organs they possess for performing this function.

1. Leaf climbers (tendrils).   Example: White Bryony.
2. Stem climbers (twining stems).   Example: Honey-suckle.

3. Hook climbers (small hooks). Example: Cleavers or Goosegrass.
4. Root climbers (rootlets on the stem). Example: Ivy.
5. Leaf stalk climbers (a " kink " or loop in their long leaf stalks). Example: Traveller's Joy.

We will now examine the hedge, and pay special attention to the examples mentioned above, as being likely to afford us a deal of interest.

II.

WHITE BRYONY—THE FOOD OF PLANTS—BLACK BRYONY— HONEYSUCKLE.

IT is evident, even to a casual observer, that those plants, which resort to climbing, have weak, slender stems. They are unable to stand up by themselves, but require a support up which they can climb, or to which they can become attached.

Note that White Bryony, for example, from the time when first it comes through the ground! You will then discover that the first leaves to appear have been formed *underground*, and that at the tip of the weak-looking stem, which has been thrust through the earth in early Spring, there are a couple of curious thin growths. What, then, are these? Continue your observations more closely, for once the Bryony starts to grow, it is in a terrible hurry to clasp everything that comes within its reach, and in a few days one can hardly recognise it for the same plant.

That it is weak may be plainly judged, for, lo! already its head is drooping, and certainly requires support. The two curious parts at the tip, previously mentioned, now come to its assistance, for, being elastic, and possessing some wonderful influence which we do not understand, these tendrils—for such they are—clasp a stem of the nearest tree or shrub and, behold, the Bryony is safely anchored! " So far, so good," you may say, " but what happens if a strong wind blows, and the anchor breaks away from its mooring? "   Pity the poor Bryony then!

If you examine a tendril a little later in the season, you will learn that it has developed into a wonderful living spiral-spring, and as the wind blows this piece of Nature's machinery, it works to and fro in a manner perfectly easy and suitable. This tendril is very sensitive, and if you touch it

Fig. 1. White Bryony, showing Tendrils and Spiral.

with your finger, it will commence to coil itself round after being stroked.

Is Bryony better off as a result of clasping its fellows, thus keeping well up in the hedge? Would it not grow equally well if it had no living springs to set in motion, but allowed itself to trail along the ground? Certainly not, for experience has taught us that plants, by lifting their stems and leaves into the air, are better able to expose them to the light, with the result that they can manufacture starch with more success.

You must not forget that all living things require food, and that trees and plants form no exception to this universal law. Let us, therefore, consider how these plants obtain

FLOWER OF BRAMBLE

WHITE VIOLETS

Fruit of Black Bryony

Honeysuckle

their nourishment.   Water is absorbed from the ground by means of the roots, and this in time reaches every living part of the plant.   In addition to this, the leaves, pierced with thousands of minute mouths called stomata, have the power of taking in air, and this, you are doubtless aware, contains what is known as carbon dioxide.   Again, leaves possess a green colouring matter, and it so happens that the

Fig. 2. Leaf and twining stem of Black Bryony.

Fig. 3. Fruit of Honeysuckle.

latter, *under the influence of sunlight,* can so act upon water and carbon dioxide as to produce starch, upon which the plants feed.   Thus you will readily understand why Bryony climbs, and how absolutely necessary light is to all such vegetation. It is worthy of note, that the starchy matter found in turnips, potatoes, rice, bulbs, roots of all kinds, and many varieties of seed, is nothing more than food stored up for the future use of the plant.

It may also be as well to remind you, that there is no connection between White and Black Bryony, although both plants bear red berries; the former climbs by means of tendrils, and has rough leaves with toothed edges; the

Black species, on the contrary, has heart-shaped leaves
with smooth edges, and climbs by means of its stem.

Close by the Bryony, firmly clasping a stem of the Nut
Hazel, is the Honeysuckle, a fine example of a stem climber.
Notice that the stem of this sweet-scented plant is always
turning to the right. See how strongly and securely it

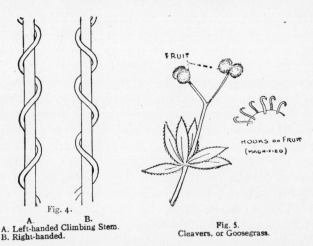

FRUIT

HOOKS on FRUIT
(MAGNIFIED)

Fig. 4.

A.   B.
A. Left-handed Climbing Stem.
B. Right-handed.

Fig. 5.
Cleavers, or Goosegrass.

grasps the stem of the Hazel. Can you guess why it is that
the Honeysuckle is so fond of caressing the Hazel in this way?
Why does it not pay as much attention to other trees and
shrubs? Probably because the stem of the Hazel is usually
very smooth, and unhampered by numerous branches. Here
then, perhaps, is the secret of the Honeysuckle's preference,
for it finds the smooth clear stem very inviting, and straight-
way climbs to the top, there to remain for life.

When next you see the Scarlet Runner Bean growing in
the garden, or the Convolvulus in the hedgerow, or the Hop
in the field, look at their twisted stems, and you will perceive

that, whereas the Honeysuckle and the Hop *turn to the right,* the Bean and the Convolvulus turn *to the left.*

III.

CLEAVERS—IVY—BRAMBLE.

NOTICE how densely crowded the hedgerow is with a very frail looking plant, whose square stem, though extremely rough, is very feeble; were it not for support, it would surely stand a poor chance of success. No difficulty will be experienced in recognising it, for the lance-shaped leaves grow in rings, and vary in number from six to nine in each ring. Some children call these plants " Sweethearts," because of the manner in which they " stick " to a person's clothing. The correct English name is Cleavers, or Goosegrass. The tiny seedlings push through the sunny bank in the earliest days of Spring, but, by the Summer, many of the shrubs that help to form our hedge are simply covered with them. They have smothered everything, and in places one might almost call this the Goosegrass Hedge.

When the plants die down in Autumn, the fruits present a curious sight. These are double, and consist of two circular lobes pressed together, and crowded with hooked spines, that cling to the fur or feathers of any creatures that may visit their vicinity. This may or may not cause some inconvenience to the bird or mammal which thus becomes decorated, but so far as the plant is concerned, all is well, since the seed, which in due time should produce a further supply of Cleavers, is scattered in all directions.

This brings us to the Ivy. Upon the bank of our hedgerow, and around the tree not far away, it is found in great quantity. This is a good example of a root climber, and to

B

understand exactly how it does its work, it will be advisable
to obtain a small sprig.   One of those pieces, which cling so
closely to a tree and which are so difficult to get off, will best
serve the purpose; but, failing this, any other will suffice.

How does the Ivy cling to its support?   Notice that the
piece you hold in your hand clings by means of a number
of short, pale brown or whitish outgrowths, which spring
only from the shaded side of the branches, that is, the side

in contact with the support, and away
from the light.   They make their appearance opposite the points where the
leaves first begin to appear, but later
on they develop all along the stem.
Now, in reality, these growths are
roots. How can we tell this? By reason
of their colour, and also because they
grow away from the light towards the
dark.

Fig. 6. Ivy, showing leaves,
stem, and roots.

Now stoop down and pull up a longer piece of the Ivy,
among which the Robin so dearly loves to hide her homestead, and lay her freckled eggs.   What can you see on its
under-side?   There you will find well-developed roots,
which serve the double purpose of anchoring the plant in the
soil and of nourishing it.   You will observe that these roots
strike downwards into the ground, and that there are root-
hairs upon them.   We see from this, therefore, that the Ivy
is really a very wonderful little plant, and that it can either
trail along the ground, forming roots as it goes, or climb,
not only a hedgerow, but a giant tree of the forest, or
wreathe an old historic castle with its evergreen leaves.

The yellow-green blossoms of the Ivy in September and
October attract a large number of insects, especially moths.
Here they assemble at nightfall, to sip the nectar within the

blossoms, and to hold high revel, as it is the last great insect feast of Nature's year. Bees also are very fond of visiting the Ivy blossoms in large numbers, and may thus be seen on a bright Autumn day.

The Bramble in the hedge cannot fail to attract attention, for it may be looked upon as the king of scramblers. Notice the prickles or hooks with which the plant is clothed for the purpose of clinging to other plants, and note also how it throws out long trailing branches, which often touch the ground, take root, and send up new shoots.

Now, although the stems are thin, they sometimes grow very long, for by using up its food for growth in length, rather than for thickening, the plant is enabled to mount the hedgerow and tower above its fellows. When the

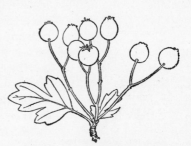

Fig. 7. Fruit of Hawthorn (Haws).

Bramble is in flower, how the insects of various kinds love to take toll from the sweet nectar found within the white or pink blossoms!

You will find, too, that some insects lay their eggs upon the leaves of the Bramble, and the larvæ (or caterpillars), when hatched the following Spring, feed upon the leaves. When they have eaten sufficient, and changed their skins several times, they are ready to pupate, or turn into a chrysalis. Later, the perfect insects emerge, and leave their chrysalis case still hanging upon the bush.

You will soon begin to think that the Bramble is really a very obliging and useful plant, but if you will inquire into the animal and vegetable inhabitants of our hedgerow or elsewhere, you will find that all, more or less, attract or depend one upon the other.

Nor must we forget the Blackberries, the well-known fruit of the Bramble. During the Autumn and Winter, various kinds of feathered friends may be looked for along the hedgerow. The Greenfinch is especially fond of Blackberries. He not only chooses the hedge as a nesting-place, but also as a convenient centre for feeding.

IV.

WILD FRUITS—TRAVELLER'S JOY—WILD ROSE—NUT HAZEL.

IT may be as well to remind you that there are several other kinds of fruits in the hedgerow, which attract a wealth of bird life. Thrushes and Blackbirds feed upon the Hips (Wild Rose) and Haws (Hawthorn); the Bullfinch is especially fond of the jet-black berries of the Privet; and our Winter visitors, the Fieldfares and the Redwings, pay their respects to the bright red berries of the Wayfaring Tree.

See how the Traveller's Joy or Wild Clematis festoons the hedgerow with its welcome blossoms. This is another fine example of a climber, and if a specimen of the stem be secured and examined, the leaf stalks can easily be noted; these, being sensitive, when they touch a support, move round so as to grip hold of it firmly. The leaves are usually composed of five leaflets, a terminal, and two pairs below it.

In some parts of the country this plant is known as Old Man's Beard, because of its greyish-white feathery " awns," or bristles, that are to be seen during Autumn and Winter; these are the seed cases of the plants. Many species belong-

FRUIT OF BRAMBLE

CLEAVERS OR GOOSEGRASS

GREATER STITCHWORT

COW PARSNIP, OR HOGWEED

ing to the Clematis family are useful in covering trellis work and unsightly places in the garden, being quick growers and of graceful habit.

The mention of the chief hedgerow trees, shrubs and other plants would be very incomplete without reference to the Wild Rose. Although we are not concerned in this book with the dry details of plant and animal life, yet the chief

Fig. 8. Fruit of Privet.   Fig. 9. Traveller's Joy in seed.

parts of a flower are so often mentioned, and play so important a part in the world of Nature, that perhaps we may be forgiven if we deal with them here. It must not be thought that every blossom is built upon one unchanging plan; on the contrary, the variations and modifications are so numerous as to be quite bewildering, especially to beginners. We, however, will only deal with a very simple case, by taking that of the Rose blossom.

Note, then, that on the outside there are five rather thick green leaves with ragged edges; these are the sepals, a most suitable name, by the way, for it means to enclose. If you desire a name for *all* the sepals taken together you must use the word calyx or cup. Within the calyx are five petals, those beautiful flower leaves which give the colour to the blossom. Here again the name exactly fits the case, for it means a leaf or a thin plate of metal; you have only to

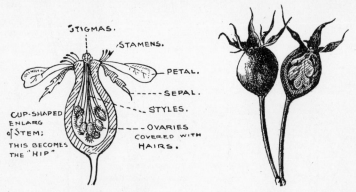

Fig. 10. Section of Wild Rose.   Fig. 11. Fruit of Wild Rose (Hips).

examine the petals of a few flowers, more particularly those of the Buttercup, to realise the truth of this.   Would you also like a name for all the petals taken together?   Then you must employ the word corolla, meaning a small crown; now look at an opening bud and see if you can suggest a better title than this.

In the centre is a cushion from which seem to spring several tiny growths somewhat resembling yellow pins with oval heads.   These are the stamens and contain pollen, the former meaning " threads " and the latter " powdered flour." Now let us deal with this central cushion, or pistil as it is called.   By cutting it through, we shall discover that it consists of a number of carpels, each of which has a minute head;

these lead down into the ovary or egg chamber which contains a tiny white ovule or seed-egg.

When a golden grain of pollen falls upon the pistil, the former sends down a tiny tube towards the ovule and passes into it; this act is spoken of as fertilisation, and it enables the ovule or seed-egg to grow and form a perfect seed,

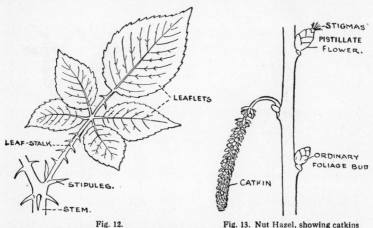

Fig. 12.
Rose, showing leaves, thorns, etc.

Fig. 13. Nut Hazel, showing catkins
and female flowers.

capable of producing a Rose plant. A most interesting subject is the study of the various methods by means of which plants become fertilised, and the numerous devices that they have adopted for enticing many kinds of insects to visit them, so that pollen may be carried from one flower to another.

Gardeners are always on the look out for what is called " Reversion," that is to say, the tendency which many cultivated plants have to go back to the type from which they sprang. This is particularly noticeable among garden Roses, and it is interesting to notice that the beautiful varieties of the queen of flowers, one sees in gardens, have been produced from the Wild Rose, which so gracefully ornaments the hedge.

What has happened may best be seen by examining a specimen of a Wild Rose and a cultivated variety. The latter possesses many more petals than its uncultivated relative. The secret is, that the gardener, in producing the cultivated Rose, has managed to convert *the stamens and pistils* of the wild species *into petals*.

If the Bramble is entitled to be called king of the scramblers, the Wild Rose is almost, if not quite, its successful rival. Where this Rose has a good chance to ramble and scramble at its own sweet will, it soon makes headway, and leaves very little room for its fellows. Yet we would not part with the Wild Rose of England, for when in flower, it makes one of the great floral shows of the country-side. The delicate petals are unfolded in the early days of June, and show up well against the dark green leaves. Later in the year, the rich red " hips," or seed cases, attract a host of feathered fowl to feed upon them.

Mention has already been made of the fondness which is displayed by the Honeysuckle for the Hazel. But are we not all fond of it too? Is it not one of the first things we look out for as soon as the New Year begins?

Even before the last of the Autumn nuts has been plucked, we may note upon the branches a cluster of little hard green cylinders, which, lengthening during the Winter months, become the familiar catkins—the so-called " Lamb's-tails "— of February. These contain the pollen, and as they swing to and fro in the breeze, the golden dust is scattered all around.

By far the greater part of it falls to the ground, and is never heard of again ; some grains, however, have a more useful career, as we shall presently see.

Look carefully at the upper part of each branch, until you have discovered some short fine crimson threads coming from what, at first sight, appears to be a leaf bud. These threads are part of the pistil, and here it is the pollen does its work of fertilisation, the result of which will be seen next Autumn, in the shape of a cluster of wood nuts.

V.

ROSE GALL AND ROSE-GALL WASP—HERB ROBERT.

IF it be Autumn you may find a gall upon the Rose bush. Probably you already know this curious growth as Robin's pincushion, but did not know it was a gall. Such it is, however, and we shall do well to obtain a specimen and examine it carefully.

Note the moss-like or fibrous-looking growth, and its bright red colour. It is formed by a Gall-fly, and this is what happens. The female Gall-fly chooses the Wild Rose bush as a spot where she may safely lay her eggs in the Spring. She does not, however, like many other kinds of insects, just merely lay them upon or under the leaf, or upon or under a branch or twig. She is far more particular than that, for she goes to the trouble of boring a number of small holes in an undeveloped leaf by means of a sharp little instrument which may be found upon the end of her body, while the leaf is still folded up in the bud. Having done this, the insect proceeds to lay one egg in each cavity, and then flies away.

You all know what happens when your finger is pricked. Irritation is caused, the blood flows out of the hole that has been made, and it is some little time before the wound is healed. Somewhat similar proceedings take place in the bud of the Wild Rose when it is pierced, but, unlike our wounded finger, it contains living eggs, which soon cause an alteration in the growth of the leaf.

Well, the sap gathers round the spot where the holes were made, a noticeable swelling is seen around the punctures, and the bark slightly cracks. From these small holes the sap escapes, and takes the form of curious moss-like or fibrous growths, spurred on either side with soft material. The eggs duly hatch, the larvæ penetrate deeper into the tissue of the leaf, and eventually, as a result of the great irritation that has been caused, an enlargement of the affected part is seen. The fibres become matted together, until at last the ball-like cluster appears like the one we are now examining.

Produce a knife and cut the curious growth open right down the centre. What do you see? Little chambers, or cells as they are more properly called, each containing a white, fleshy, legless grub. This, then, is the little fellow which has come from the egg laid in the Spring, and, having passed through various changes, found himself very snugly tucked up in a nice apartment until we disturbed him. Several cells may be found in the interior, and it will be noticed that the nearer one gets to the centre the harder the growth becomes.

What is the object of the eggs being laid in this way? So that the young may be safely sheltered during the Winter. How does this little fly know she must adopt such a marvellous provision for her family? This question, and others concerning the insect creation, have in vain taxed the brains and the ingenuity of some of our greatest men.

You may count two or three dozen of the cells in the centre of a good gall, and every cell will be tenanted by a lively grub, which twists and coils as if very much upset at our interference with its domestic affairs.

In this snug position, then, the grubs pass the long Winter days, secure from the rigours of king frost. When the Spring days arrive once more, the grub makes preparation for the final change to a chrysalis, and at length the perfect insect —the Rose-gall Wasp, to give it its true name—proceeds to work its way out of the mossy home, and takes to flight during June.

As we stepped across the ditch to the bank to reach the Rose gall, there at our feet the bright pink petals of Herb Robert attracted attention. The herbage upon the bank is so luxurious that we hardly noticed the plant before. It belongs to the family of Wild Geraniums or Crane's Bills, of which there are a number, some of them being rather difficult to identify. The Dove's Foot is a very common one, but Herb Robert is perhaps the commonest of them all. They are all easily recognised when in fruit, by reason of the long seed vessel, which has earned for them the names of Stork's Bill and Crane's Bill.

Herb Robert is not a particular plant, and any obliging hedge bank will suit it well. It seems to thrive in the sun as well as in the shade. When the May blossom is almost ready to burst into milk-white bloom, and give to the hedge one of its fairest garments of the whole year, then one may expect to see the bright pink petals of the plant we are looking at, peeping out from the grass-tangled bank.

The plant has a strong smell which some people consider unpleasant. It grows from one to two feet high, and the red colour of the hairy stem cannot fail to attract attention. Towards Autumn the leaves, which are divided into five or fewer leaflets and then sub-divided, assume the same hue.

Notice how beautifully the petals, usually pink in colour,

are veined with deep red. These veinings are honey guides, and attract insect visitors to the flowers, and thence to the storehouse within.

The seed vessel of Herb Robert is a splendid artillery-man, for it can disperse the seeds an extraordinary distance; indeed, it has been known to throw its seeds a distance of at least thirty feet, so that we must certainly look upon it as one of the best shots of the hedgerow. Why is it called Herb Robert? Because it is said to be named after Saint Robert, a Benedictine abbot to whom April 29 is dedicated; the plant is usually at that time just about to bloom.

It is a good plan to spend a whole ramble along the hedge when the wild fruits and seeds are at their best. A collection may be made of the commoner kinds, and an examination of them afterwards will prove both interesting and instructive.

VI.

WILD ARUM OR CUCKOO PINT—SWEET VIOLET—DOG VIOLET.

ONE of the most interesting of the hedgerow plants is the Cuckoo Pint, or Wild Arum. This is a typical specimen, and is, perhaps, far better known as Lords and Ladies. Notice how boldly it stands up in the Springtime, showing the purple club-like spadix inside the green hood-shaped spathe.

Why is it that the Wild Arum makes itself so prominent? What good purpose is served by its so doing? It has been proved that small insects, attracted by the carrion-like colour and odour of the spadix, climb into the hood. They then proceed downwards for the purpose of securing food, but when they have arrived, they find themselves imprisoned

SNAILS ON DOCK LEAF

LONG TAILED FIELD MOUSE

WILD ARUM BEFORE SPATHE
IS UNROLLED

WILD ARUM SHOWING
LOWER PART OF SPATHE
CUT AWAY

FRUIT OF WILD
ARUM

by long hairs, which permit of easy descent but prevent return.

After a time, the plant sheds its pollen, the hairs wither, and then the little insect prisoners find themselves free. They climb up the fleshy spadix and make good their escape. Very soon, however, the insects feel hungry again. Away they go on their mission, and, finding another Wild Arum, go through the same programme, but in this case, however, their bodies having probably become dusted with pollen from the plant previously visited, they aid very considerably in carrying the precious pollen from one plant to another, and so help to bring about fertilisation.

The green spathe, its work accomplished, gradually withers away, and we really do not notice the plant again until the Autumn; for by this time, as our photograph shows, nothing remains but a mass of berries of a vivid scarlet colour, these being clustered around a short green stump, all that is left of the original plant.

There upon the bank, amidst the long grass and herbage, sheltered from the winds and the glare of the sun by the overhanging bushes, flourishes the Sweet-scented Violet. This, perhaps, is one of our most highly-prized wild flowers, not only because of its fragrance, but because it is among the very first to greet the Spring.

The leaves are heart-shaped and slightly downy, especially underneath, and the edges are somewhat wavy. The flowers vary in colour from deep purple and lilac to pale rose colour, or even white, but all these tints may sometimes be discovered on the same bank. The root stock is perennial, that is to say, it lasts many years; and from one root spring several runners.

The petals are unequal in size and shape, there being two pairs and one odd one; the latter is the largest, and has its narrow end shaped like a round tube, which, instead of being hidden in the sepals, stands out beyond them like a spur. It is in this spur that nectar is secreted and, as a consequence, it is here that the Bee pays his visits.

There is another species called the Dog-Violet, but this, unfortunately, has no scent, although it is a charming flower in other respects. Generally speaking, the leaves and the stem are smooth, and do not possess those soft hairs so characteristic of the Sweet Violet. The word "Dog" is often used as a prefix when dealing with flowers, and means worthless, but in this case, as in many others, the suggestion is an unjust one.

When the Spring season is over, the Violet no longer produces flowers for show, but develops buds which remain closed, and which have no petals, apparently with the sole object of strengthening the stamens and pistils, and thus producing perfect seed. It then adopts a most interesting plan for the dispersal of this seed. The ovary splits open into three parts, each of which, by bringing its edges together, shoots out its smooth glossy contents with such force as to scatter them for a distance of several yards.

VII.

GREATER AND LESSER STITCHWORTS—GERMANDER SPEEDWELL—COW PARSNIP.

ANOTHER common, but very beautiful flower to greet the Spring, is the Greater Stitchwort, which may be looked for when the Primrose, the Wild Hyacinth, and the Wood Anemone are in bloom. Each of its pure white blossoms gleams like a clear cut star. At first sight one would imagine there were ten petals, but more careful examination will prove that there are only five, each of which is cleft almost to the middle.

The brittle grass-like stems have lines of short bristles running up each side, and the tips of the pointed narrow leaves usually curl back. This grass-like form enables it to hold its own against its neighbours, for it can fill up gaps where plants with wider leaves would be starved.

There is another species of Stitchwort that blooms later in the year than the one we have just been looking at. It is known as the Lesser Stitchwort, because it has a smaller flower than that of the Greater species. It grows in companies, and, when the flowering period is at its height, the effect of the pretty little white stars peeping out of the hedgerow is very charming.

Earlier botanists studied plants from a medicinal point of view, and it was thought that nearly all had some healing power; hence we are constantly coming across such words as Wort and Bane, both of which suggest a remedy against a disease or pest; thus we have Woundwort, Lousewort, Milkwort, Pennywort, Fleabane, Henbane, and Leopard's Bane.

But what is that cluster of bright blue flowers which look so like the Forget-me-not? Those are the Speedwell, but since at least sixteen distinct species of this plant are known to flourish in the British Isles, we shall confine ourselves to the particular type we are now examining, which, to give it its full name, is the Germander Speedwell.

It is a slender wiry plant, and its stem sometimes creeps along the ground and takes root again before growing upward. Its dark green leaves, thickly covered with soft silky hairs, are egg-shaped, coarsely toothed, and have very short stalks.

Now look down upon the blossom and count the four bright blue petals. Notice also the small circle or zone of

white, which, with the tiny green seed vessel, forms the centre
of the flower; here we have the reason why some people
call this flower Bird's Eye, and others name it Cat's Eyes.
Those dark blue lines, running down each petal towards
the centre, merely indicate the road to the nectar, and it
is thought that insects are thereby assisted in finding this
sweet juice.

Another plant of the hedgerow, specially deserving of

mention, is the Hogweed or
Cow Parsnip. Its leaves are
woolly, large, and very irregular in shape; they are
covered with rough hairs, and
more often than not with dust
too. Cattle feed upon it in large
quantities and seem to thrive
thereby, and this fact, perhaps, may have given rise to
its names.

Fig. 14. Umbel of Cow Parsnip.

It has a thick, hollow, rough,
and hairy stem, which often
grows to a height of four, or even five feet. Near the top
of this are the branches, so arranged as to make one think
of the ribs of a Japanese umbrella. Indeed, when the plant
is in full bloom, an excellent shelter is provided, such as
might do duty for elves and fairies in time of rain. This
umbrella-like arrangement of flowers is termed an umbel,
a word derived from the Latin, and meaning a screen. The
five white or pinkish heart-shaped petals, of which each
flower is composed, are irregular in size.

Can you guess why this umbel has all its blossoms massed
together in such a way that it looks like a flattened bouquet?
It is only another method of attracting insect visitors, and

thus of ensuring fertilisation; for you must always remember that the final work of a plant is to reproduce its kind by means of seed.

During the Winter the dry hollow stems of the Cow Parsnip may still be seen standing erect, but, although deprived of their former glory, they still afford a welcome shelter for very small insects; the tiny holes, which the latter have bored to gain admission, may easily be found.

VIII.

FOXGLOVE—HUMBLE BEE—WHITE DEAD-NETTLE— HONEY BEE.

A FOXGLOVE stands up sentinel-like, as if it, at any rate, will not consent to die without a bold struggle for existence.

A fine show it makes in the hedgerow, as it stands from two to six feet high, with its lower leaves wrinkled and somewhat downy; whilst higher up the stem are numerous purple bell-shaped flowers. It is not out of place to speak of the flowers as fairy bells, as we find that originally

Fig. 15. Humble Bee.

the name of Foxglove was " Folks'-glove," that is " Fairies'-glove."

One need not watch the Foxglove very long before getting on intimate terms with other inhabitants of the hedgerow, for the Humble Bees dearly like to visit the storehouses of honey secreted in these fairy bells.

Indeed, wherever there is a hedgerow decked with wild flowers, there, sure enough, one may look for the Humble or Bumble Bee. And what brings him here this bright Summer morning? Listen to his humming! Does he not make a

C

fuss and a commotion? Truly a fussy and bustling individual is the Humble Bee, but what a sweet pillage is his
among the flowers. Why does he come to our hedgerow?
The stately Foxglove growing there is the secret. See how
he visits one by one every fairy bell as yet open. In and
out of the thimble-like corolla he goes upon his pilgrimage,

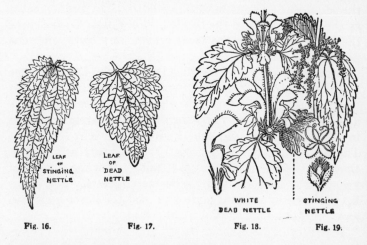

Fig. 16.　　　　Fig. 17.　　　　Fig. 18.　　　　Fig. 19.

bringing his body now and again against the stamens with
their stores of pollen, and thus doing the same service for
the Foxglove as the Hive, or Honey Bee, does for the Dead-
Nettle.

Watch our friend the Humble Bee now. How unsteady
he seems. What can be the matter? Is he damaged in
any way and finding flight difficult? Now he has fallen to
the ground, and lies there on his back, buzzing loudly and
struggling violently. Leave him alone, and he will soon
recover. He has taken more nectar than was good for him,
and has become intoxicated.

The Dead or Stingless Nettle is also a prominent hedgerow plant, and is easily distinguished by its square hollow stem from the Stinging species, whose stem is round and solid. It rarely, if ever, appears to be throttled by its companions, but blooms throughout almost the whole year. There are three common kinds of Dead-Nettle. One, the Red Dead-Nettle, is a somewhat dwarf species and has a purple corolla; the second is of a most beautiful yellow colour, and is known as the Archangel; and the third is pure white. Of the three the latter is certainly the most upright in growth, and also perhaps the commonest.

Now pick a piece of the White Dead-Nettle, for preference a complete plant. You will at once observe that it does not " sting," the stalk is square, the pointed serrated leaves are arranged in pairs, and the white, scentless flowers are borne in whorls or rings, and are situate in different " stories." The hairy character of the Dead-Nettle flower will by this time have been noted. Why is it hairy? For the purpose of keeping out unbidden and useless insect guests. The upper lip protects the stamens and pistil, and the lower lip serves as an alighting platform for a Bee.

If possible, a Bee should be carefully watched when entering a flower. It will then be seen that, having alighted upon the " platform," the insect at once proceeds to dive into the interior, and work its way down the corolla tube. During the course of its movements, the body comes into contact with the long pistil, upon which the Bee unconsciously deposits some of the pollen gathered from a flower previously visited.

As the Bee proceeds towards the interior of the flower, thrusting its body well into the tube, the hind portion is brushed several times against the stamens at the top of the flower, and so it gets dusted with pollen again. In this way the

White Dead-Nettle, and other plants claiming kinship, become fertilised.

You will now understand more clearly why it is that the Dead-Nettle so often flourishes on the bank of a hedgerow; why it is that it contrives to grow in such a stately way, and how distinctly useful the plant is to the insect, and the insect to the plant.

IX.

DOCK—SNAIL—TIGER MOTH—GREEN-VEINED WHITE BUTTERFLY—HEDGE GARLIC.

YONDER Dock, with its large strong leaves and roots so firmly embedded in the earth, forms but another of the countless examples illustrating the dependency of the animal upon the vegetable world.

Although we find it growing by the hedge, many of this species prefer watery places. They have great tap roots, and are with difficulty expelled when once they have taken occupation of a piece of ground, not only because of the firm anchorage exercised by their roots, but because they multiply so rapidly from seed.

But though these plants are detested by the farmer, the Snail is not quite so difficult to please. Often we may find him making his way over the sturdy leaves, especially in warm, damp weather, when he dearly loves to crawl among the vegetation and low-growing foliage. How often have we turned our backs upon these silent, slow-moving creatures, without once giving them more than a passing thought, and yet how intensely interesting they are!

Let us first of all examine one of their shells, and look

1   2

3

4

5

LIFE HISTORY OF SMALL TORTOISESHELL BUTTERFLY

1. BATCH OF EGGS HIGHLY MAGNIFIED   2. LARVA, OR CATERPILLAR
3. PUPA, OR CHRYSALIS   4. PERFECT BUTTERFLY RESTING ON BARK
       5. SET SPECIMENS SHOWING UPPER AND UNDER-SIDES

GREEN-VEINED WHITE BUTTERFLY

TIGER MOTH AND PUPA CASE

for those numerous lines running parallel to the edge; these are termed lines of life, and mark the successive positions occupied by the free edge during growth. If we are fortunate enough to discover a Snail, which has only recently added to the size of its shell, we shall learn that the newly formed part is very thin, and can be easily bent; but in the course of a few days this hardens and becomes as strong and firm as the original.

But what are those black spots at the ends of the two long horns? Touch them gently with your finger, and watch them disappear as if by magic. These black spots are the eyes of the Snail, and can be withdrawn into the body until the horn assumes the shape of a finger of a glove, which has been pulled down into the glove-hand.

Now place the Snail upon a piece of glass, and feed it with a small portion of moist bread. If it be hungry, you can, by inverting the glass, watch its method of eating. The ribbon-like tongue—properly called the radula—may be compared to a minute rake or harrow, for it is covered with rows of very small teeth which point backward and act as a rasp.

If during the months of July and August—the spawning season—we search the moist places beneath the dead leaves or loose stones, we may chance upon patches of the eggs of these creatures. Each egg is protected by a rounded leathery shell, measuring about one-sixth of an inch in diameter. Before the approach of Winter, these eggs will hatch out, and then the Snails, both old and young, having each closed the door of its house by a thin, porous lid, seek shelter from the cold and frost in some cosy nook, or even in the earth itself.

Snails are not the only guests which pay a visit to the Dock leaf, for the "Woolly Bear" caterpillar may often be seen enjoying a good meal off this and the neighbouring Nettle leaf. This furry-looking creature is the larva of the Garden Tiger Moth, and at times is so plentiful as to become a pest.

The Tiger Moth, one of the commonest but most highly coloured of its kind, is so called because of the peculiar tiger-like markings on its ample wings; and although one very rarely finds two specimens exactly alike, yet a glance at the picture opposite page 47 will give you a good idea of its general appearance, and prove that its name is well deserved.

Do you know the difference between a moth and a butter-

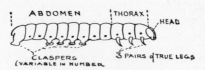

Fig. 20. A Larva or Caterpillar.

fly, so far as its shape is concerned? If not, compare the Tiger Moth with the Green-veined Butterfly illustrated, and you will notice that whereas the horns, feelers, or antennæ of the moth taper to a point, those of the butterfly are clubbed. This simple fact will nearly always enable you to distinguish the one from the other, unless you are dealing with those found in foreign countries, when this rule will not hold good. Many male moths, however, are provided with saw-like or comb-like feelers, while those of the females are simple.

Should you desire to know more of the Green-veined Butterfly, you must first search for its pale eggs, which are laid singly on the leaves of Hedge Garlic or plants of a similar type. Keep these until the caterpillar comes, when it will be noticed that it is green above and whitish-grey beneath; those not in captivity may be found any time from June to September.

But one of you may exclaim, " We don't know what this Hedge Garlic is like! " Then look out for a tall, erect plant with a smooth stem measuring from two to three feet, and with heart-shaped leaves having toothed edges. Some of these can be seen at the top of the coloured picture of the Greater Stitchwort opposite page 27. Perhaps the best

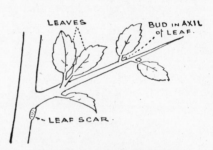

Fig. 21, Leaf of Hedge Garlic.   Fig 22. Hawthorn, showing Leaves, etc.

way of making sure you have discovered the right specimen, is to rub one of its leaves between your fingers, and you will at once note a strong, garlic-like odour.

The flowers are white, and grow in a cluster at the end of the stem; the four petals are arranged crosswise, like those of its cousin, the Wallflower. Some people call this plant Jack-by-the-hedge, while others christen it Sauce-alone.

X.

CHAFFINCH—LONG-TAILED TIT—GARDEN WARBLER—HEDGE
SPARROW—THE YOUNG CUCKOO—YELLOW BUNTING.

ONE side of the hedge is very sheltered from the cold winds
of early Spring, and it is here that the sheep and lambs lie at
night. They get as close to the hedge as they can, and
there the Bramble, the Wild Rose, the Blackthorn, and
other prickly plants rob them of some of their wool.

It so happens that the Chaffinch builds its mossy cup-
shaped cradle near by, and this wool is largely used in building it.

An old stump not far away is covered with moss, an Oak
tree with lichen; both of these are visited by the Chaffinch
in turn; thus with the wool, moss, and lichen, a few sticks
and grasses from the hedgerow perhaps, hair shed by a horse
or cow, and even cobwebs, the bird constructs its wonderful
model homestead.

There are probably only two or three other birds which
build such a lovely nest as that of the Chaffinch, and these
are the Goldfinch, Goldcrest, and Long-tailed Tit. The
latter bird constructs a most remarkable homestead, and
has been known to use over two thousand feathers in one
nest, each feather representing a separate journey. Whilst
we may perhaps find the nest of this active little bird in the
hedge—a Black or White Thorn bush being a favourable site
—it is also fond of Furze bushes, and there perhaps we had
better search for it.

We are, however, bound to meet with a party of Long-
tailed Tits along the hedgerow at some season of the year,
for they dearly love to hunt together for food in this way.
Possessing, as these birds do, a soft flight, a little rounded

body, a very long tail, most active and engaging ways, and an agreeable querulous note, they cannot fail to attract attention when seen. They are, however, so quiet in their movements, so light and buoyant, and so engaged in their work searching for insects or larvæ, that one has to look out for them most carefully before they can be seen.

A little company of a dozen or more may be in possession of a certain part of the hedgerow, sedulously searching every

Fig. 23. Long-Tailed Tit.

nook and corner for insects; but apart from a chattering there is very little to indicate the presence of such a number of birds. As the feathered acrobats—for such they are—hang head downwards, it is most interesting to watch them, so much so that they have been called "little monkeys in feathers."

The Tits will not mind in the least being watched. They still pursue their feeding operations, moving on when they are ready, and not before. A whole hedgerow is worked by these birds in this way, and the number of insects of which they rid the land must be enormous. When they fly, the long tail may be very plainly seen. The flight is jerky and not long sustained.

Another bird, that may be found in the hedge, is the Garden Warbler. It often builds its flimsy nest in a Bramble bush, and is thus hidden among the leaves, and well protected by the prickles.

Should there be a Sycamore tree along the hedgerow this bird will delight to hide among its leaves. Here, too, it secures an abundance of insect food, singing the whole time sweet plaintive music. Although it is comparatively common, yet it is but little known, probably because it is rarely seen or heard unless one looks or listens for it. Although called Garden Warbler, it is not found solely in gardens; but in a dense hedge, or little coppice, it dearly loves to make its home. It is brownish-yellow in colour, much lighter on the breast than on the back.

This bird is one of our Summer visitors. It spends the Winter months in Africa, but as Spring draws near it leaves that country, and, by easy stages, commences to travel over land and sea until it reaches England.

The wonderful subject of the migration of birds has been studied and described by many naturalists, who have spent much time and thought on the matter. The most remarkable points in connection with bird-migration seem to be that birds, who have never left this country before, find their way unaided to unknown lands, and that a wonderful instinct guides these feathered wanderers back to the old home again.

A pair of Swallows, for instance, upon which a watch was kept during the Summer, returned the next Spring to the same house where they had previously nested. The Nightingale, and many other birds of passage, return to the same haunt year after year, and although we have learned a great deal concerning these migration movements of the feathered tribe, much remains to be accomplished. In this good work every young naturalist can help, for, by continuous observation of bird movements, a story of much importance may be pieced together.

Listen! Do you hear that low plaintive " cheep, cheep," uttered by a bird of some kind? Peep into the Bramble and you will see its nest. It is wrongly named Hedge Sparrow, for it belongs to the Warbler family, and is not a Sparrow at all. It sings a cheerful little song, and is often spoken of as the Hedge Warbler. It is an elegant-looking bird in its steel grey and brown dress, something like a Robin without a red breast; it builds a mossy nest lined with wool, hair, and feathers, and lays beautiful pure pale blue eggs.

It is interesting to notice that in England the Hedge Sparrow's nest is the one often chosen by the Cuckoo in which to place her egg. It is well known, of course, that the Cuckoo does not build a nest of her own.

Fig. 24. Yellow Bunting.

In Scotland the Meadow Pipit seems to be the favourite foster-parent, and, although many other birds' nests are chosen in both countries, the Hedge Sparrow is easily first favourite with us, and the Meadow Pipit in Scotland. Perhaps we may find a Cuckoo in the hedge, for she may be there for the purpose of depositing an egg in a nest, or searching for food, such as the hairy caterpillar of the Tiger Moth, which we have already seen inhabits the hedgerow.

Very few birds eat hairy caterpillars, and thus the Cuckoo, by feeding upon these, performs good service in keeping the same in check. When the young Cuckoo is hatched the Hedge Sparrows have to search diligently and unceasingly for food wherewith to feed their foster-child, for it has an enormous appetite. It is necessary the young Cuckoo should be well fed because, up to the time he is about ten days old, he has the habit of turning out of the nest in which he is born either the eggs, or the young birds, belonging to the rightful owners. As a consequence, his strength is often exhausted, and doubtless the countless caterpillars he has so greedily devoured assist him to repair that loss.

Many people consider that in throwing out the eggs or young birds of the rightful owners of the nest, the young Cuckoo should be condemned as a vagabond in feathers, but, after all, there is a good deal in Nature we do not understand, and this may be one of the mysteries which the future will explain.

Near by is the Yellow Bunting, or Yellow Hammer. This is really one of the most beautiful British birds, but although one meets with it elsewhere, it prefers to haunt a hedge-row, and in the tangled mass of grass near, or upon, the ground, weaves its homestead; this consists of dead grasses, moss, and hair. The white eggs are marked in such a curious way that the bird is called the Scribbling Lark in some country districts; these markings are purple to purplish-black in colour.

Whilst the Hedge Sparrow feeds almost exclusively upon insects, with perhaps scraps in Winter, the Yellow Bunting is to a great extent a seed eater. The male bird has a song that is very sweet, although it only consists of a few notes, and these are often jokingly translated as being like " A-little-bit-of-bread-and-no-cheese." He pays remarkable attention to his little wife, and takes his turn in hatching the eggs.

NEST AND EGGS OF GARDEN WARBLER IN BRAMBLE

NEST AND EGGS OF GREATER WHITETHROAT

YOUNG OF GREATER WHITETHROAT

In the Winter, various kinds of Buntings associate in small flocks, and visit farmyards and other places, while the Hedge Sparrow does not flock, but resorts almost exclusively to the hedgerows, shrubberies, and gardens.

XI.

GREATER WHITETHROAT—STINGING NETTLE—SMALL TORTOISESHELL BUTTERFLY—ROBIN.

DID you not notice, as we walked along, a small brownish bird fly out noiselessly from a clump of Nettles? It was a Common or Greater Whitethroat. See, there the male bird is suspended over the topmost branches of the hedgerow. Notice his curious antics as, flying about in a jerky manner, he seems suspended by an unseen wire.

Listen to his snatchy and somewhat harsh song, for although it is by no means sweet, it is delivered with great energy. Now he is uttering a note of defiance, a still harsher sound, and seems to declare his refusal to be outdone by other birds.

Let us examine the spot from whence this bird flew. Brush the Stinging Nettles on one side, and do it carefully if you would avoid being " stung." Our efforts are rewarded, for there, deftly hung between the Nettles, and fairly low down, is the Whitethroat's nest. It is a very frail structure, composed of the thinner portions of dry grasses, and lined with a little hair.

There are five eggs in the nest, and these are greenish in ground colour, marked with grey, chiefly at the larger end. Though the nest be fragile, one cannot but admire its neat appearance. Cover the homestead up again carefully and do not leave any trace of your visit behind, for this is a useful bird, feeding as it does upon insects, and deserves protection.

The full number of eggs has been laid, therefore in a week or so you may pay a return visit and see the baby chicks, and perhaps you may then see something like that shown opposite page 57.

We have already mentioned the Stinging Nettle in connection with the " Woolly Bear " caterpillar, but this is by no means the only insect that looks to these plants for a supply of food.

In April, May, and again in July, search should therefore be made on the upper parts of this plant and under the young leaves. If you are vigilant, your efforts may be rewarded, for there the eggs of three beautiful butterflies are laid, namely, the Small Tortoiseshell, the very handsome Peacock, and the Red Admiral. The eggs of the Tortoiseshell and the Peacock are laid in clusters, but those of the Red Admiral are solitary. The full life history of the small Tortoiseshell is shown in the pictures, but it should be stated that the eggs are very highly magnified, and much smaller objects than those shown must be sought for.

The egg is at first green, but after a time becomes tinted with yellow, the ribs standing out clear and transparent. It is only possible to see these eggs of butterflies and other insects to perfection under a magnifying glass, and when thus examined they often reveal much beauty both in form and texture.

When the eggs hatch, the larvæ or caterpillars feed upon the Nettle leaves, thus explaining why the instinct of the female Tortoiseshell led her to lay her eggs in such a well-chosen and protected spot.

It has already been stated that these eggs are found in companies, and when thus located the larvæ are known as gregarious. The larva is yellowish in colour, covered with black specks and short hairs. Down the back there is a black line, and, on each side, this is bordered with clear yellow. The black, hairy head is speckled with this same colour.

When the larva has cast its skin several times, it shows signs of changing into another form. It becomes less active and eventually pupates, that is, turns into a chrysalis. The shape of this will be seen from the illustration. It is grey or pinkish in colour, but sometimes the top and other portions bear a metallic lustre. When the chrysalis has performed its remarkable change to a perfect butterfly, a very handsome insect presents itself for our admiration.

It will be noticed that the general colour is reddish orange, marked with patches of yellow, black spots, and blue crescents, a very beautiful combination. Watch the insect carefully, for it may take to flight at any moment. It has now closed its bright wings, and the colour of the under-side is quite different from that of the upper. The under-side is dull coloured, and this well protects the insect when it has settled upon the ground or some other similar object, for it is difficult to detect which is the insect and which its resting-place. Suddenly, however, it has taken flight once more, and now has its wings fully extended. Quick as thought a bird darts out of the hedge, hovers for a second or two in the air just over the butterfly, snatches up the latter in its beak, and flies back to the spot from whence it came. What bold intruder is this that has so unceremoniously snatched off and swallowed the little insect we have been watching?

Let us explore the spot where the bird went in. Has he gone? No, there he goes, none other than Cock Robin himself! The rascal! Who would have thought that he could be guilty of such a crime? It is not often we have caught the

Redbreast thus engaged, for he more often feeds upon Ear-wigs, Spiders, Caterpillars, Earthworms, Daddy-long-legs or Crane-flies, and other creatures.

Search the spot from whence Cock Robin rose, especially among the tangled grasses and between the Ivy. Yes, there is his nest. Is it not a snug homestead? How many eggs are there in it? Five? That is probably all that will be laid, and the female, which is very similar to Cock Robin himself, will soon begin to sit.

The eggs are white in ground colour, freckled with light brown, mostly at the larger end, and will probably take from ten to fourteen days to hatch. At first, the young Robins are covered with black down, but as they grow they improve in appearance, and after a time they have spotted breasts like a young Thrush. Indeed, young Robins are often mistaken for Thrushes, for, until after the first moult, they do not have the cherry-red breast of the full-grown bird.

In habits, Robins are domineering and pugnacious, and are only found in pairs; they often come near dwelling houses in the Autumn, and also when forced to do so by severe weather. Their song is sweet and plaintive, and is uttered at a time when most song birds are silent. Then it appeals to us, but is not much noticed when other songsters abound.

XII.

WEASEL—LONG-TAILED FIELD-MOUSE—BROWN RAT— HEDGEHOG.

WHAT is that moving as quickly as lightning? It is a Weasel. What is he doing here in the hedge? He dearly loves birds and their eggs, and as a consequence ground-nesting birds, including the Partridge, often suffer from his visits. More often, however, he prefers larger prey, and hunts with great courage and wariness. When we saw him he was just pouncing upon a Long-tailed Field-mouse.

Yes, there are many tragedies in wild life going on in the little hedgerow we are watching, but this is true of each of Nature's communities.

The Long-tailed Field-mouse does a good deal of damage to crops, and the Weasel is, therefore, a friend to the farmer in ridding him of this troublesome visitor, and consequently should be encouraged. The Weasel also feeds largely upon the Brown Rat, which is acknowledged to be one of the worst pests we have in this country. The haystack further along the hedge is almost riddled by it; but if the farmer would only encourage the Weasel, and get one to take up its abode in the stack, he would not for long be troubled with Mr Rat, for it will not stay when the Weasel has come into residence.

Fig. 25. Head and Foot of Weasel.

This mammal is much smaller than its near relative the Stoat. It is reddish in colour on the back, and pure white below, and measures about eight and a quarter inches over head and body. The female is smaller than the male.

The Weasel is not the only animal which is attracted to the hedgerow by reason of a good hunting ground, for to the list must be added the Hedgehog, or Hedgepig, as it is sometimes called. If this animal were not found in a hedge, where else would one expect to find it? True enough names stand for little or nothing in many cases, but in this instance one has not much cause for complaint.

Although we may meet with this interesting creature on hunting expeditions in woods, plantations, and sometimes in

D

open country, yet it specially loves a hedgerow in which to wander, and it is there, at any rate, we may search for its nest, although it has a preference for the hollows of a tree or crevices in a rock.

Where the hedge-bottom is well supplied with dead leaves, there you may search for the Hedgehog with a hope of being successful. It is a nocturnal or night animal, and although we may come across it several times during the day, it is obvious that it is for the most part a species which hunts very largely during the silent hours.

When the day breaks it rolls itself into a ball, and thus rests, being splendidly protected by a spiny outer-covering. These spines are about an inch in length, and, being remarkably firm and elastic, will act as a cushion to break the creature's fall from a great height.

Some time in early Summer the nest may be found containing from two to four young ones. At first the baby Hedgepigs are clothed in soft white spines and are quite blind. The spines, however, soon harden, the eyes open, and, this accomplished, the youngsters hunt about for food on their own account.

There is an abundance of this in the hedge, for besides the eggs of Partridges and Pheasants, the Hedgehog will eat young birds, and has even been known to enter poultry houses for this purpose. A large variety of insects, as well as Frogs, Toads, Snails, Slugs, Earthworms, and even Snakes, are also eaten. It is very useful in a garden or house infested by Cockroaches. That it does a deal of damage to game is undoubted, but, taken all round, probably the animal does more good than harm.

It is a shy creature, and hates being watched. It has, as our coloured picture shows, a Pig-like face, small black eyes, and short legs and feet. It measures about ten inches in length, and is clothed on the back and sides with the well-known spines. These are calculated to serve the Hedgehog well, and no animal, except man himself, preys to any extent upon it. When hunting for food, the Hedgehog reminds one very strikingly of a Pig sniffing here, there, and everywhere after anything of an eatable kind.

During the Winter it makes a cosy nest of dead leaves in some sheltered ditch under a hedge, or at the bottom of a tree. There it tucks itself up snugly and securely, and thus remains all through the dark days of Winter. It does not feed during this time, but as soon as the Larks are carolling overhead in early Spring, and the Primroses are peeping out of their leaf-strewn beds, it awakens from its slumber, and loses no time in making preparations for family affairs.

XIII.

DORMOUSE——COMMON PARTRIDGE.

THE Dormouse is another creature which inhabits the hedge. Why is it there? For one thing, this really beautiful little animal loves to hang its round nest of dead grasses in a Blackthorn or Whitethorn bush; and then again the Dormouse finds food in plenty all around, for he feeds, for example, very largely upon nuts, such as can be obtained from the Hazel bush.

In the Winter months, or early in the Spring before the bushes have become covered with leaves, it is a good plan to examine a hedge, and search for the old nests. Most of them will probably belong to the Song Thrush, Blackbird, Greenfinch, Chaffinch, Yellow Bunting, and Hedge Sparrow, but care should be taken to look inside, because the Dormouse, or some Field-mouse, may have built its own cosy

quarters within the bird's old homestead. It may be, however, that you will discover a small round ball of dry grass
hanging there. You should gently tap the grass ball to see
if anyone is at home.

It is more than probable, if it be early Springtime, a Dormouse will pop its head out of the front door to see who
is about and, in less time than it takes to tell the story, the
active little creature will have disappeared
among the undergrowth.

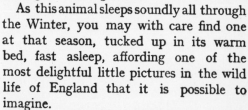

As this animal sleeps soundly all through
the Winter, you may with care find one
at that season, tucked up in its warm
bed, fast asleep, affording one of the
most delightful little pictures in the wild
life of England that it is possible to
imagine.

Our photograph of a Dormouse asleep
will give a much better idea of what
the little creature looks like than any
written description, but should you be fortunate enough to
find a living specimen, put the slumberer back in its grassy
home, so that it may pass the Winter quietly and peacefully.
Then it will awaken one mild Spring day and choose a wife.

Fig. 26. Fruit of Nut Hazel.

A bird of some kind—and a large one, too—was disturbed from the hedge just now. What a noise it made!
A " whirr " of wings, and then 'twas gone! Let us go to
the opening in the hedgerow and look over. Yes, there is
the bird we disturbed, feeding quite unconcernedly in the
adjoining meadow. It is a Common or English Partridge,
the most plentiful of all game birds in Britain.

Let us search for its nest. Be careful where you tread, or you
may quite unintentionally put your foot upon it. You must
not expect to find a nest such as that built by a Blackbird

or a Thrush, and doubtless, if you are lucky enough to locate it, you will be somewhat disappointed.

What shall you look for? Just a few dead leaves upon the ground, hurriedly gathered together, and looking as if an animal of some kind had been sitting upon them, or resting there. You can see several little clusters of leaves that answer the description. True, but you need a practised eye to find a Partridge's nest.

The hunt becomes quite exciting, knowing, as we do, that a number of eggs lie secreted somewhere in the hedgerow and yet we cannot discover them. Pass your finger gently over each little company of leaves, and see if you can feel anything underneath. You can! Let us see what you have unearthed. An egg? Bravo! You have found the missing homestead! Now feel for more eggs under the leaves, and tell us how many there are. Thirteen! The Partridge always covers her eggs over in this manner, *until she commences to sit,* so that it is probable more eggs will yet be added to the number.

The female is rather smaller than the male. The upper parts of both are ash-grey, finely marked with brown and black. The male may be distinguished by a horse-shoe patch upon the breast.

We must return on another occasion and see what further has happened. Then, if we find the mother bird at home, some such picture as that shown opposite page 66 will be seen, and if we carefully put her off the nest we shall discover the eggs nicely packed together, as depicted in the photograph on the same plate.

You would be interested to see the young Partridges soon after they are hatched. They do not stay in the nest like most young birds, for it is necessary that birds building upon the ground, being exposed to numerous four-footed and other enemies, should, soon after hatching, be able to run about and take care of themselves.

Many young Partridges and Pheasants have been helped into the world by having their shells gently broken open. No sooner have the little chicks been set free than they have run about in a pretty and most active way, and have soon become strong enough to gain their own living.

XIV.

OIL BEETLE—SYCAMORE—COMMON MAPLE—ORANGE-TIP BUTTERFLY—HEDGE MUSTARD.

WHAT curious-looking individual is this that comes blundering across the pathway towards the hedge? She is in no hurry to get out of sight, that is plainly to be seen. Stop her before she is lost to view in the thick herbage by the side of the bank.

Now pick her up and examine her closely. The body looks too big for her. She is about an inch and a half long, dull blue-black in colour, the surface closely pitted, and the wing-covers looking too small for the hind part of the body. Pick her up if you would learn why the name of Oil Beetle has been conferred upon this handsome, if somewhat cumbersome, species.

Now see, a globule of yellowish oil has come from between the joints of the legs. What purpose does this serve? As a means of warning various animals which might otherwise eat her, that she is of an offensive nature; indeed this Beetle possesses no other defence of any kind.

She has been tempted from her hiding-place. What is she doing? Hers is a wonderful mission. Early in the Spring she selects a warm spot on a sunny bank, and deposits a very

COMMON PARTRIDGE SITTING ON NEST

NEST AND EGGS OF COMMON PARTRIDGE

ROBIN ENTERING NEST

NEST AND EGGS OF ROBIN
(Photographed at close quarters to show eggs large and in detail)

large number of eggs in a crevice in the earth.   Having laid them, she, like nearly all other insects, takes no further heed of them.   The eggs hatch in due season, and from each there comes a tiny grub, active in disposition.

Each grub then undertakes a journey into the very heart of a flower of some hedgerow plant, and waits.   Presently a Wild Bee comes along to gather honey or pollen for her young ones.   She dives into the rich storehouse of the flower, and, whilst sipping up the sweet nectar or busily engaged gathering pollen, the grub of the Beetle seizes its opportunity, climbs among the hairs upon the Bee's body, and waits patiently for the latter to fly away bearing it with her!

Fig. 27. Oil Beetle.

The Bee returns to her nest, and proceeds to fill one of the empty cells with pollen, for the use of the Bee larva.   But the industrious creature has reckoned without her host, for the Beetle grub eats both egg and Bee-bread.   Soon the intruder casts its skin, and in so doing its active legs are got rid of, it having no further use for them.   Eventually the outer case of the pupa, or chrysalis, breaks, and the perfect Oil Beetle comes forth triumphant, after having passed through what must really have proved a very exciting period.

The hedge contains at least two kinds of Maples.   The Sycamore we have already referred to in connection with the Garden Warbler, but it is as well to notice that this beautiful tree is a near relative of the Common Maple.   It is sometimes called the Great Plane, and lives from 150 to 250 years.   It is a rapid grower, and is now largely distributed throughout the country.   This is the more remarkable when it is remembered, that as recently as the fourteenth century, it was looked upon as a rare tree from abroad. Two of our old writers have written of the Sycamore that " it specially is planted for the shadow-sake."

The Common Maple is mostly found growing in thickets and hedgerows. It flourishes along a dry hedgerow, and will also grow under the shade of other trees. The leaves are much smaller than those of the Sycamore, and the bark is very corky, and brown in colour. The wood is soft, close grained, but beautifully veined, and looks very handsome when polished.

The leaves which are broad at the base, and have five main lobes, are often attacked by Mites. These little creatures produce the small pimple-like red galls which have perhaps attracted your attention.

Look, quickly, there flies the first Orange-tip Butterfly of the season. Does he not look a picture as he pursues his way along, for it is the male which possesses the orange-tips on the wings, those of the female being blackish-grey. Let us follow him closely and see exactly what he is like, and learn what business he has to transact at this spot.

Here is the Orange-tip settled upon a Bramble bush. Is he not a fine fellow? Notice his fore-wings. These are white, or creamy-white, with a patch of orange, but the tip is blackish. The greenish markings on the under surface of the hind wings often protect him, for they make him appear so like the surrounding vegetation that his enemies fail to see him very easily. The female is of a more sombre colour, and still more difficult to discover when her wings are folded; we may find one resting along the hedgerow which could not possibly have been seen had we not stooped down to look at something else, and thus chanced to see the butterfly.

Look! there goes a female Orange-tip, and see she has

settled on a somewhat tall-growing plant bearing small yellow flowers. This is the Hedge Mustard, and if we search the clusters of blossom of this plant, or the Cuckoo Flower in June, the eggs may be found, for these are placed upright on the leaf-stalk. They are whitish when first laid, with a faint tinge of green, but soon turn to yellow, later to orange, and then dark violet.

If eggs of a dark violet colour are found, the caterpillar

Fig. 28. Leaf of Maple.

Fig. 29. Leaf of Hedge Mustard.

may soon be expected. This is dull bluish-green, with raised dots and warts. Whitish hairs proceed from the dots, and from the warts arise long blackish hairs. Along the sides of the body there is a line, or stripe of white, and the body underneath is greener than the back.

The caterpillar is very well protected, as you will readily agree when you commence to search for it. It so nearly resembles the seed pods of the plant upon which it feeds that it is often only by chance discovered. The next time you see a plant of Hedge Mustard, bearing what you consider more than a full complement of seed vessels, just examine it, and see if the caterpillar has deceived you.

The larva also feeds upon other plants, besides those on which it is born, such as Charlock, Hedge Garlic, Water-cress, Horse Radish, and Rock Cress. The eggs, however, must be sought for upon the Cuckoo Flower or the Hedge Mustard.

It should be noted that the Hedge Mustard and the Hedge Garlic, although first cousins, are very different, and can be readily distinguished one from the other (see page 49). The Hedge Mustard has small pale yellow flowers which are borne on a long slender spike. It is a strong wiry plant and often becomes quite bushy.

When the flowers have gone the curious long and narrow seed vessels press closely to the stem, and somewhat resemble green caterpillars creeping up each side. The hairy leaves grow mostly towards the base and are somewhat like those of the Dandelion.

XV.

GROUND IVY—GLOW-WORM.

THERE is still another hedgerow plant that we must see before we leave, and this is the Ground Ivy. It must not be confused with the Common Ivy, for, although both are growing together, they are in no way connected.

The Ground Ivy is an early bloomer, and sometimes before March is out, the purple or blue flowers brighten the hedge-bank in a beautiful way. The flowers are borne in whorls or circles at the axils of the leaves, that is, at the place where the latter meet the stems. In shape, these blossoms some-what resemble those of the Dead-Nettle, for the petals are

A Pair of Hedgehogs

DORMICE AWAKE

DORMOUSE ASLEEP

united in the form of a tube. The leaves are kidney-shaped, rough, and have scalloped edges.

It is in its creeping habits more than anything else, that the present plant interests us, for as its square stem makes its way along the ground, it sends down a tuft of fibrous roots wherever it puts forth a pair of leaves. Thus, like the Strawberry, it is able to spread and take possession of the ground.

The juice of the plant is aromatic and bitter, and it is

Fig. 30. Ground Ivy, showing roots.

interesting to notice that in olden times it was used in brewing, as Hops are to-day.

It is the gloaming-hour now; the time when the Bats, the Owls, the Cockchafers, the Moths, and many other creatures commence their revels. It is almost dark, but how quiet and beautiful everything is! And, look, the hedge is still a lovely place, for the insect lamplighters have come out and set their lamps burning brightly.

Are we in Fairyland or England? What is the meaning of this brilliant lighting up of our hedgerow, the bottom of which now seems set with sparkling gems? What means this?

It is the gloaming, and also the Glow-worm's hour. That is the secret of this electric effect of the hedge-bottom. Every moment the lights increase, until the place is simply aglow with living green fairy lamps.

Try and catch one of the creatures if you can. See, it is not a worm at all, but a beetle. This is without doubt a female, because her colour is of a dull black, her body is soft and flexible, and she has no wings. The male possesses less

MALE   FEMALE

Fig. 31. Glow-worms.

power of producing this curious glow, and he may at once be known by his wings and wing-covers. He flies at night, and is guided in his wanderings by the bright signal given off by his mate in the hedge-bottom.

The "lantern" is simply a luminous spot on the abdomen, and as the insect moves about, the light appears, disappears, and re-appears, producing a most charming effect.

Beyond this, the female has the power of increasing or diminishing or putting out the light altogether. When there is more electricity in the air than usual, the brightness of the light increases. If the insect be placed in warm water the light is much brighter; cold water puts the lantern out entirely.

The larva or grub of this remarkable insect has to celebrate more than one birthday before it reaches the adult state.

Snails form its chief diet, and here we have still another example of why we find it in our hedgerow. The larva is a wonderful little creature, for it has a sort of brush at the end of the body, and by means of this, it is not only able to move along, but can also clean its body from the slime of the Snail.

The hours have sped all too quickly, while we have been wending our way along this pleasant hedgerow, but we trust that the time has not been spent in vain. And if " in Nature's infinite book of secrecy a little can you read," it should but entice you to return again and again to those marvellous pages, and glean for yourselves more and more of the ways and doings of Nature's wild children.

MADE AT THE TEMPLE PRESS LETCHWORTH IN GREAT BRITAIN

CALENDAR AND NOTES

OF

ANIMALS AND PLANTS

COMPILED BY C. S. COOPER, F.R.H.S.

I. BIRDS

CHAFFINCH.—In England all the year; also many visitors from Norway and Sweden in Winter. *Male bird:* chestnut-brown; forehead black; head and neck ashy grey; breast red; some white tail feathers; length 6 inches. *Female:* ashy brown; some wing feathers yellow; breast pink; length 6½ inches. *Nest:* April–July; in bushes, branches, or small forks of trees; moss, hairs, feathers, roots, and lichens; *eggs* 4–6, ashy grey with reddish and bluish tinge, spotted with brown and black. *Food:* insects and larvæ in summer; seeds and beech mast in winter. *Call-note:* "pink, pink"; begins to sing in February; full song in April.

CUCKOO.—Spends Winter in Africa and India; arrives here in April; leaves about end of July. *Male bird:* general colour above leaden-grey; under surface white, barred with black; length 14 inches. *Female:* very similar to male; length 12½ inches. *Nest:* none; *eggs* placed in nests of other birds; usual colour reddish-grey or greyish-green, speckled and mottled with darker shades. *Food:* insects and their larvæ; believed to be the only bird which eats the "Woolly Bear" larva of the Tiger Moth. *Call-note,* "Cuckoo" uttered by male bird; female utters a "whittling" or "water-burbling" cry; begins to sing in April, "in May he sings all day, in June he alters his tune."

79

GARDEN WARBLER.—Spends Winter in Africa; arrives here about beginning of May; leaves again in September. *Male bird :* general colour greyish-brown above, tinged with olive; throat and breast brownish-white; length 6 inches. *Female :* similar to male, but rather paler. *Nest :* May–September; low down in a bush, or near ground amongst herbage; dry grasses and rootlets, wool and moss, lined with fine roots and hair; *eggs* 4 or 5, greenish-white, mottled, spotted, and streaked with light grey and olive brown. *Food :* insects, grubs, and soft fruits. *Song :* soft and rich, somewhat like that of the Blackbird; seldom sings in the open or from a perch.

GREATER WHITETHROAT.—Spends Winter in S. Africa; arrives here early in April; leaves at end of September. *Male bird :* general colour greyish-brown above, breast dull white, tinged with rose; length $5\frac{1}{2}$ inches. *Female :* duller brown above, under surface whiter, rose tint less distinct. *Nest :* May–July; in bramble-bushes and coarse herbage close to ground; dry grasses, lined with hair; *eggs* 4–6, greenish-white, spotted and speckled with greenish-grey and brownish-grey. *Food :* insects and soft fruits, large numbers of Daddy Longlegs. *Song :* loud and lively, with a few harsh notes; warbles from sunrise to sunset, usually from top of hedge, even during rain and storm.

HEDGE SPARROW.—In England all the year. *Male bird :* general colour above brown, throat and breast slaty-grey, shading off into dull white; length $5\frac{1}{2}$ inches. *Female :* similar to male. *Nest :* March–June; in hedges, brambles, shrubs, stacks, ivy, etc.; twigs, grass, moss, wool, and hair; *eggs* 4–6, blue, without spots. *Food :* worms and insects, with seeds or scraps in Winter. *Sings* all through the year.

LONG-TAILED TIT.—In England all the year round. *Male bird :* black, white, and brown, flushed with rosy-red, length $5\frac{1}{2}$

inches. *Female:* similar to male, slightly smaller. *Nest:* March–June; in hedges and furze bushes; moss, wool, lichens, spiders' webs, and lined with feathers; *eggs* 6–10, white or pearly-grey, sprinkled with light red dots, with a few faint purple marks. *Food:* almost entirely of insects. *Song:* a low and delicate trill, with the zi-zi peculiar to the Tits, and a " churring " note of its own.

PARTRIDGE.—In England all the year. *Male bird:* general colour above brownish-buff, with wavy cross-bars and lines of black; breast grey, mottled with black, with large horse-shoe-shaped chestnut patch; length 12½ inches. *Female:* with buff cross on some of the wing feathers; in some parts the horse-shoe patch is indistinct or entirely absent. *Nest:* May and early June; a slight hollow in the ground, roughly lined with a few dry grasses; *eggs* 10–20, pale olive-brown. *Food:* grain, seeds of weeds, worms, caterpillars, beetles, young leaves. *Cry:* a powerful, metallic, far-reaching note.

ROBIN.—In England all the year round; also many visitors from the continent in Autumn. *Male bird:* general colour dark olive brown; cheeks, throat, and chest orange-red, bordered with bluish-grey; centre of breast and abdomen dull white; length 6 inches. *Female:* almost similar to male. *Nest:* early Spring to late Summer; in many situations, amongst ivy, a hole in a wall or tree, old cans and utensils, etc.; dead leaves and moss, lined with rootlets and hair; *eggs* 5–7, white, freckled with red. *Food:* worms, insects, and scraps. *Call-note:* clear and musical; cry of distress, a long-drawn shrill note; sings all the year except during the moulting in Autumn.

YELLOW BUNTING.—In England all the year. *Male bird:* brown above; under surface yellow, with tinge of green; breast and sides chestnut or bay; crown yellow; length 7 inches. *Female:* less brightly coloured; yellow on crown concealed; throat and breast striped; length 6¼ inches. *Nest:* April–August; low down in a hedgerow, bush, or bank; moss, rootlets, cobwebs, and lichens, lined with horse-hair and down; *eggs* 3–4, generally 3, dingy white, streaked and veined with dark purplish-brown, with spots of same colour. *Food :* insects and caterpillars, with grain in Winter. *Song :* two or three chirps like "chit-chit," followed by a long "chirr-r-r,"—said to resemble "Bit o' bread and no chee-e-e-se."

II. INSECTS

BRIMSTONE MOTH.—April–September; most plentiful in May and June; can be taken on palings during day; flies in the evening, and comes to light. *Wings :* sulphur-yellow; front margin of fore wings spotted with red. *Eggs :* June–September. *Larva :* June–September; twig-like, brownish tinged with greenish or purplish, 14 legs; feeds on Hawthorn and Blackthorn.

DRINKER MOTH.—July and August; may be found at rest among coarse grasses in lanes and ditch-sides; comes to light. *Male :* dull reddish brown, antennæ very feathery, abdomen slightly tufted. *Female :* yellow, abdomen thick. *Eggs :* white with bluish grey markings, laid in clusters on grass stems. *Larva :* dull slaty grey inclining to blackish with tufts of black, white, brown, and yellow hairs; feeds on coarse grasses from August to October, hybernates through Winter, feeds again from April to June; likes its food to be sprinkled with water.

GLOW-WORM.—May–September. *Male :* has brownish wing-cases (elytra) covering a pair of wings; five-twelfths inch long. *Female :* grub-like, wingless; two-thirds inch long. *Larva :* hybernates through Winter, changes to pupa in April or May; feeds on snails.

GOLD-TAIL MOTH.—July and August; may be found at rest on the foliage of bushes, branches of trees, and palings, looking like a fluffy white feather; attracted by light. *Male :* white, usually a black mark on the fore wings, under sides black, tuft yellow, expands one and one-third inches. *Female :* white, expands one and five-sixths inches; golden hairs of tail used for covering eggs. *Eggs* laid in batches in August. *Larva :* black with a double red line down the back, a white line beneath, and a red line on the sides, small humps on three segments; hybernates through Winter in a silken case, recommences feeding in Spring, in May separates from its companions, a common object on Hawthorn hedges; feeds on Hawthorn, Apple, Oak, and other trees.

GREEN - VEINED WHITE BUTTERFLY. — April – August. *Male :* one black spot on fore wings. *Female :* two spots and a black dash. Under side of both yellow with greenish veins. *Eggs :* May and August. *Larva :* June and September; green; feeds on Water-cress, Hedge Garlic, and others of Wallflower Family.

LACKEY MOTH.—July and August; is attracted by light. *Wings :* varying from pale yellow ochre, through pale brown to reddish or dark brown; generally two lines across the fore wings. *Eggs :* July and August, greyish brown, in a ring cluster around a twig, remaining exposed through the Winter. *Larva :* hatch in April, and live till June under a common silken tent-like web; full grown caterpillar is many-coloured, slaty blue above, with a bluish white line, bordered by a reddish-orange-lined black stripe, with various other stripes below; head slaty blue, with two black eye-like spots; feeds on Hawthorn, Blackthorn, fruit trees, and forest trees, doing very great damage to the foliage; chrysalis enclosed in a double cocoon, the inner being covered with a sulphur-like powder.

OIL BEETLE.—April and May. *Male :* wingless, elytra covering about two-thirds of body. *Female :* wingless, body often much swollen, elytra covering about half the body. *Eggs :* laid in the ground. *Larva :* parasitic in nests of Bees, feeding on food prepared for Bee larva.

ORANGE TIP BUTTERFLY.—April–June. *Male :* tip half of fore wings deep orange. *Female :* without orange mark. Under side of hind wings in both white chequered with yellowish green. *Eggs :* May, on Cuckoo Flower and Hedge Mustard. *Larva :* July; green, white stripe on each side, spiny; feeds on Cuckoo Flower, Hedge Garlic, Hedge Mustard, and others of Wallflower Family.

PEACOCK BUTTERFLY.—March–May and July–September, hybernating through Winter. *Wings* dull deep red with an eye-like spot on each. *Eggs :* April and May. *Larva :* June and July; black with white dots, spiny; feeds on Stinging Nettle.

RED ADMIRAL BUTTERFLY.—August–October, hybernating through Winter and reappearing on sunny days in Spring. *Wings* black and red with white spots near tip of fore wings. *Eggs :* April and May. *Larva :* June and July; yellowish-grey with a pale yellow line, spiny; feeds on Stinging Nettle.

SMALL TORTOISESHELL BUTTERFLY.—March–September, hybernating through Winter. *Wings* reddish-orange with black spots, border marked with blue spots. *Eggs :* April, May, and July. *Larva :* May, June, and August; yellowish grey, striped with black and brownish-yellow; feeds on Stinging Nettle.

TIGER MOTH.—July. *Fore wings* brown, with white interlacing bands; *hind wings* and abdomen dark red, with blue-black spots. *Eggs :* July. *Larva :* September–May, hybernating through Winter; black, with long white hairs along back; reddish brown hairs along the sides and on the 2nd, 3rd, and 4th segments; feeds on Stinging Nettle, White Dead-Nettle, and many low plants.

III. MAMMALS

BROWN RAT.—Introduced from the Continent early in the 18th century. *General colour* greyish brown above, whitish beneath. *Length* of head and body about 9 inches; tail $7\frac{1}{2}$ inches. *Inhabits* drains, sewers, buildings, granaries, banks of canals, and rivers. *Feeds* on almost anything.

DORMOUSE.—A native of Britain. *General colour* of upper parts light tawny, paler and yellowish beneath. *Length* of head and body, about 3 inches; tail 2½ inches. *Inhabits* hedgerows, woods, and plantations, and sometimes met with in fields. Sleeps through Winter in a nest, generally in the stump of a Hazel Tree, sometimes on the ground, or even in deserted bird's-nest. *Food :* Acorns, Hazel-nuts, seeds of Hornbeam and other trees, grain, and fruit.

HEDGEHOG.—A native of Britain. Back and sides protected by spines; face and under parts clothed with yellowish-white hair. *Length* of head and body, about 10 inches; tail 1½ inches. *Inhabits* hedge-banks and thickets, hiding during the day, and seeking food at night. Sleeps through the Winter. *Food :* Slugs, Snails, Worms, Beetles, Frogs, Snakes, eggs, and young birds.

LONG-TAILED FIELD MOUSE.—A native of Britain. *General colour* of upper parts bright reddish-grey; under parts whitish, with patch of light brown on breast. *Length* of head and body 4¼ inches; tail 4 inches. *Inhabits* hedges, thickets, corn-fields, and gardens during Summer; in Winter hides in barns, out-buildings, and corn-stacks. *Food :* corn, bulbs, nuts, acorns, small seeds, insects, and grubs; stores up large quantities of food for Winter, underground, in deserted birds'-nests, or in hedge-banks. *Natural enemies :* Kestrel, Owl, Stoat, Weasel, and Fox.

WEASEL.—A native of Britain. *General colour* of upper parts reddish-brown; under parts yellowish-white. *Male :* length of head and body 8¼ inches; tail 2½ inches. *Female :* length of head and body 7 inches; tail 2 inches. *Inhabits* hedgerows and woods, fields and pastures, pursuing its prey into barns, granaries, and corn-stacks. *Feeds* on Voles, Rats, and Moles, and sometimes small birds and eggs.

IV. TREES AND FLOWERING PLANTS

NAME.	Time of Flowering.	Colour.	Height.
Hazel . . .	Feb.—April	Male catkin, yellow; female catkin, tuft of red stigmas	Tree
Ground Ivy . .	Mar.—June	Blue	Creeping
Sweet Violet . .	,, —May	,, or White	,,
Dog Violet . .	April—June	,,	,,
Greater Stitchwort .	,, — ,,	White	1–2 ft.
Red Dead-Nettle .	,, —Oct.	Reddish Purple	6–12 ins.
White Dead-Nettle .	,, ,,	White	6–18 ins.
Lords and Ladies (Arum)	,, May	Purple	6–12 ins.
Germander Speedwell .	May—June	Blue	1–2 ft.
Hedge Garlic . .	,, ,,	White	2–3 ft.
Sycamore . . .	,, ,,	Green	Tree
Maple . . .	,, ,,	,,	,,
Hawthorn . . .	,, ,,	White	,,
Black Bryony . .	,, —July	Yellowish Green	Climber
Herb Robert . .	,, —Sept.	Pink	1–2 ft.
Lesser Stitchwort .	,, —Aug.	White	1–2 ft.
White Bryony . .	,, —Sept.	Whitish Green	Climber
Dog Rose . . .	June—July	Pink	3–6 ft.
Hedge Mustard . .	,, ,,	Yellow	1–2 ft.
Cleavers . . .	,, —Aug.	White	1–5 ft.
Cow Parsnip . .	,, — ,,	Pinkish White	4–5 ft.
Greater Bindweed .	,, — ,,	White	Climber
Honeysuckle . .	,, —Sept.	Creamy Yellow	,,
Foxglove . . .	,, — ,,	Purple	2–5 ft.
Stinging Nettle . .	,, — ,,	Green	1–4 ft.
Blackberry . .	July—Aug.	White or Pink	3–10 ft.
Traveller's Joy . .	,, — Sept.	Greenish White	Climber
Dock . . .	,, — ,,	Reddish Green	2–5 ft.
Ivy	Oct.—Nov.	Green	Climber

The Pond I Know

THE
POND I KNOW

EDITED BY

W. PERCIVAL WESTELL, F.L.S.
& HENRY E. TURNER

General Secretary of the School
Nature Study Union

WITH

14 COLOURED

& MANY BLACK AND WHITE
ILLUSTRATIONS

LONDON
J. M. DENT & SONS LTD.

" The grass, the trees, the flowers, the earth, the air, swarm with innumerable kinds of active living creatures; every stone upturned reveals some insect wonder; nay, the stagnant ditch discloses a world wherein incalculable myriads pass their lives, and every drop swarms with animated atoms . . ."

CONTENTS

LIST OF ILLUSTRATIONS

COLOURED PLATES AND HALF-TONES

ILLUSTRATIONS IN THE TEXT

9

THE POND I KNOW

I

HOW A POND IS FORMED

NOTES UPON CLAY—FIRST IMPRESSIONS—A BIRD'S-EYE
VIEW—THE PURIFYING OF THE WATER

" MARK what happens when a heavy shower of rain falls
upon dry ground. If the latter be formed of hard and solid
rock, such as Granite, the rain, after wetting the surface,
runs off in all directions, some finding its way to the nearest
streamlet, whence it flows sooner or later into a river, and
some finding lodgment in little hollows of the rock, where
it collects in pools, which are slowly dried up by wind and
sunshine.

" But if the rock, instead of being hard like Granite, is
soft and porous like Sand or Chalk, the water will then sink
into its substance, and may even pass out of sight before
the surface of the thirsty soil is thoroughly wetted.
Rocks which thus allow water to filter through them are
said to be permeable, while those—such as Clay—which
refuse to allow the water to soak in, are described as im-
permeable." [1]

There may exist in some of your minds a doubt as to
what a rock really is. At the first mention of the word we
think of a towering mass of stony matter, against which the
Elements appear to act in vain. But you must take a
broader view than this, and include under the heading of

[1] Professor Huxley's *Physiography*. p. 21.

rocks " all constituents of the Earth's crust, whether hard
Granite and Sandstone, or soft Clay and Gravel."

It may interest you to know that water is constantly
acting upon the hardest rocks, decomposing them into
Sand and Mud, which the running streams carry down, and
later spread out in layers, not only in the estuary, but also in
the sea beyond. In course of time the shrinking of the
earth, caused by its cooling, forces these layers above the
level of the sea, and they become dry land. What was
formerly known as Mud is now called Clay.

Thus we see that Clay was originally a fine sediment,
and this accounts for the fact that in no other rocks are
fossils so well preserved; if we examine these fossils, we
shall discover that they are the remains of creatures which
were of common occurrence on those parts of the sea-bed
where mud is nowadays being carried down.

Clays differ in colour, and may be red, blue, brown or
grey, according to the colouring matter they contain.

The surface of our country is by no means smooth or
flat, and one has not very far to travel before meeting with
a natural hollow or cup-like depression; here water will
readily collect, and should the bed be of a clayey nature,
and should there be no outlet for all the water, a pond or
small lake will be the result.

This in time becomes one of Nature's most interesting
colonies; above and below its surface will be found all kinds
of life; flowers will spring up near its waters, and as the
years roll by, even trees and shrubs will make their appearance. Let us therefore pay this pond a visit, and observe
for ourselves some of those wonders which will more than
repay us for our trouble.

When visiting the hedgerow we were struck, if you

remember, with the abundance of things that climb. The pond, however, conveys an entirely different impression, and as we come to consider each environment or colony, we shall find that it presents a new set of animals and plants for us to study. Does not the pond convey an idea of stagnation, a suggestion of things that are still and dormant? First impressions, however, are often wrong; indeed, if we stay long enough thoroughly to explore a pond, we shall find it is far from being such a stagnant place after all.

Having arrived at the pond we have decided to visit, what first attracts our attention? Probably each of us will find a special interest there, and no two will think exactly alike. We have already learned how it was formed; now let us discover what animals and plants have been attracted thither, for what purposes they came, what they are doing there, and so on.

Evidently the pond has been here some time, for on its banks various trees have made their home, and these bear marks of old age. Then again, the margin of the water is garnished with a number of Rushes, Sedges, and kindred plants, among which birds and other animals find a safe hiding-place.

Fig. 1. Alder Fly in flight and at rest.

Just let us walk round the pond to start with, and take a sort of bird's-eye view of it. We have casually noted its bed, its trees, and plants. A closer examination will reveal an abundance of bird and insect life, whilst countless tiny creatures may be observed disporting themselves over the green surface scum, which we shall study in detail a little later.

Watch the water closely, for there are many things in and around a pond which, unless looked for, are sure to escape attention. What do you see? Bubbles are arising which burst on reaching the air; these may be formed of the gases which are thrown off by the various kinds of matter decomposing below, but are probably bubbles of oxygen.

Look! there, in the sunlight, a number of fish and other aquatic creatures may be plainly seen!

" But," you will ask, " how is it possible for any animal to live in a pond which is covered with a green scum, and from which, as we have already seen, gases are arising? Surely these would kill any creature living below the surface? "

Now the green scum is in reality a very minute plant; this, and other vegetable growths, help to aerate or purify the water, as you may see for yourself by carrying out the following simple directions.

Obtain some pond weed from a neighbouring pool and put it in a glass jar filled with water. The American Pond-weed will best suit your purpose; this is easily recognised by its small oval leaves, which are arranged in groups of three along the whole length of the stem; failing this, however, you must take what first comes to hand, so long as the plant be in a healthy condition.

Now place your jar near the window, where the sun's rays can act upon the weed, and watch the result. Almost immediately a continual stream of tiny bubbles of oxygen will be set free, apparently from the plant itself. Here you have an illustration of what is constantly taking place in our pond during the Summer months, but, of course, on a much larger scale.

To understand the why and wherefore of all this, a

knowledge of chemistry is required; so, for the present, you must be content with knowing that the sunshine and the green colouring matter in the plant are the two great agents which act upon the carbon dioxide dissolved in the water, and set free the oxygen; the latter purifies the water, and all is well for those that dwell within.

II

TREES ROUND THE POND

ALDER—WILLOW—POPLAR

Having considered how our pond came here, we cannot help being interested in learning how and why the various inhabitants, which now go to make up one of Nature's most interesting colonies, first took up their residence.

There, for example, are the sturdy Alder, the nodding Poplar, and a row of stately Willows, standing sentinel-like, as if they, the pond and its inhabitants, had been living together for generations.

All these moisture-loving trees arouse our interest, long before they put forth their fresh green leaves in the early Spring, for all are Catkin-bearers. This strange-looking word is said to mean a little cat or kitten, and is so called from the fact that the Catkin often resembles the tail of one of those fluffy creatures. You have only to think of the Catkins—the " Lambs' Tails "—of the Hazel to realise the truth of this.

But we must not speak of them as tails, if we wish to understand what part they play in the life of a tree.

Briefly then, a Catkin consists of a spike, which in some cases stands erect, but in others hangs down like the pendulum of a clock, and is then described as pendulous. This spike bears a number of small flowers, which are always of one sex; that is to say, *all* the flowers of any *one* Catkin are either those which produce pollen,[1] or those which bear seed. In addition to this, we shall find that the flowers are usually protected by small shields, or bracts, to give them their real name.

With the exception of those of the Willow, the flowers forming the Catkins do not secrete nectar, and are therefore not visited by insects; thus they have to depend upon the wind for fertilisation. The Pollen Catkins, having shed their golden dust, die off, and have usually disappeared even before the leaves burst from their Winter quarters. The Seed Catkins, however, persist during the Summer, and flourish until the Autumn, when they, too, perform their allotted task and pass away.

It is interesting to inquire, before we pass on, how these trees came to grow around our pond. Two of the three kinds—Poplar and Willow—have fruits possessing a downy attachment whereby they are borne through the air on the wind. The seed falls to earth in various places, and may perhaps germinate, eventually establishing itself as a tree in such a position and situation as best suit it. The Willows, and indeed the Alder and the Poplar, too, are lovers of the water-side, and hence here they are, round the margin of our pond, flourishing exceedingly. In some such way as this, or through the seeds being carried by birds for the purpose of lining their nests with the down, these trees have probably become the monarchs of this Nature colony.

[1] See *The Hedge I Know*, p. 28.

FORGET-ME-NOT

FLOWERING RUSH

WATER LILIES

But now let us pay special attention to the Alder.

In the month of March the small cone-like female Catkins may be noticed, and by then the male Catkins, from two to four inches in length and dark red in colour, have become more pendulous, or drooping; the bracts enclosing the stamens [1] open, and the pollen is dispersed. If examined, the shield-like scales will be seen to be beautifully arranged so as to protect the little boxes containing the pollen from rain and winds, until the flower has sufficiently developed to cast the powdery dust into the air, to be borne by the wind upon its all-important mission.

The Seed Catkins are about an inch long, reddish-brown in colour, and resemble small Fir-cones. These remain on the tree long after the ripe seeds have been discharged, and at such times still more closely resemble miniature Fir-cones.

Fig. 2. Catkins and Leaf of Alder. A, Male catkins; B, Female catkins; c, Female cones of previous year.

Let us examine a leaf of the Alder; notice that it is roundish, that the margins are slightly cut up and wavy, and that the stalk is very short. Examine, if you can, a young leaf and one of an older growth. It will then be seen that the young leaf is hairy and sticky, whilst the older one is glossed with dark olive-green both above and below.

Where the Alder fringes our streams and ponds it beautifies the surroundings in a very charming way, and perhaps looks best when it has been pollarded, for then the tree sends up several stems, which give it quite a bushy appearance.

[1] See *The Hedge I Know*, p. 28.

One thing we shall notice concerning the Alder, as also of the other plants that flourish by our pond, and that is, they retain their leaves longer than those growing in dry situations.

In general outline the Alder is stiff and rigid, and its branches are not nearly so graceful as some of its near relatives.

It seems to delight in flourishing where there is stagnant water, and if the immense mass of roots be examined, it will be seen that the tree is well able to anchor itself in the soil. The bark is almost black.

The wood is soft and, when in a living condition, white in colour, but when newly felled it becomes red where the axe severed the limb, as if the branch had shed blood as a sort of final gasp and a protest against its destruction. In olden days the wood was largely used for making boats, piles, or posts, and other purposes. One great feature concerning the wood of this tree is that it does not warp, so that it is a favourite among those who have to work upon it, and, being soft, it does not split.

We might refer at far greater length to this, the first resident near the pond we have set ourselves out to examine, but let us pass on to the next clump of trees arranged like a row of soldiers standing at attention. What, then, are these? Just pull down a branch and look at the leaf. It differs greatly from that of the Alder in being linear or long. This, then, is the Willow.

The group of trees known as Willows is a very large one, and we cannot hope, on the present excursion, to make acquaintance with many.

Those boys who play cricket will at once recognise the Willow as a friend, for from the wood of this tree the cricket

bat is manufactured. Beyond this, it is important to
notice that some of our Willows are made into paper pulp,
and others make the best kinds of charcoal crayons; the
bark is most useful for tanning; and a valuable medicine,
known as Salicine, is largely obtained from the same. The
Willow Catkins may at once be distinguished from those of
the Alder and the Poplar by their growing more erect.

Most of you are familiar with the Sallow, which is the
earliest of all the Willows to flower,
and to which the Bees hasten for their
first supply of the sweet-scented nectar.
The gold (male) and silver (female)
Catkins appear before Easter, and
branches bearing these flowers are sold
as " Palm " in large quantities in our
cities, although they have no connection with the Palm Tree whatever.

The Willows vary greatly as to the
positions in which they grow, for not
only may Sallow be found flourishing
right in the water, but it may also be
met with growing luxuriously in a
high and apparently dry hedge.

Fig. 3. Catkins and leaf of
Willow. A, Female cat-
kins; B, Male catkins.

There are over ninety forms of Willow in this country,
but the White Willow, which so gracefully ornaments
our pond, can hold its place among them all. Notice
that the specimen leaf you hold in your hand tapers considerably, and that it is very shiny underneath. Observe
also the smooth, green, flexible twigs.

When Willows are pollarded, as shown in the first
coloured picture in this book, various kinds of birds build
among the topmost branches, and there one may find the

nest of the Marsh Tit, the Tree Creeper, the Wryneck, and even our newly introduced British bird, the Little Owl.

Some of these fine old pollarded Willows may be seen in a state of decay, and when the wood becomes rotten, many of our birds find cracks and crevices in which to hide their cradles. The tree is often attacked by various sorts of insects, but perhaps the greatest enemy of all is the caterpillar of the Goat Moth. This is one of the largest and most destructive of British moths, and the larva lives in the wood of Willows, Poplars, and other trees. After two or three years it makes a cocoon of chips of wood in which to pass the pupal or chrysalis state, and emerges as a perfect insect in June or July.

Fig. 4. Larva of Goat Moth.

The larva, or caterpillar, is reddish-brown on the upper part of its body, and yellowish underneath; its head is small and of a glossy black. It gives off a very disagreeable smell, something like that of a he-goat, which may be one of the means it adopts for protective purposes.

Probably very few boys or girls will have any difficulty in recognising a Poplar tree, such as, for example, the one that graces the border of our pond. Although these trees prefer a moist soil, yet one may meet with them in all kinds of situations.

Like all trees which have a rapid growth, the Poplars are of little use as timber, except in such industries as box-making, when the whiteness and softness of the wood are greatly appreciated.

Usually the leaves are heart-shaped or triangular, and

have serrated or toothed edges, but they vary according to the species. It is a remarkable thing that, owing to the unusual length and flattened form of the stalk, the leaves of all Poplars are alike in their restlessness. This is specially the case with the Aspen. Even when there is scarcely a breath of air stirring among the branches, the ever-moving, ever-nodding leaves refuse to take a rest. One can almost imagine them keeping up an unending conversation, whispering of the past, and planning for the future. If only they could speak, what wonderful tales they would have to tell!

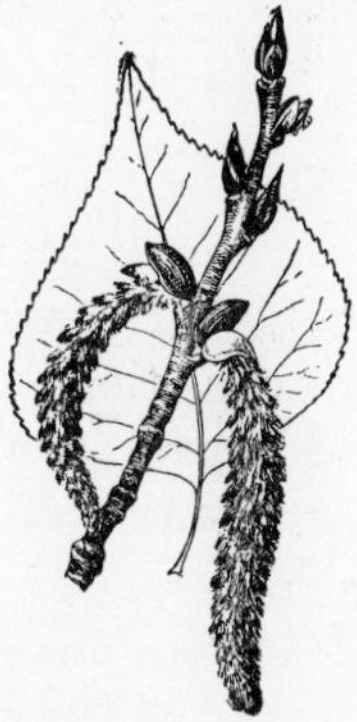

The White or Cotton Poplar, perhaps, is one of the most interesting to children, for not only are the buds, young leaves, and shoots covered with a soft, downy substance, but when the seeds are scattered in the Autumn, tiny white threads are attached to them, too, and make the surrounding vegetation appear as though

Fig. 5. Catkins and leaf of Black Poplar.

sprinkled with minute fragments of cotton. Maybe the fairies hold their sewing classes there!

The dark red Catkins of the Black Poplar also form a never-to-be-forgotten sight. They entirely alter the appearance of the gaunt, bare branches, and the showers of bright golden pollen which they throw out, when swung to and fro by the wind, can leave no doubt in the mind of the beholder as to the lavishness of Mother Nature in this direction.

III

WILD PLANTS ROUND THE POND

FLOWERING RUSH — FORGET-ME-NOT — WATER PLANTAIN—
PINK PERSICARIA—BRANCHED BUR-REED—WATER MINT

MANY of the aquatic plants that are found around the pond need searching for, as the vegetation is very luxuriant, and some of the smaller kinds are entirely hidden among their larger fellows. It was the same in the hedgerow, you will remember, and is mostly true of all such communities, some plants being more prominent than others.

We cannot fail to be attracted by the beautiful Flowering Rush, both by reason of the delicate pink colour of the flower and the upright habit that this typical water plant possesses.

It is first cousin to the Water Plantain growing almost next door, but is easily distinguished by its light rose-coloured flowers. It will be difficult for us to obtain a good specimen, as the ground is very marshy here, but, after all, the plant looks best as it is growing, and there is not a great deal for close examination.

The coloured plate will give you a good idea of what to look for. The pink flowers grow in a cluster at the end of a long upright stalk, which measures from five to six feet. The leaves, which are sword-shaped, all spring from the root stock and fold each over the other at the base.

MOORHEN ON NEST

NEST AND EGGS OF MOORHEN

WATER SCORPIONS

GREAT BROWN WATER BEETLE

But see! There is a bed of dainty Forget-me-nots!
These well-known flowers flourish wherever there is plenty
of water, and often give the only splash of colour to a
neighbourhood which would otherwise be a dull, dreary
place.

The slender, spoon-shaped leaves grasp the upper part
of the stem, and in ancient days were thought to resemble
the ear of a Mouse; hence the other name for this plant
" Myosotis," which is nothing more than
a Greek word meaning " Mouse-Ear."

Like most flowers that dwell by the
water side, the Forget-me-not has a weak,
juicy stem, and this usually rises to a
height of one foot. The most charming
feature of the flower is the pure blue of
its fairy-like blossoms, each of which has
five small round petals lying open like
a wheel, with a bright yellow eye in the
centre.

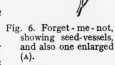

Fig. 6. Forget-me-not,
showing seed-vessels,
and also one enlarged
(A).

If we compare the Water Forget-
me-not with its cousin of the wood, we
shall find that the former is the smoother of the two; that
is to say, it is almost destitute of hairs and hooks such as
are found in other specimens.

Can you guess the reason of this? Does not the water
protect the plant from the inroads of Ants and other foes?
Protective hairs are therefore no longer necessary. Does
not the water also act as the agent for seed dispersal?
Hooked fruits are, as a consequence, not required.

Towering above our azure friend is the Great Water
Plantain, with its large stem, often three feet in length;
this is triangular in section, a shape specially fitted to give

it the strength to resist the varying currents so common to our streams.

The leaves have smooth edges, and are very large, often nine inches in length; these are borne upon long stalks, which spring direct from the root, and overlap each other at their base. They are somewhat like those of the ordinary Field Plantain, but, in spite of name and leaves, there is no relationship between the two.

The flower-bearing branches are thrown off in rings from the central stem, and somewhat resemble a circular hat-stand. Each flower consists of three rose-coloured petals supported by three green sepals.

Do not omit to notice the firm leaves and the upright growth of both this plant and its cousin, the Flowering Rush, for these serve various water insects in a manner we shall see later on.

You cannot fail to espy another treasure, namely, Pink Persicaria, growing in great quantity almost all round the pond, but not nearly so tall as the Flowering Rush, or so delicate in colour. This is a very remarkable plant, for, although showing a great liking for damp situations, it can be met with growing abundantly in a dry stony roadway, together with the Willow Herb and many other plants, which seem strangely out of place. Indeed, waste places, but more especially those of a marshy nature, seem to be the more usual habitat, or home, of this plant. That it flourishes around our pond may be plainly seen, for, see how the young Moorhens are playing hide-and-seek among its leaves and blossoms at this very moment.

Let us procure a specimen, since it is so plentiful, and examine it. There, now you have one, but it was quite an exertion to secure it, for the Pink Persicaria has a freely branching stem and is a great lover of plenty of room.

Notice that the stem is quite brittle and that it is reddish in colour. What do you say? You think the head of flowers looks more like a cluster of red seeds? As these compact and tiny blossoms are found at the tip of the flower stalk,

Fig. 7. Great Water Plantain.
A, Enlarged flower.

Fig. 8. A, Pink Persicaria.
B, Enlarged flower.

and do not all open at the same time, there is some reason for your remark.

The fine pink colour of the flower produces a splendid effect when a number are seen together, especially if the sunlight be playing upon the water, or it be towards sunset.

The Persicaria is a lover of hot weather; hence we find it in bloom during July and August. The leaves are long and usually have a dark spot in the centre; those at the top of the plant, you will notice, almost clasp the stem, but those at the bottom have short stalks.

Near by we find the Branched Bur-reed, which, at a distance, might be mistaken for the Iris, the plant ordinarily known as Flag. Although it belongs to one of the highest orders of British flowering plants, yet it is not too proud to make its home in a muddy ditch or pond.

The leaves, which are sometimes five feet long, remind one of a bayonet, a shape which is often adopted by our aquatic plants. The reason of this is not far to seek, for plants living in the water should offer as little resistance as possible to the flowing stream.

The flowers are arranged in rounded heads along a spike, and look something like " burs; " those at the upper end produce the pollen, whilst those below bear the seed. This is somewhat interesting, for it is contrary to the common practice in force in Nature's kingdom, where the loftier flowers are usually those containing the " seed-boxes." It is certainly true in the majority of cases that pollen grains, which are carried off by moderate winds, at first soar upwards; even when the air is still, the flowers themselves seem to give an upward force to their pollen grains when scattering them.

But what plant is that throwing off such a strong scent? Why, we are actually treading upon it and did not notice it! That, too, is the reason we suddenly discovered the odour it emitted, for, when bruised, the Water Mint is very aromatic indeed.

You know the Mint that grows in the garden, and which Mother finds so useful in preparing vegetables for the table? The Water Mint is a near relative, but our Garden Mint appears to be hardier and, unless in large clumps, flowers much less than the Water species, probably because, being in such request, it is so often picked.

The pale lilac flowers of the Water Mint are of a rather delicate nature, and the whole plant is somewhat shy and unlikely to arrest attention. It makes up for

Fig. 9. Branched Bur-reed.

Fig. 10. Hairy Water Mint.

this, however, by its pungent odour, which is due to the presence of a special kind of oil stored away in the leaves.

Botanists believe that all such plants as Mint and Thyme have adopted this method of secreting oils as a means of protecting themselves against the ravages of plant - eating insects and mammals. Whatever be the reason, however, the fact remains the same that our per-fumers gain thereby.

IV

"GREEN MANTLE OF THE STANDING POOL"

THE DUCKWEED

FOR some time you have been looking at the green coating upon the surface of the pond, and you are eager to find out something about it.

Notice how the surface of the water is covered in dense masses by this minute floating plant. Shakespeare refers to this as the

"Green mantle of the standing pool."

The little plant which, when massed together, makes such a pretty green covering for our pond, is sometimes called Lemna, and you shall now learn how this name has come about. Here is the story.

Over two thousand years ago there lived in Greece—a mighty country in those days—a certain philosopher who, like Pliny and Aristotle, devoted a portion of his time and talent to the study of Natural History. This Grecian sage was Theophrastus, and he wrote a book on plants somewhere about B.C. 300.

This same Greek was acquainted with a certain water plant, and to this he gave the name of Lemna. For what reason, you may ask? Because it is believed that the name was probably suggested to Theophrastus by the little Island of Lemnos in the Ægean Sea, the island apparently reminding the Greek philosopher of a plant floating in the water.

Let us now examine this tiny plant, which even an eminent Greek scholar did not consider too small or too insignificant to notice.

It is the Duckweed, a minute floating plant which is able to multiply and increase at an enormous rate by a quick and plentiful production of off-shoots. It flowers but rarely, preferring to reproduce its kind by means of these off-shoots. It harbours many insects, and they and it are greedily devoured by Ducks.

Now of what service is this little plant to the pond and its inhabitants? The water is its home. There it flourishes abundantly, and has a definite task to perform.

During the heat of the Summer sun there is, of course, a large amount of evaporation from the surface of a pond, and, if it be a small one, it is usually dried up towards the end of August. In many cases, however, the " green mantle of the standing pool " protects the water and acts as a barrier against the sun's rays.

Fig. 11. A, Lesser Duckweed; B, Ivy-leaved Duckweed.

Then again, how grateful must be the cool shade of these tiny plants to the multitude of animals which disport themselves in the water beneath the green canopy. Have you not yourselves felt as grateful lying in the depths of some wood in Summer, watching the sunlight glinting on the leaves above?

Put a stick in the pond and make a division among the countless plants of Duckweed here congregated. See, no sooner has the stick been withdrawn than the plants all close up towards one another again, evidently firm believers in the motto that " Union is strength."

It has already been shown how certain plants keep the water pure in which they live, and the Duckweeds must be included among this number.

When the little plant has gone to seed in the Autumn, the fruits sink to the bottom of the water, and remain buried in the mud during the cold Winter months. In the Spring time they rise to the surface again, where the sunlight and warm breezes tempt them to germinate, and soon the pond presents an appearance similar to that of the preceding Summer.

V

MORE PLANTS IN THE POND

WATER CROWFOOT—CANADIAN PONDWEED—WATER LILIES

LET us move round to the further side of the pond, where we can see a most beautiful sight, like so many white and yellow stars peeping out from the dark surface of the water. What floral treasures are these? Procure a specimen, for no harm can be done by so doing, since the plant grows in great abundance.

You will have to exercise some amount of care and ingenuity in securing specimens of these water plants, for they are difficult to get out of the water in their entirety, even if not securely anchored in the bed of the pond. They appear to possess some power of adhering to their environment, as it were, and fight bravely against every effort to dislodge them from their watery home. There, now we have secured a fine specimen.

"How like a White Buttercup," you will probably remark, and you are not far wrong, for the Water Crowfoot, as it is called, belongs to the same family.

LARVA OF DRAGON FLY

DRAGON FLY JUST EMERGING

DRAGON FLY, Great Water Plantain (on left), Rushes,
and Water Crowfoot

Let us carefully examine the blossom. It consists of five white glossy petals, each of which has a yellow patch at the base; this mark is said to be a sign to the flies, bees, and beetles that honey is to be had within. The insects then visit the flowers in search of this nectar, and in so doing, carry the precious pollen from one blossom to another. You will find the five green sepals folded right back against the flower stalk.

Another interesting fact connected with the Water Crowfoot is its habit of raising its flowers well above the level of the surrounding water; this action is, of course, common to many such plants, and is necessary to ensure that the pollen shall have an opportunity of being scattered in all directions, either by the insect visitors recently referred to, or by the wind.

The leaves of this aquatic plant are sure to attract your notice, because those which float upon the surface of the pond Fig. 12. Water Crowfoot. are kidney-shaped, whilst those that grow lower down, and are accordingly submerged, are divided into fine hairs which are forked at the end. If the Crowfoot possessed heavy and entire leaves below, it would probably be much more easily wrenched from its moorings during storms and heavy winds. The submerged leaves, being finely cut up, permit the water to pursue its action, and the plant to be swayed to and fro without any undue violence.

The study of some of the members of the Buttercup family will amply repay any boy or girl, or even grown-up persons. The various changes in colour from yellow to red, the attempts of certain individuals to alter their number of petals and sepals, and of others to store up food in their underground roots, are all points worthy of close attention. One member of the Buttercup family has turned climber, and its sensitive leaf-stalks and scented flowers show great progression and almost reason.

A slight reference has already been made to American Pondweed. Very often it is spoken of as Canadian Water-weed, but either name will suffice. It has not always

Fig. 13. Canadian Pondweed.

Fig. 14. White Water Lily.

grown in this country, but a few pieces were brought from North America about seventy years ago, and since then it has spread all over England.

The stem is very brittle, and every piece broken off is capable of forming a new plant. New buds are continually being formed, and the plant is said to grow better here than in its native Canadian waters. So quickly does it form a dense, tangled mass, that in some canals and rivers it almost prevents boats and barges getting along. Water fowl, especially Swans, are said to be very fond of it. Fishes, too, eat it in large quantities.

If you have any Gold Fish in a tank, you cannot do

better than grow some of this weed in the water. It will
grow without soil, but will do best in a small flower pot
filled with earth and hidden among the rocks and stones at
the bottom of the tank. The Gold Fish will eat the tender
shoots with great relish, and this, with an occasional Blood-
worm, will serve for all the food they require.

The Water Lily is closely related to the Water Crowfoot,
and delights in making its home in stagnant or slowly-
running water. It is a perennial, that is to say, once it has
obtained a footing, it comes up regularly year after year.

Fig. 15. Yellow   Fig. 16. Seed vessel of   Fig. 17. Seed vessel
Water Lily.   Yellow Water Lily.   of White Water Lily.

There are two common kinds, the White and Yellow
Water Lilies, but many varieties have been introduced
which, although very pretty, do not strike one as being in
keeping with the surroundings of a pond in this country.
Both the white and yellow species may be sought for in
bloom during July and August, and present a delightfully
cool and refreshing appearance.

The leaves of both kinds are roundish and are all floating. There are no finely divided submerged leaves as in
the case of the Water Crowfoot. Some of the larger leaves
measure from five to ten inches across, and these are
attached to a long, round stem, which reminds one of

india-rubber, and which absolutely refuses to be dislodged from its anchorage.

The flowers of the White Water Lily rest on the water during the day and stand out prominently at such time. If, however, you were to visit our pond at nightfall, you would probably imagine that some one had stolen the flowers. But this would be a wrong explanation, for at the approach of night, the flowers droop or collapse, and sink beneath the surface, there to remain until the following morning.

The flowers of the Yellow Water Lily, which are of comparatively little beauty, do not rest upon the surface of the pond, but are raised by their stalks above it.

If ever you have an opportunity of looking at the seed vessel of the White Lily, note what a curious thing it is. Between its two outer coats is a layer of air, and this makes it buoyant, and able to float on the water. Thus it stands a chance of getting dispersed by the action of the wind.

But what is that small black and white bird which walks with measured tread over the leaves of the Lily, flicking his long tail as he goes? What bird is this that has the courage to trust itself on these floating green rafts? Let us follow and see for ourselves.

VI

BIRD LIFE OF THE POND

PIED WAGTAIL—MOORHEN—COOT—LITTLE GREBE—
MARSH TIT

THE black and white bird that is so sedately walking from
lily leaf to lily leaf is a Pied Wagtail, and is one of the
smallest birds that walk.

He visits the pond for the purpose of quenching his

Fig. 18. Pied Wagtail.

thirst—and birds are far more fond of drinking than many
people imagine—and in this respect it is interesting to keep
watch at a pond some hot Summer's day, and notice the
many kinds of birds which come to drink. The bird also
finds insect life abundant at the pond, and may be seen
running hither and thither after some winged denizen of
the air.

The Pied Wagtail, as you will have seen, is dressed in
black and white. It has a long tail, and delights in
moving it rapidly up and down. This, together with the
bird's active and lively disposition, and its black and white
plumage, cannot fail to attract attention.

c

There, the bird has now taken to flight. Hearken, do you hear his cheery alarm note? Something like " tisit, tisit, tisit," and not at all unlike one of the notes uttered by the Swallow when upon the wing.

Its nest is made of dry grass and moss, with an inner covering of wool and feathers, and may be found in the holes of a wall, or under bridges, or beneath the rock near a stream.

Fig. 19. Head and Foot of Moorhen.

Have you not noticed, every now and then, a sound something like " croo " or " crook "? The noise was made by a Moorhen as she hid among the rushes. Let us peep into the herbage round the pond, and see if we can find her nest.

Be on the look-out for the stump of a tree, or the low branches of a bush overhanging the water, for there the Moor or Water-hen dearly loves to make her home.

Come here on tip-toe and peer over the rushes, for there

sits the mother bird upon her nest. The latter is a sort of lightly-made rush-basket, and is quite flat, so much so that the female almost covers it as she sits upon it. In some instances it is found simply floating in the water, but the bird then takes the precaution to make a firmer foundation for the structure, so that, in the event of flood or a rise in the water, her home may be protected.

Note the bird carefully, for she sits perfectly still, thus allowing a good view of her. It will at once be seen that she is dark olive-brown, with the exception of a bright red forehead. The legs are greenish-yellow below and red above.

Now she has slipped off the nest and is playing hide-and-seek, " croo-ing " as she goes. Keep perfectly still, and she will come out into the open more, and then a few white feathers will be seen near the tail. Now

Fig. 20. Young Moorhen.

we can examine the nest. See, it is made of dry rushes and reeds, and is lined with finer portions of the same. Count the large eggs. How many are there? Eight. As the bird was sitting quite tight, those are probably all that will be laid, but ten or twelve are sometimes found.

Their colour, as you will note, is reddish-white or yellowish, blotched with orange-brown.

One day a Moorhen's nest was being photographed. It contained nine eggs, but before the photographer had time to get the camera in position, five of the eggs hatched, and the little black babies jumped straight into the water and swam beautifully during the first moment of their lives.

What a sudden transformation this must have been for them! One moment hidden in a shell, shut out from the world; the next swimming around our pond with all the confidence of the parent birds.

See, there is another bird at the far end of the pond. Is this also a Moorhen? No, it is a Coot, first cousin to the Moorhen, but to be at once distinguished by having a white patch on the forehead in place of the red.   The Coot

Fig. 21. Coot.

Fig. 22. Head and Foot of Little Grebe.

is a larger bird, too, measuring eighteen inches in length, and has slate-grey plumage on the upper parts and sooty-black underneath. There is, you will observe, a thin white bar across the wing, and the legs and feet are dark green.

The nest is somewhat similar to that of the bird we last discovered, but the eggs—as might be supposed—are larger, dingy stone-colour, and speckled with dark brown.

This pond is also just the very spot where we should find the Little Grebe, or Dabchick, as he is often called.

Let us take a quiet saunter round, keeping our eyes well

COMMON FROG

COMMON TOAD

FROG SPAWN

TOAD SPAWN

open so as to observe any movement taking place. Do you see anything?

You thought you did! Your eyes have not deceived you, for in the middle of the pool, there, sure enough, is a Little Grebe having a fine game, bobbing first under and then out of the water, for he is the most expert of divers.

There he is again; now he has gone. Is it not difficult to follow him, as he bobs up and down so quickly and so unexpectedly? It is really trying to our patience getting a good sight of the restless creature, but we are in no hurry, so wait and watch.

Now the Grebe has tired of his manœuvres and we can see him to more advantage. Notice that he has a dark brown head, neck, and upper parts; that he is greyish-white below; that his cheeks, throat, and sides of neck are reddish-chestnut, and that his bill is horn-coloured.

You cannot see his legs as they are hidden in the water. These are dull green in colour, and in shape as shown in the little sketch here given. It is as well, perhaps, that he stays in the water, for although he is a graceful swimmer, his movements on land are ungainly in the extreme.

Some country people call this bird Tom Pudding, but what relation he has, strictly speaking, to that useful article of diet, we do not pretend to know!

The nest is somewhat like that of the Moorhen, but is not so large. Nests are often found which apparently do not contain any eggs, but be careful Mrs Tom Pudding does not deceive you, for, like the Partridge we found in the hedge, she often covers the eggs over when leaving the nest.

The eggs are from four to six in number and are white when first laid. An idea of the shape may be gained from the accompanying sketch. The wet feet of the bird, and the stain from the damp herbage, soon soil the eggs and make them appear to be almost black.

The three kinds of birds we have been fortunate enough to see at the pond feed upon various herbage, as well as snails, worms, and insects. The Little Grebe is more particular, however, and partakes of larger fry as well, such as tadpoles, frogs, and fish.

If you ever hear the Grebe singing, don't take the bird too seriously, for its song has been compared to the creaking of a rusty hinge on a wooden gate.

Do you see that little grey bird with a black head creeping about the Willows, now hanging head downwards like a feathered acrobat?

Fig. 23. Nest and eggs of Little Grebe, showing Eggs about half natural size.

That is the Marsh Tit, a near relative of the Long-tailed Tit which we found in the hedgerow.

As we approach the bird more closely, we see that it has dull white cheeks, throat, and breast.

This active bird builds its nest in the holes of rotten tree stumps, usually in marshy places, and the homestead is made up of moss, wool, rabbit's fur, and down from the ripe catkins of the Willow. The eggs number from six to eight. They are quite small, and white in colour, faintly marked with red-brown.

We have now seen from these few birds how admirably the pond suits them for hiding, nesting, and feeding, and we must ever be on the look-out to discover why various animals—and remember this term includes all living things that are not vegetables—make their home in certain places.

VII

ANIMALS IN THE POND

WATER BOATMAN—WHIRLIGIG BEETLE—WATER SCORPION— GREAT BROWN WATER BEETLE—FRESH-WATER SHRIMP

As we pursue our operations, we shall find that not only do trees and smaller plants grow in and around the pond, and birds hide, nest, and feed among the vegetation, but, if we insert a net into the hidden depths underneath the green mantle, we shall bring to land a whole host of curious and interesting creatures.

Let us now use our net. You must be prepared for several failures before you are fortunate enough in landing the wished-for specimen; in fact, one whole day's fishing may only end in disappointment. Insert the net gently, work under and around the water plants, and then withdraw it. Look now at the many wonderful animals we have succeeded in catching!

Our first dip has been crowned with great luck. There is stock enough to start a small aquarium of our own. Some of the creatures wriggle, and seem much upset at being suddenly taken from their watery home; others are more sluggish in their movements.

We will now examine a few of our captives, and learn what we can concerning them. Here is a yellowish-brown insect with long, hairy hind-legs, and rejoicing in the name of Water Boatman. Its body is smooth and glossy, and if the wing-cases be lifted, the wings may be seen, for during the night it often takes to flight.

By means of its hind-legs this interesting pond creature " rows " through the water, using its limbs as oars, whilst floating on its back! Let us put him into the water again,

and watch him closely. See, his back is shaped in the centre somewhat like the keel of a boat.

Is not his body well suited for darting through the water? Notice, too, the fringe of hairs which clothe certain parts of his person ; when the insect arrives at the surface of the water, air bubbles get entangled among these hairs, and later on serve the Boatman for breathing purposes.

Fig. 24. A, Whirligig Beetle gyrating, and below enlarged ; B, Water Boatmen.

There he goes, wonderful little oarsman, rowing and floating, rowing and floating, until eventually he sinks below and is lost to view.

In reality he is a bloodthirsty monster, and preys upon the other inhabitants of the pond; he seizes these with his fore-legs, while he eagerly sucks out their juices.

Let us turn attention to our next specimen. What curious creature is this? It is the Whirligig Beetle, an insect about a quarter of an inch long, with a shining, dark bronze body.

We will now put the creature back into its element, for its movements can be plainly seen, since it is one of those insects which dwell upon the *surface* of the water and not below it. Notice that the Whirligig moves about in circles.

or curves, and that the specimen we were examining has now joined some of its comrades on the pond.

Quick of sight, this insect has eyes for seeing both above and below, each eye being divided in two by a sort of partition. With the upper eye the Whirligig can see objects above the surface of the water, and with the lower those objects beneath it. If we wished to catch our little friend again, we should have to be very quick, for it was only by accident the specimen we secured got into our net.

Let us try our hand! But remember they have the habit of giving off a most disgusting odour, which serves them as a protection. This is caused by a milky fluid which exudes from between the joints. There! The Whirligigs have all dived below the surface, carrying their air bubble with them. This they will do when-

Fig. 25. Larva of Water Scorpion.

ever they are scared, and will remain hidden until the danger is past. Search should sometimes be made for the yellow oval eggs, which are laid in parallel rows on the leaves of various water plants.

The next thing to attract our attention is a curious-looking insect, brown on the upper part of its body and red underneath. It is the Water Scorpion, and its slow, sluggish ways form a strong contrast to those of the Whirligig. Place it in this jar of water, and pay special attention to the two long processes which extend from the extreme tip of the abdomen.

These curious tail-like appendages form the breathing apparatus. When a fresh supply of air is necessary, the Water Scorpion comes near to the surface, puts out the tips of the breathing tubes, takes in a fresh supply of air, and then dives below again to pursue the ordinary course of its life.

By far the most active parts of the body are the two
long fore-legs, which somewhat resemble those of a Scorpion.
With these it seizes its prey, for which it will lay in wait
long and patiently.   Once it has captured some unfortunate
creature, it never leaves go until all the juices are sucked
from the body.   It can hold its own against nearly all

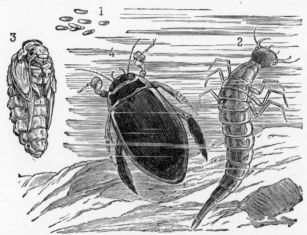

Fig. 26. Great Brown Water Beetle.
1. Eggs; 2. Larva; 3. Pupa; 4. Adult Insect (all natural size).

comers, and is even ready to try its strength against that of
a Stickleback.

But what is this handsome Beetle, oval in shape and
olive-brown in colour, which we have now succeeded in
capturing?   It is the Great Brown Water Beetle, one of
the worst cannibals of our pond and the " lord of water
insects."

We are fortunate in getting it, for this is a wary creature
and very quick, diving to the bottom at the first sign of

danger and remaining there, clinging to some stone or weed. If it did not do this it would be obliged to rise to the surface, for, being lighter than water, some sort of anchorage is required to enable the insect to keep below.

The margins of the middle part of the body and the wing-cases are marked with a yellow band, and when the Beetle opens its elytra, or wing-cases, and takes to flight, it presents a wonderful sight.

At night-time it often flies from one pond to another, but is somewhat unguarded in its movements, as it has been known to mistake a glass house for water, dash down upon the roof, and come to an untimely end.

It is a strong swimmer, and the oval shape of its body assists it in this respect. It captures its prey with amazing cleverness; this consists of small fish, tadpoles, and insects of various kinds, including its own kith and kin. That is why we called it a cannibal.

The female has her wing-cases furrowed, whilst those of the male are smooth. There are other differences which need not detain us here.

The female makes a slit in some water plant by means of a contrivance called an ovipositor or egg-placer, and then lays her eggs. These hatch in about a fortnight, and each larva will eventually be about two inches long. So voracious is this larva that it has been called the Water Tiger. It is dirty brown in colour, cylindrical in shape, and tapers gradually towards the head and tail. There are three pairs of legs, and these act as oars when the larva wishes to swim about. Near the end of the body are the spiracles or breathing holes, by the aid of which the rapacious larva respires atmospheric air.

If you see one of these Beetle larva be sure to notice the

terrible-looking jaws. By means of these it is able to secure and suck the juices of its captives.

Here is another tenant of our pond which, by reason of its shape, might be mistaken for the larva of the Great Brown Water Beetle by those unacquainted with the two animals. What, then, is it? It is the Fresh-water Shrimp.

Although very fond of a clear stream not fast-running,

this little creature also resorts to ponds, and if a handful of water plants be secured and shaken, a good specimen may fall out.

It will then be seen how curious its movements are, for the Shrimp lies on its side and then commences twisting or screwing in a very extraordinary way. This has resulted in the name of Fresh-water Screw being also given to this species.

Fig. 27. Fresh-water Shrimp.

This is one of the scavengers of our pond, for it feeds upon various kinds of waste matter, and helps to make the water pure. Fish are very fond of it, and eat it whenever they have the opportunity.

If kept in an aquarium with a Water Snail, the Shrimp will, on the death of the former, make a home of the Snail's shell.

From time to time the Shrimp sheds its horny case, and this is often mistaken for the living animal, in the same way as the shell of the Shore Crab.

The female carries her eggs underneath her body, and in this position the little ones remain some time after they are hatched. Dark-reddish is the usual colour of the parents, but in some waters the animals are quite black.

DEVELOPMENT OF FROG

1. Tadpole during early life.
2. Tadpole showing eyes and hind legs.
3. The same but more advanced.
4. Tadpole showing hind legs well formed.
5. The little frog is surely coming!
6. Tail almost disappeared.
7. The perfect little frog.

CRESTED NEWT

SMOOTH NEWT

VIII

THE DANDY OF THE INSECT WORLD

THE DRAGON-FLY

DURING the hottest days of Summer a number of different kinds of insects may be seen around our pool, darting through the air, or skimming over the surface of the water; chief among these is the dandy of the insect world, the Dragon-Fly.

Almost every one knows this glorious creature by sight, but few are aware what a really wonderful life-history is revealed, when one comes to inquire into its past.

There are nearly fifty species of Dragon-Flies in England alone, but whilst the young Nature-lover cannot hope to become acquainted with many of these, there are a few common sorts which may be found after a little searching.

The Dragon-Fly, it should be stated, is also known as the " Horse-Sting " or " Horse-Stinger," but it is quite a mistake to suppose that this insect can sting. It certainly looks very formidable as it skims through the air, and its large globular eyes add to its strange appearance, but it has no organ, excepting a strong pair of jaws, with which to " sting." When made captive, it attempts to reach with its tail the hand that has seized it. This may possibly account for the " stinging " theory.

It may also be that the male Dragon-Fly, when seen with the claspers situated at the end of the abdomen of its gaudily-attired body, does strike terror into the hearts of those who know not its habits, but when it is remembered that these claspers are used by the male Dragon-Fly for the purpose of carrying off a wife, the idea of its being able to sting must at once be dismissed.

The male seizes his lady-love round the neck with the claspers, and thus leads her away as his own. If the season be a favourable one, several pairs may be seen around our pond flying in all directions, and united in this manner.

These wonderful creatures—the Eagles of the insect world as we may also call them—are divided by naturalists into three sections.

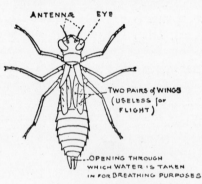

Fig. 28. Larva of Dragon-Fly.

The members of the first family may be recognised by their large and almost hemispherical heads, by their very large eyes, which meet on the forehead, and by their long and rather slender bodies. They keep the wings stretched out when at rest.

The members of the second family are very similar to those of the first group so far as concerns their head, eyes, and wings. The bodies, however, are generally broader, shorter, and flatter.

The commonest among this second class is perhaps the one known as the " Horse-Stinger." It is about two inches in length and has a broad, flat body. The male is covered with a beautiful violet-blue powder, whilst the female is yellowish-brown on the abdomen, with yellow spots upon the sides.

Those belonging to the third family of British Dragon-

Flies are the smallest, the most elegant, and the most
delicate-looking of all.

So graceful are these creatures that the French call
them and all their relatives " Demoiselles." The eyes are
separated from one another by a wide crown, the abdomen
is cylinder-shape, very slender, and flattened a trifle at
the end.

Both the first and second families extend their wings to
the fullest *when at rest*, in striking contrast to the members
of the third family, which place their wings close together.

Let us now, in imagination, follow the doings of a female
Dragon-Fly. She seeks out some silent pool and lays her
eggs, either singly or in bunches, in the water, or very close
to its edge.

Females have frequently been seen beating their tails
on the surface of the water in rapid succession, until the
eggs formed a mass like a bunch of minute grapes.

On some occasions the eggs may be found attached to
the stems of water plants, and sometimes, so it is said, they
are inserted by the females of some species in small holes
made in aquatic weeds by means of an instrument called
an ovipositor.

Again, a female Dragon-Fly has been seen to crawl
beneath the water, where she herself once made her home,
proceed along the stalk of a suitable plant, and then lay her
eggs.

When the egg hatches, the grub, or larva, is usually
dark brown, and there is good reason for this, as the larva's
body matches the mud in which it crawls about, and it is
thus protected from numerous enemies.

The Dragon-Fly larva is one of the most untiring hunters
among all water insects, and when it becomes a chrysalis

or pupa, its appetite and its ravenous disposition are still more noticeable. Yet it is interesting to notice that, although so greedy, the larva of this remarkable inhabitant of our pond has the power of fasting, and has been known to live for some considerable time in apparently perfect health without eating.

Let us insert our net and see if we can procure a larva for examination. Sweep well the bottom of the pond with the net, or insert a hook tied on to a stick or piece of cord, and fish out a tangled mass of weeds.

After many attempts we have at last secured a quantity

Fig. 29. Larva of Dragon-Fly.

Fig. 30. Pupa or Nymph of Dragon-Fly.

of pond weed of various kinds, and see how it is peopled by crawling creatures. We are fortunate in our haul, for here is a larva of a Dragon-Fly, in a great state of excitement because it has been so suddenly dragged from its watery home.

Now look at the picture opposite page 34 where you will see a photograph of our friend, and this will give you a good general idea what to look for when you go pond-dipping.

If several specimens are found, it will be noticed perhaps that they are not all alike. They will be seen to be of different shapes, sizes, and ages.

Some of them ought perhaps to be called pupæ rather than larvæ, because signs of wings can be seen in their cases. This shows us that these specimens have arrived at what is called their nymph stage, and before long they will leave their watery home and change to the perfect insect.

If we had been specially fortunate we might have had the rare luck of discovering among our weeds a larva belonging to each of the three families already discussed.

Here, perhaps, would be a strong and bold-looking animal with three pairs of legs, a formidable head, and prominent segments upon the body. This is the larva of the first family we referred to on page 58.

Another insect, which is very similar to the last, but of stouter and clumsier build, might next claim our attention.

Fig. 31. Larva of Dragon-Fly.

Fig. 32. Pupa or nymph of Dragon-Fly.

The eyes are smaller and further apart, the head is not so rounded, and the larva will sometimes be covered with various matter from the bed of the pond. This, then, is a representative of our second family.

We now come to the third family, and this larva will be found to be much slenderer than either of the last two, and instead of spine-like projections at the end of the body there will be seen some beautiful leaf-like appendages—often of great length. All these larvæ are alike, however, in their greediness, and if food is scarce they do not hesitate to eat one another.

You remember the spines we saw at the extremity of the bodies of the two larvæ belonging to the first and second families; these can be opened or shut as the creature

D

desires, and it is by means of these organs that water is drawn into the hinder part of the body. Then, by means of a breathing apparatus that is placed there, the larva extracts all the oxygen the water contains and discharges the remainder through the same opening by which it entered.

Sometimes the waste water is shot out quite gently, but at others a forceful expulsion is made. When this quick movement takes place, the body of the larva is driven through the water at great speed, and this is the only way it can propel itself along, except when crawling about at the bottom of the pond or among weeds.

The Dragon-Fly larva has a curious organ called a " mask." This partly covers the lower part of the head, and is a kind of insect-catching trap. This wonderful apparatus is so arranged as to be folded and hidden beneath the head. Fixed on to the tip there will be found a pair of strong curved hooks with teeth, and when the larva wishes to secure its prey, it rapidly thrusts out the " mask," and the victim is secured by means of the hooks.

The larva moults several times, and after each shedding of the old body-covering the wings increase in size; the latter, however, cannot be compared with the beautiful appendages of the adult Dragon-Fly.

At last the larva has—so we believe—a longing to leave its old home in the pond; it loses its voracious appetite, and commences to climb some aquatic plant or other object, which will aid it in its progress.

Having found a suitable resting-place, it clings securely to it by means of its claws, the head being held uppermost.

Soon after this a great change takes place, for the eyes become bright and clear, the old body-covering splits along the back, and the creature gradually extracts itself from its worn-out garment. The middle part of the body and the head are first to be seen coming out, and last of all the legs.

Thus, by much patience and care, the creature finds itself clear of its former covering, and if you turn to the picture opposite page 34 you will see exactly how the Dragon-Fly looks when it is thus free.

Then the insect rests; the body dries, and the wings are spread out and become ready for flight. At first the newly-emerged insect is in a most helpless condition, but fresh air and the sunbeams soon work wonders on the weak form. The wings expand and stiffen, and eventually the gorgeous creature finds itself able to fly through the air, capturing insects of other kinds as it proceeds.

The long abdomen permits it to turn and twist in the air in a remarkable way; the large round eyes, composed of some thousands of lenses or facets, help it to find its prey, and its powerful jaws aid it considerably in snapping at passing denizens of the air and tearing them to pieces.

Thus the Dragon-Fly, free from its watery home, seems to revel in its rapid flights; but courting, mating, and feeding, it only lives some three months as the perfect insect.

IX

MORE ANIMALS IN THE POND

FRESH-WATER WHELK—RAMSHORN SNAIL—HORSE LEECH —WATER SPIDER

SHALL we renew our search among the reeds and weeds, and see what further wonders the pond has to show?

Here, for instance, upon this large leaf is a quantity of spawn of the Fresh-water Whelk, which is well shown in the accompanying photograph, and below it are two of the animals themselves.

There are a large variety of Snails in our fresh waters—some very small, and others of a larger type—but few are more elegant than the Fresh-water Whelk, as it is called. The body is yellowish-grey in colour, tinged with bluish-green, and mottled with brown and white. The shell is about one and a half inches long, and greyish-white or yellowish horn-colour. There are from six to eight whorls, the house proper in which the creature lives being much larger than the smaller whorls towards the end.

Here is another Snail of an entirely different construction, the shell being flat-coiled, as may be seen by referring to the photograph facing page 74.

This is a handsome, hardy, and large species of Pond Snail, which may not inaptly be called the Ramshorn. Although found in slow-running or stagnant water, we are somewhat fortunate in discovering it upon our present expedition. The shell is yellowish-brown, usually paler on the lower side; sometimes, however, it is almost quite black.

This is the largest member of the family to which it belongs. It is not an active species, and, when irritated, has the habit of pouring forth a plentiful stream of red-coloured liquid. It crawls with a jerky sort of movement, and is fond of floating on the surface of the water. The body of the Ramshorn Snail is black above and slightly grey below.

The egg-capsules or clusters, as we may call them, are oval or roundish in form, and colourless; but occasionally they are of a pale pink colour. In each cluster from twelve to forty eggs are placed, and the young ones hatch in about fifteen days, according to the temperature of the water.

PERCH

TENCH

SPAWN OF FRESH-WATER WHELK

FRESH-WATER WHELKS

Many of our Snails, although they enjoy a meal off the fresh green pondweed, will live on the waste matter to be found in their neighbourhood, and therefore act as excellent scavengers.

What curious creature is this crawling about the plants still left in our net? It is a Horse Leech, and a very clear picture of it may be seen among our illustrations. This Leech is about four inches long and half an inch broad.

The body becomes rather wider towards the tail end; its mouth, as will be seen, has a protruding upper lip, and contains from eighty to ninety minute teeth with which it bites its prey before sucking the blood of the unfortunate creature. It is greenish-black above and yellowish-green underneath, and from time to time it casts this slimy outer coat. Although it looks strangely out of place stranded on the ground, yet, when in the water, it is a graceful swimmer, and may often be seen near the surface.

You would hardly expect to fish out a Spider from our pond, but that this has been done is plainly evident from the creature which is now disporting herself in our glass jar.

There are several kinds of so-called Water Spiders, so that it is necessary you should take careful heed of the species we have before us.

Like its relatives upon land, this is an interesting and intelligent creature. But, remember, it is *not* an insect, because, firstly, it has no division between its head and thorax; secondly, it has no antennæ or feelers; thirdly, it has four pairs of legs instead of three, and fourthly, its body is not divided into segments. Then, again, the Spider does not pass through the same stages as an insect, for when the eggs hatch, young Spiders are seen, not caterpillars or grubs.

Our true Water Spider is about half-an-inch long, and

is therefore rather a large species. It is dark reddish-brown in colour, with olive-brown on the abdomen. Of its

four pairs of legs the first and last are longer than the two middle pairs.

Now note the hairs on the back part of the body. " What purpose do these serve? " you may ask. They help to repel the water, and prevent the creature from getting wet, so that it may pursue its operations in the water without any harm or hindrance.

Fig. 33. Water Spiders and Nest.

Let us now place the Water Spider back in our jar. As its body is immersed, it will be observed that the hinder portion of it looks as if it were covered with silver. This is caused by the air bubbles, which have become entangled among the hairs.

Do you know that this industrious little animal constructs a wonderful nest under the water? This is how she does it. She selects an aquatic plant, and between the lower branches below water weaves a web. When the web is completed, the Spider goes to the surface, puts the end of its body out of the water, and then, by means of a quick motion, it obtains a bubble of air. This it holds between the hind part of its body and its crossed hindermost legs.

Down into the water goes the Spider with its precious burden, and having reached its web, discharges the air bubble within it. Many more such journeys are undertaken, until at last the little nest is filled with air and looks something like a lady's thimble. When making these journeys the Spider runs like a little steeple-jack up and down a thread, which it has taken the precaution to erect between its nest and the surface of the water.

In this beautiful little home Mrs. Spider spends most of her time, but when the hour arrives for egg-laying, she either makes the nest larger, or builds a new one. Mr. Spider often builds a nest of his own, not far from his industrious little wife.

The eggs are enclosed in a sort of cocoon, and then fastened inside the nest. In about fourteen days the young Spiders make their appearance, and no sooner have they left their home than they commence to build little nests of their own, and fill them with air in the manner already described.

These interesting creatures feed upon various animals, not only those found in the water, but those which dwell on land too, and will often leave their watery fastness for this purpose.

X

AMPHIBIANS IN THE POND

FROG—TOAD—NEWTS

So many people shudder at the sight of a Frog that one would imagine the poor creature was poisonous. Let it be stated at once that Frogs, Toads, and Newts are quite harmless. Indeed they are very useful creatures, living for the most part upon injurious insects. In spite of stupid legends, they can neither " sting," " spit," nor " bite." Toads haven't any teeth wherewith to do this, so that you need not in future pay any heed to such ridiculous fables.

A most curious sight is to watch a Frog when feeding. Its tongue is fixed to the middle part of the lower jaw, but is quite free behind. Thus the tongue can be easily " shot out " of the mouth almost to its full length, and woe betide the luckless insect that comes within its reach!

This pond of ours is a very favourite resort of all three animals, and during the Spring one may spend some very happy days in Frog, Toad, and Newt-lands.

The life of one species answers fairly well for all three, and the several pictures of these amphibians will give a splendid idea of how they start life, how they develop, and what they look like when they are grown up.

Now what is an amphibian, or amphibious animal? Be careful how you apply the word. A Duck, for example, is not an amphibian. An amphibian is an animal which, like the Frog, Toad, and Newt, spends the first part of its life entirely in the water and takes to the land when its transformation is complete.

During the Summer—and especially when there has been a shower of rain—you may meet with a Newt along a roadway, but, generally speaking, it is a much greater lover of water than either the Frog or Toad, except when the latter are spawning. The Frog and Toad, however, are met with in many different places, and at a long distance from water.

In the two pictures shown opposite page 47, you will see very clear illustrations of the spawn of the Frog and the Toad. You will notice that the spawn of the former is laid in a mass, whereas that of the latter is laid in long chains. When first laid the eggs are quite small, but they soon swell when in the water, and at last the globules of jelly are about the size of a pea. As many as two thousand eggs have been known to have been laid by one Frog.

The little dark brown speck in the centre of the jelly-

like substance is the true egg, the covering around protecting it from enemies, helping it to float at the surface, so
that the sun may aid in hatching; the jelly also prevents
overcrowding of the eggs.

Now the Newt is much more particular as to her eggs
than either the Frog or the Toad, for she wraps each one
carefully in the leaf of some water-plant by means of her
hind-legs.

The egg is quite small, and is surrounded by a gummy
substance. Sometimes the mother Newt will take the leaf
and egg in her mouth
and then give them a
grip, so as to make the
precious contents more
secure.

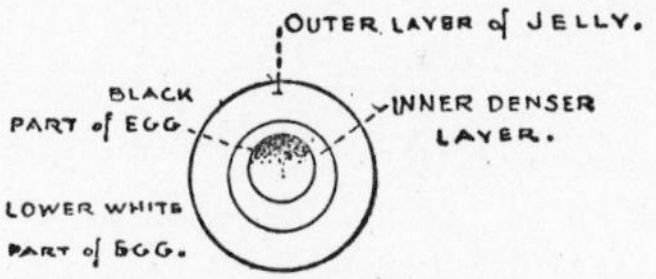

As the little one

Fig. 34. Egg of Frog.

within hatches and begins to grow, so the leaf unfolds,
until, at last, the young Newt comes forth as a Tadpole,
and is free.

During the breeding season the male Newt is ornamented with a very fine crest along its back.

Sometimes Newts are mistaken for Lizards, but a careful
examination will prove that there is an enormous difference between them. Newts, for example, have no scales
on their body, and no nails on their toes, whereas Lizards
are covered with scales and have their nails strongly developed. Then again, the flattened tail of the Newt, so
useful in swimming, is in strong contrast to the rounded
tail of the Lizard.

To return to the eggs of the Frog and Toad. Having
distinguished one from the other, next look at the series of
photographs shown opposite page 54, and there you will

see a fairly complete life-history in pictures of the Frog, and
these will serve also for the Toad.

It should be pointed out, however, that before the little
Tadpole—as it is known to most people—appears, it passes
through various changes, and you should carefully note
these for yourselves by keeping some spawn in a jar of fresh
water placed near the light and supplied with a sufficient
quantity of pondweed. The Toad Tadpole is darker than
that of the Frog, whilst that of the Newt
retains, instead of loses, its tail.

It is interesting to notice that when
in the Tadpole stage, these animals breathe
like a fish by means of gills. After a time,
however, a great change takes place both
within and without the little creatures;
they must surely for many days wonder
whatever is going to happen to them next.

Fig. 35. Newt Tad-
poles. A, Legs un-
developed; B, Fore
legs developed; c,
Fore and hind legs
developed.

The tail of each is absorbed within the
body; the little legs appear; the gills dry up; a great change
takes place inside; and at last the animal comes to land,
and is then found to breathe by means of lungs, just like an
ordinary being, although it can still respire by means of
its skin.

Have you ever considered what respiration really is?
Why do we breathe, and why cannot we live without air?

The great object of all this is to purify the blood, and
" it matters little whether the blood vessels are spread out
on the walls of a lung which is open to the outer world, or
on the large surface of a feathery gill which is washed by
water, or in the moist skin." What does matter is that the
blood shall have regular opportunities of absorbing oxygen
and throwing off carbon dioxide; this constitutes respiration.

Even when grown up the Frog is a fine swimmer, but the Toad, although an expert climber, is a much more sluggish creature, more ungainly in its movements, preferring to crawl rather than hop; although very useful as a destroyer of insects, it does not appeal to one so much as the active Frog.

The latter is smaller and much more brightly coloured than its slow-moving relative, which, in its turn, possesses shorter and thicker legs, a more wrinkled and wartier skin, and a more bulldog-like head. Another point of difference is that the Toad prefers the night, and becomes more active as the daylight wanes.

Have you ever seen a Toad swallow its skin? If not, you have a curious sight in store. One was recently watched in Covent Garden market. The poor old warrior was most upset because his old body-covering would not slip off easily, but at last his efforts were rewarded—slow but sure being an excellent motto. It is said that he then partook of a meal by swallowing his old coat. This accomplished, he moved across to another side of the glass aquarium in which he was kept, and went to sleep. We wonder what his dreams were like?

One of the prettiest sights of all in Frog-land is to come across an army of little Frogs, which have just left their watery home, and are commencing to migrate and distribute themselves over the surrounding country.

Some of the little fellows are no larger than one's smallest finger-nail; yet they all keep together in one large battalion, like the well-disciplined soldiers of the King's own army.

XI

FISHES IN THE POND

PERCH—TENCH—ROACH—PIKE

How quickly the time has passed during our pilgrimage round the pond we have been visiting! How much and yet how little we have seen and heard! Doubtless many things have escaped our notice, for we have been able to peep at just a few only of the countless creatures which go to make up this Nature community.

It would ill become us, however, if we left the water without learning something about its fish-life. When we were examining the pond earlier in the day, you must have surely noticed how we espied some fish sunning themselves near the top of the water.

You will probably wonder how any fish could get into this isolated pond, and this has often caused others similar thought. Sometimes we find fish have been placed in ponds by their owners; in other cases, however, places that are low-lying are swamped in flood time, and some fish from a neighbouring river get into the deep holes, and when the waters subside the scaly visitors find themselves stranded.

Let us first of all pay attention to the Perch.

This is a handsome species, with bright red fins, a beautiful bronze-green body, shading into yellow on the sides. It is also banded with a darker colour, and possesses a very prickly dorsal fin along the back. It usually goes about in shoals, feeding on insects, worms, small fish of other kinds, young water-birds, and water voles.

In May search should be made among the reeds for the

COMMON HORSE LEECH

RAMSHORN SNAIL

ROACH

PIKE

spawn. These minute eggs are laid in long strings during the Spring, and are attached to the water-weeds.

This fish attains a weight of seven or eight pounds, but a specimen turning the scale at three or four pounds may be looked upon as a good one.

It is a voracious feeder, and one that affords much sport to the angler, being very powerful, and making a bold bid for liberty when caught with rod and line.

The Tench, which belongs to the Carp family, simply revels in mud; in fact, it rests there during the Winter months; it is therefore quite at home in our little sheet of water. When taken from a muddy pool and put into clear fresh water, one can hardly recognise it as the same fish, so bright and trim has it become.

It is dark green in colour, and whitish on the under parts. It will, like the Eel, live for quite a long time out of water, and can exist for many hours in wet moss. It feeds on insects of various kinds, as well as vegetable matter.

The scales upon the Tench are very small; it is slimy to the touch, has two barbels, or small fleshy threads, at the corner of the mouth, and a flattish tail, which is not forked.

We find the Roach—and indeed all four fish upon our list—in the stream as well as in the pond, and this may add weight to the theory as to how the pond obtained its fish population. The Roach, which is also a member of the Carp family, is a common and very beautiful fresh-water fish.

It is dark blue or green on the upper parts, lighter on the sides, and silver below. The lower fins are red. It lives mostly upon insects and small molluscs, or minute shellfish, and attains a weight of some three pounds. The angler, however, who lands a fish weighing two pounds, considers he has obtained a prize.

Did you notice just now a splash made in the water? If you had looked in the direction from whence the noise proceeded you would have seen a fish darting away at full speed. It was a Pike, and the voracious creature had just made a dart at a small shoal of Roach, which were at the top of the water sunning themselves.

Well, the Pike, what of him, cunning fish that he is?

He is one of the monarchs of our little pond, and whenever he moves through the water, many of the smaller animals are terrified beyond measure, and make haste to escape before being gobbled up. The little Tadpole, the water insects we have seen, the baby Moorhens, and many other inhabitants, very often only just escape with their lives when Master Pike is particularly hungry and does not much mind what he has for breakfast.

He has also been known to seize young Ducks, Water Voles, various kinds of water fowl, and even the head of a large Swan. This latter resulted in the death of both the bird and the monster fish, for the bird's head and neck choked the fish, and the fish strangled the bird. Both were eventually secured, still firmly grasped in one another's clutches. It is, therefore, easy to understand why the Pike is sometimes described as the River or Water Wolf.

A young Pike is called a Jack, and there are several little ones in our pond. They may often be seen quite motionless—just passing the hours away in sheer idleness. At times it is quite difficult to rouse the sluggish creatures from their dulness, but it is quite another tale when Master Jack is hungry, and his hunting expeditions cause much commotion.

MADE AT THE TEMPLE PRESS LETCHWORTH IN GREAT BRITAIN

CALENDAR AND NOTES

OF

ANIMALS AND PLANTS

COMPILED BY C. S. COOPER, F.R.H.S.

I. AMPHIBIANS

COMMON FROG.—*Body :* broad and flat; length 3 inches; skin greenish-yellow or reddish-brown with dark spots, toning with its surroundings, smooth, moist, cast in pieces and swallowed; teeth in upper jaw; hind legs long. *Eggs :* laid in a mass. *Larva or tadpole :* hind legs appear first. *Food :* insects, slugs, worms, snails. *Habits :* walks, leaps and swims; passes the Winter in a torpid state in the mud under water; lives 12–15 years.

COMMON TOAD.—*Body :* broad and squat; skin usually a livid grey, spotted with brown and yellow, puffed out, especially underneath, glandular warts secreting an acrid juice, cast and swallowed; no teeth; hind legs not much longer than front ones, only slightly webbed. *Eggs :* laid in a string. *Larva or tadpole :* resembling that of Frog. *Food :* insects, worms and snails. *Habits :* hops and crawls; seldom takes to the water; hybernates in holes and under stones; lives to a great age.

EDIBLE FROG.—Found in the East of England. *Body :* resembling Common Frog in general shape; length 3 inches; skin greenish, somewhat warty; head triangular, eyes prominent, male with a globular sac on each side of head; hind feet very much webbed. *Habits :* croaking much louder and more musical than that of Common Frog, being produced by the globular sacs placed near the angle of the mouth.

GREAT WATER NEWT.—Also called Crested or Warted Newt. *Body :* long and narrow; length nearly 6 inches, of which tail constitutes about one half; skin usually blackish or olive-brown with darker circular spots above, rough and warty, yellow or orange-red with black spots of marbling beneath, sides speckled with white, cast in pieces and eaten; jaws furnished with minute teeth; male when mature has a beautiful serrated crest along the back and tail. *Eggs :* laid singly, wrapped in the leaves of a growing water-plant. *Larva or tadpole :* resembling tadpole of frog and toad; fore legs first developed. *Food :* insects, frog spawn and smaller Newts. *Habits :* takes three years to come to maturity; after that passes much of its time on land, preferring moist situations, such as a damp cellar, hybernating in Winter; in Spring of third year the male develops the serrated crest, and the colours on its body are very brilliant, this lasting for about three months.

NATTERJACK TOAD.—*Body :* length 3 inches; skin yellowish or olive-brown, with a bright yellow line along the middle of the back; eyes prominent; hind limbs short, toes not much webbed. *Habits :* prefers dry spots; can run quickly and climb well.

PALMATED NEWT.—*Body :* length 3 inches; skin marbled with olive-grey and white, head speckled with black, female usually paler; hind feet slightly webbed; male with a straight crest edged with black in the breeding season.

SMOOTH NEWT or EFT.—*Body :* length 4 inches; skin light brownish-grey, inclining to olive on upper parts, the under parts being yellowish; both sexes are spotted, and the male becomes orange coloured beneath in Spring; male with a continuous crest; two patches of pores on the head. *Habits :* both adults and young are fond of wandering about on land, often finding their way into damp cellars.

II. BIRDS

COOT.—In England all the year round. *Male bird :* general colour above cindery-grey with a slight olive shade on the back; under surface slaty-grey; bill pale lavender with pinkish tint; frontal shield ivory-white; length 14½ inches. *Female :* similar to male; length 14 inches. *Nest :* April onwards; in the shallow water near the edge; flags, reeds, rushes, on a foundation of reeds below the water. *Eggs,* 7–10, dingy stone-colour, speckled and spotted with dark brown. *Food :* worms, small fish, and young shoots of water-plants. *Call-note :* clear-ringing, often repeated, like " crew " or " kew."

LITTLE GREBE or DABCHICK.—In England all the year round. *Male bird :* general colour above sooty black, with slight greenish gloss; cheeks, throat and sides of neck chestnut; bill black with yellowish tip; legs and feet olive-green; length 8½ inches. *Female :* similar to male; length 8 inches. *Nest :* March to July or August; generally a mass of reeds and water-plants floating on the surface; sometimes in shallow water with a foundation of weeds. *Eggs* 4–6, bluish-white when laid, but soon becoming stained a dirty yellow. *Food :* tadpoles, frogs, fish and water-insects. *Call-note :* likened to a stick being drawn across a rail.

MARSH TIT.—In England all the year round; also some visitors on the East coast in Winter. *Male bird :* general colour above ruddy brown; crown blue-black; cheeks white; sides buff; length 4½ inches. *Female :* similar in size and colour. *Nest :* end of April and on to June; in holes of tree-stumps; moss, wool, hair and willow down. *Eggs* 6–8, white, thickly spotted with red and reddish-brown. *Food :* principally insects and their larvæ; also fruit, seeds, buds, and fat when suspended from a tree in the garden. *Song :* a constant " che-chee," " tzit, tzit," with a shrill " cheep," and a metallic " twink."

MOORHEN.—A resident all the year round. *Male bird :* general colour above dark olive-brown; head and neck slaty-grey; sides of body streaked with white; frontal shield and part of bill deep lake-red, tip greenish-yellow; legs olive-green, garter lake-red; length 12½ inches. *Female :* similar in colour, but with flank streaks not so broad; length 11½ inches. *Nest :* March to August; among reeds or rushes near or in the water, sometimes on an over-hanging branch, or even in a high branch of a tree; dry rushes and reeds, lined with dry grasses and sedges. *Eggs,* usually 7–9; reddish-white, sparingly spotted and speckled with reddish-brown. *Food :* worms, insects and seeds. *Call-note :* a deep " crr-o-ok-crr-o-ook."

PIED WAGTAIL.—In England all the year round, but many leave the country in the Winter. *Male bird :* Summer plumage: black above; throat and fore-neck black; breast and abdomen white; sides ashy-grey; Winter plumage: back grey; throat white, with black band across the fore-neck; length 7¼ inches. *Female :* resembling male, but not so black; body a dingy grey, mottled with black feathers; length 6⅘ inches. *Nest :* April onwards; in holes in walls, roofs of buildings, stacks, and crevices of every description; grass, roots and moss, neatly lined with hair, feathers and wool. *Eggs* 4 or 5, bluish-white or stone-grey, speckled with purplish-brown, often resembling those of House-Sparrow. *Food :* entirely of insects. *Call-note :* a sharp chirp resembling " chiz-zit "; song a hurried warble.

III. FISH

PERCH.—*Body :* broad, somewhat flattened laterally; dorsal fin spiny. *Colour :* bronze-green, shading to yellowish or golden-white on sides; 5–7 dark transverse bands on back; lower fins and tail bright red. *Weight :* up to 8 lbs., average 2–3 lbs. *Eggs :* about 250,000; laid in May; in a band-like mass on leaves of aquatic plants or roots of trees not far below the surface of the water. *Food :* principally young fish, worms and insects. *Habits :* a very voracious feeder; fights hard for liberty when caught.

PIKE.—*Body :* long, flattened on the back, tapering abruptly towards the tail; teeth very numerous, and exceedingly sharp-pointed; length of body 4–6 feet. *Colour :* green and brown above, lighter on sides, white below; fins and tail reddish brown. *Weight :* up to 60 lbs.; average 15–25 lbs., small specimens (2–4 lbs.) are called Jack. *Food :* fish, frogs, water-voles, water-fowl. *Habits :* the most voracious and destructive of fresh-water fishes, devouring with avidity anything that comes in its way; lies suspended in water perfectly motionless till its prey is within reach; has been known to live for over 260 years.

ROACH.—*Body :* somewhat plump; average length about 10 inches. *Colour :* dark blue or green on upper parts, lighter on the sides, and silver below; lower fins red. *Weight :* up to 3½ lbs., average 1–2 lbs. *Food :* insects and water-snails. *Habits :* nibbles at a baited hook in a very delicate manner.

TENCH.—*Body :* short and thick; slimy to the touch; small barbels at corner of mouth; dorsal fin without spines; tail flattish, not forked. *Colour :* dark green; whitish below. *Weight :* up to 12 lbs., average 5–8 lbs. *Food :* insects and young shoots of water plants. *Habits :* loves the mud; lies buried in it during the Winter, sunk in a deep torpor.

IV. INSECTS

DEMOISELLE DRAGON-FLY.—June–August. *Male :* body very slender, 1½ ins. long, deep blue; wings with black patches, expanding 2 ins., raised when at rest. *Female :* body and wings green. *Larva* and *pupa* (*nymph*) live in water and feed on aquatic insects and their larvæ. *Food* of Dragon-fly consists principally of insects.

GOAT MOTH.—June and July; may be found resting on tree-trunks and palings. *Wings :* pale brown, clouded with whitish, with wavy irregular lines. *Male :* expanding 2¾ inches. *Female :* expanding 3¾ inches. *Eggs :* July. *Larva :* pinkish, inclining to reddish-brown on back; head small, black and glossy, lives in wood of Willows, Poplars, Ash and other trees; takes 3 to 4 years to mature; when full grown is 4 inches long; has disagreeable smell, something like that of he-goat. *Pupa :* 1½ inches long; cocoon made of decayed wood; empty pupa-case somewhat resembling a lobster.

GREAT BLACK WATER BEETLE.—*Male :* 1¾ ins. long; wing cases (elytra) blackish-olive with margin of bluish tinge. *Female :* very similar to male. *Eggs :* 50–60 in a turnip-shaped silken cocoon fastened to the stem of a water-plant. *Larva :* body 3 ins. long, very fat, dusky in colour; feeds on snails and insects. *Pupa :* in an oval cocoon in the soft bank. *Food* of Beetle mainly vegetable matter.

GREAT BROWN WATER BEETLE or PLUNGER.—Nearly all the year round, hybernating in Winter. *Male :* 1¼ ins. long; wing cases olive-brown, almost black, with yellow margin, smooth; first and second pairs of legs armed with suckers. *Female :* wing cases dark brown with duller yellow margin, furrowed. *Larva :* body 2 ins. long, tapering, yellowish brown; head large, armed with powerful hollow jaws for sucking juices of snails, larvæ, etc. *Pupa :* resting as a chrysalis in the soft bank. *Food* of Beetle consists of insects, worms, small fish, etc.

GREAT DRAGON - FLY. — June – August; usually found near streams. Length 3 ins.; body and thorax marked with stripes of golden-yellow; wings expanding 4 ins., extended when at rest, each with a dark spot on the outer edge; three simple eyes set in a row. Life-history as in Demoiselle.

HORSE-STINGER.—April–November. *Male :* length $1\frac{7}{8}$ ins.; body broad and flattened with delicate bluish tint; wings expanding $3\frac{1}{4}$ ins., extended when at rest, each with a dark spot on the outer edge, and a large chestnut-brown spot at the base; simple eyes set in a triangle. *Female :* body yellowish-brown with yellow spots on sides. Life-history as in Demoiselle.

WATER-BOATMAN.—$\frac{3}{4}$ inch long, wing cases yellowish-brown, smooth and glossy. *Eggs :* laid on water-plants. *Larva* and *pupa* resembling the perfect insect in outward form. *Food :* aquatic insects, the juices being sucked from the victim by means of a strong beak.

WATER SCORPION.—Body $\frac{7}{8}$ inch long, flat and leaf-like, wing cases blackish-brown; two bristle-like filaments at end of body; first pair of legs used for seizing prey. *Eggs :* oval, with seven horn-like projections arranged in a circle at the base, and bending backwards so as to form a circle of hooks around the upper end of the egg. *Food :* aquatic larvæ, from which juices are sucked.

WHIRLIGIG BEETLE.—$\frac{1}{4}$ inch long, wing cases blue-black with greenish margin. *Larva :* resembling a Centipede in appearance; body one inch long, dirty-white, head armed with powerful jaws; six long legs, and long slender filaments from the body-segments. *Pupa :* in a small grey cocoon on a water-plant above the surface. *Eggs :* yellow, oval, in parallel rows on a water-plant. *Food :* principally small flies, beetles and other insects.

V. MISCELLANEOUS

FRESH-WATER SHRIMP.—*Body:* dark-reddish, $\frac{1}{2}$ inch long; seven pairs of thoracic legs. *Eggs:* carried by female under her body. *Food:* waste matter (carrion of the pond). *Habits:* swims on its side when in the water; young brood follow the parent about; horny case shed several times.

FRESH-WATER WHELK.—*Shell:* thin, greyish-white, horn or brown-coloured; spiral, elongated, $1\frac{1}{2}$–2 inches long, whorls 7 or 8, body whorl occupying nearly $\frac{3}{4}$ of the shell, spire acute, mouth oval, large. *Body:* yellowish grey, tinged with bluish-green, mottled with brown and white; two tentacles with eyes at base; about 110 rows of minute teeth, about 12,000. *Food:* vegetable matter and refuse, rather preferring animal substances. *Habits:* occasionally rises to the surface to breathe, gliding along foot uppermost, at times suspended by a glutinous thread, after the fashion of a Spider.

HORSE LEECH.—*Body:* about 4 inches long, $\frac{1}{2}$ inch broad; greenish-black above, yellowish-green underneath; consists of a number of rings; jaws comparatively blunt, only able to cut through soft mucous membrane; slime oozes from little round pockets in sides of body; blood is red. *Eggs:* laid in cocoons of gummy slime in holes and clay of the banks. *Food:* the juices of snails, grubs, and fish. *Habits:* is a graceful swimmer; casts its slimy coat from time to time; derives its name from the fact that it attaches itself to the mucous membrane of the mouth in horses whilst drinking; hybernates in mud during Winter.

RAMSHORN SNAIL.—*Shell:* reddish-brown, glossy, nearly opaque; flat-coiled, $\frac{1}{2}$–1 inch diameter, whorls 5 or 6, mouth semilunar. *Body:* black above, slightly grey below; foot short, oval; tentacles two, slender, eyes at their inner bases. *Eggs:* laid in oval or roundish clusters of 12–40, colourless or pale pink. *Food:* mainly vegetable matter. *Habits:* crawls with a jerky movement; floats on surface of water; pours out a purple fluid when irritated.

WATER SPIDER.—*Body:* $\frac{1}{2}$ inch long, dark reddish-brown, abdomen olive-brown, hairy. *Eggs:* 100 or more in a silken cocoon inside dome. *Web:* dome-shaped, made of silk, filled with air. *Food:* water insects.

VI. TREES AND FLOWERING PLANTS

Name.	Time of Flowering.	Colour.	Height.
Alder . . .	Mar. April	Male catkins, red; female catkins, reddish brown	Tree
White Poplar . .	,, ,,	Catkins, red	,,
Black Poplar . .	,, ,,		,,
Sallow . . .	April May	Male catkins, golden; female catkins, greenish	,,
White Willow . .	,, ,,	Greenish	,,
Water Crowfoot . .	May—Aug.	White	Floating
Flowering Rush . .	June July	Rose-pink	3–4 ft.
Branched Bur-reed .	,, ,,	Greenish	2–4 ft.
Ivy-leaved Duckweed .	,, ,,	,,	Floating
Water Forget-me-not .	,, —Aug.	Blue	12–18 ins.
Water Plantain . .	,, — ,,	Purpled-pink	2–3 ft.
White Water Lily .	July ,,	White	Floating
Yellow Water Lily .	,, ,,	Yellow	,,
Lesser Duckweed .	,, ,,	Greenish	,,
Pink Persicaria . .	,, —Oct.	Pink	1–2 ft.
Water Mint . .	Aug. Sept.	Lilac	1–4 ft.

THE WOOD I KNOW.

THE
WOOD I KNOW

EDITED BY

W. PERCIVAL WESTELL, F.L.S.
& HENRY E. TURNER

*General Secretary of the School
Nature Study Union*

WITH
12 COLOURED

& MANY BLACK AND WHITE
ILLUSTRATIONS

J. M. DENT AND SONS LTD.
BEDFORD ST. LONDON W.C.2
TORONTO VANCOUVER
MELBOURNE WELLINGTON

" If thou art worn and hard beset
With sorrows, that thou wouldst forget,
If thou wouldst read a lesson, that will keep
Thy heart from fainting and thy soul from sleep,
Go to the woods and hills! No tears
Dim the sweet look that Nature wears."

LONGFELLOW.

PRINTED IN GREAT BRITAIN

CONTENTS

LIST OF ILLUSTRATIONS

COLOURED PLATES AND HALF-TONES

ILLUSTRATIONS IN THE TEXT

THE WOOD I KNOW

I.—INTRODUCTION

ANCIENT WOODS—THE VALUE OF TREES—ARBOR DAYS—
TRANSPIRATION—THE SILENCE OF THE WOODS

As we wander through the countless streets of our crowded cities, we can scarcely realise that ages ago Britain possessed enormous woods, and that her people lived and hunted and fought in the dark recesses of those ancient forests.

There the Druids performed their mystic and often cruel rites, for they deemed it an insult to their gods to enclose their sacred altars in buildings erected by man; the forest was therefore their temple, and a rough unhewn stone their altar. Each wood had its special god, to whom prayers were offered and sacrifices made.

How different is the England of these modern days! Great belts of forest land have been cleared, and where once the sturdy Oak and stately Beech reigned supreme, we now find rich pasture lands and fields of waving corn.

Much the same kind of thing is at present going on in Canada, for history is ever repeating itself. The early settlers found themselves in a land of trees; civilisation had taught them the need of cattle and the necessity of corn; thus the woods have been supplanted by farms, and the ring of the axe has given place to the swish of the plough.

" But the axe was laid at the roots of the trees with a vengeance, and the forests were felled without any regard to the future; present necessity was the sole thought in the minds of the early settlers." Men are now wiser, and although the impossibility of living in an endless wood is self-apparent, yet it is generally admitted that " when we plant a tree, we are doing what we can to make our planet a more wholesome and happier dwelling-place for those who come after us, if not for ourselves."

Are you satisfied with this bald statement, or do you require an explanation? Well, the reason is not far to seek. The carbon dioxide exhaled by animals, and which to them is nothing less than poison, is inhaled by plants and forms part of their natural food. This silent machinery of Nature is ever in motion, and by it the atmosphere of our planet is purified. Thus there exists a kind of co-operation between animal and plant, the one being dependent upon the other.

Then, again, treeless areas are not suitable for the retention of moisture, so necessary for the nourishment of vegetation; the rain that falls on these areas either flows away quickly, because it meets with no resistance, or is rapidly evaporated; whereas, forest lands, rendered porous by the roots which pierce the soil, and shaded by the foliage, are far more retentive.

Then we must not forget the great commercial importance of our trees. Many of our trades are practically dependent upon the supply of suitable timber; thoughtful men therefore view with alarm the wholesale disappearance of forests, and the lack of provision made for replanting them. In order to solve this problem, various governments and societies are engaged in the work of re-afforestation, and the encouragement of Arbor or Tree Planting Days. Londoners have only to travel as far as Hainault, near Epping, to see for themselves this most interesting experiment, which has been in full swing since 1903.

So much then for forests in general; now let us deal with our wood in particular. Have you ever approached it on a hot Summer's day, when the dusty glaring roads threw back the heat, so pitilessly pouring down upon them? Have you experienced the refreshing influence of the trees even before you reached their grateful and welcome shade? One might almost have imagined that the strong branches had become huge fans, and were cooling the air for the sake of perspiring humanity.

Yet the explanation is simple enough! The trees take in moisture by means of their roots, and the flow of the sap is upwards towards the leaves. The latter possess countless tiny pores or stomata, which open under the genial influence of light and heat, and from their minute mouths the superfluous water escapes in the form of vapour. This process is known as Transpiration, and it is this which cools the air, and the effect is felt even beyond the borders of the wood.

Then as we enter the wood, with its dim subdued light, with here and there a shaft of golden sunshine making its way between the leafy arches, with the irregular, far-stretching aisles wandering between the stately columns of giant trees, can we not imagine we stand in one of Nature's vast Cathedrals? Indeed, we are told it was here our first architects obtained their ideas, and merely reproduced in stone what first they had learned to love in Nature.

There is no better plan, when penetrating into the heart of a wood, than to remain perfectly silent for several minutes. Gradually there dawns upon you the fact that the place teems with life; and the countless sounds, that charm the ear or arouse the wonder, will make you yearn to know something of the creatures from whom these sounds proceed. Noise tends to silence the inmates of a wood, for they are easily frightened, and, unlike human beings, desire to see rather than be seen. Their chief aim is to keep out of sight, and remain unobserved, for therein lies safety and protection from enemies which surround them on all sides.

II.—DECIDUOUS TREES

OAK—BEECH

How do you propose to study the trees beneath whose branches we are now walking? Shall you be content to know merely their leaves and fruits, and thus distinguish them one from the other? Surely this is a most unsatisfactory plan, and one that will fail you in Winter time, or when trying to name a tree in the distance. Oliver Wendell Holmes thus decides this point: " What we want is the meaning, the character, the expression of a tree, as a kind and as an individual."

Take yonder Oak for instance! Its noble rounded crown and lower horizontal branches make it unique among the giants of the forest. No other tree seems to have the pluck to hold its strong arms straight out, as if in defiance of the power of Gravity. Mark, too, its sturdy trunk, expanding towards the base, giving it that appearance of endurance and strength which suggested to Smeaton his plan for the construction of Eddystone Lighthouse.

The light grey bark, so useful to the tanner, is deeply furrowed from top to bottom, and affords shelter to hundreds of insects, which, in return, thanklessly prey upon the tree, and sometimes strip the branches of all their leaves. To see these branches to full advantage, one must pay them a visit in Winter time, when the foliage no longer hides them from view. Crooked and zigzag in shape, they form numerous " elbows " or " knees," and this peculiarity makes them extremely useful in boat building.

The wavy outlines of the lobed leaves are known to all, and need no further description here. But as these leaves emerge from their Winter quarters, the pollen-bearing Catkins are also beginning to make their appearance. These consist of hanging stalks, and, when full grown, measure from two to three inches in length; along them the male flowers are arranged in tiny groups. Being green in colour, they do not show up well against their background of leaves; but the wind does not fail to mark them out, and in due season the grains of pollen are wafted hither and thither,

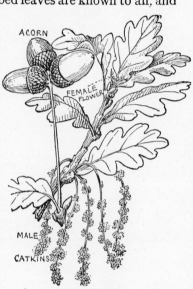

Fig. 1. Oak.

some to perform their allotted tasks, but the majority to fall by the way.

The fruit-bearing Catkins are fewer in number, and should be sought for where the leaves meet the young twigs. They may be difficult to find, but later on, in the Autumn, when the egg-and-cup-shaped fruits—so dear to the heart of a Squirrel—appear, no such difficulty will be experienced. In many countries, such as Russia, where large belts of Oak forest exist, huge numbers of pigs roam among the trees to fatten on the ripe acorns, which so plentifully bestrew the ground.

No tree is more subject to the attacks of insects than the Oak. Among these the Gall Wasps are very notice-able, and all parts of the tree—leaves, twigs, buds, and even roots—are liable to be visited. The female pierces the tissue of the selected spot, and in the cavity thus formed de-posits her eggs; it is astonishing how she will seek for a place difficult of access, or favourably situated for the food supply of her offspring when in the larval stage.

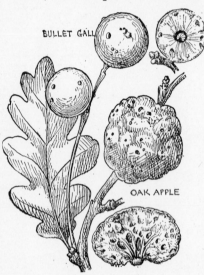

BULLET GALL

OAK APPLE

Fig. 2. Oak Galls.

Sometimes the Gall be-gins to form as soon as the egg has been laid, but in the majority of cases the " swelling " does not take place until the larva has been hatched, *i.e.*, in the Spring time. Two of these Galls form the subject of our illustration; one, the rosy-cheeked but spongy Oak Apple, is even now worn on May 29 in honour of Charles II.; the other, harder in texture and of a much smoother surface, is known as the Bullet Gall, and is useful in the manufacture of certain kinds of ink.

Time was when the Oak was specially grown to supply the needs of our ever-increasing Royal Navy, as the Forest of Dean can bear witness; now, although we still love to

PRIMROSES.

WILD HYACINTHS.

WOODRUFF.

WOOD SORREL.

think of our Dreadnoughts as " Hearts of Oak," teak and
steel have supplanted the former favourite.

It is not a far cry from " The King of the Forest " to
" The Mother of Forests," and if we take the trouble to
climb to the top of yonder rising ground, we shall see her in
all her glory. The Beech—for
that is her everyday name—
loves an elevated position,
and should the soil also be of
a limy nature, then indeed is
the tree in a happy condition!

But why has she been
christened " The Mother of
Forests "? The reply is thus
given by Mr. Step: " Its drip
destroys most of the soil-
exhausting weeds, its shade
protects the soil from over-
evaporation, and the heavy
crop of leaves enriches it by
their decomposition." Thus
the way is prepared for young
and tender saplings by this
forest nurse.

Fig. 3. Beech.

Even in the name of the
tree there is an interest, for it is said to mean a book. In
ancient times the tribes of Northern Europe—the Goths,
etc.—wrote upon blocks of wood cut from the Beech tree;
these are now known as Runic Writings, and thus the tree
came to be associated with books.

As we climb the hill we stumble over the spreading roots,
for the Beech obtains most of its nourishment from the upper
soil, and does not burrow so deep down as do its neighbours.

When at last we sight our clump of Beeches, what a glorious scene they present! The massive rounded trunks so smooth and grey, many of them forking into clusters of smaller columns, carry our minds back again to Nature's Cathedral, and this idea is strengthened by the almost entire absence of undergrowth.

Should the season be Winter, the long pointed buds in their brown envelopes cannot fail to attract attention; indeed they are to be reckoned among some of the most pointed of all our tree buds except, perhaps, those of the Fig.

Spring and Summer will work wonders on the tree, and soon the oval, glossy leaves, with their wavy edges, will afford a most complete shade. Search a young leaf for its fringe of delicate silky hairs; these protect it against the cold, and help to conduct any excess of moisture from off its surface. They also lessen Transpiration as mentioned on page 13; if the tree be on a dry soil, this act is very necessary, as the tree cannot afford to part with too much moisture.

The pollen-bearing flowers, which appear about May, are purplish brown in colour, and present the appearance of tassels tipped with yellow. The female flowers are clustered in a cup-like form. The bristly seed box opens in the Autumn by splitting into four sections, and discharges its three-sided fruits, which more often go to form food for the Badger, Squirrel, Deer, Mouse, and even the Pig, than to produce fresh trees.

The wood of the Beech is not very valuable, and is used chiefly for chair-making; several districts, such as High Wycombe, owe their prosperity to this and kindred trades, which sprang up on account of the abundance of Beech trees in that particular neighbourhood.

Nearly all our British trees lose their leaves in the

Autumn—the "Fall," as it is called in Canada. They are grouped together under the title of "deciduous," a most suitable name, for it means "fallen." The few remaining trees are evergreens.

III.—MORE DECIDUOUS TREES

HORNBEAM—ELM—WILD CHERRY

MOST people, meeting with the Hornbeam for the first time, are struck with its resemblance to the Beech, but closer inspection soon proves that there are many points of difference. The trunk or bole, although smooth and grey, is more gnarled and twisted than that of the Beech. Its branches, also, are usually of more slender proportions, and they have a curious habit of reuniting several feet from their point of separation and again forming one stem.

The edges of the oval leaves are serrated like those of the Elm, are somewhat rough in texture, and do not possess that smooth, glossy surface enjoyed by the leaves of the Beech. Even in Winter there is no need to confuse one tree with the other, for the buds of the Hornbeam are fairly short and thick, and nestle up close to the twigs, in striking contrast to the lean, outstretched buds of the Beech.

In nearly every part of the country this unfortunate tree has been maimed by the pruning knife, and disfigured by constant pollarding. This practice consisted of cutting back the branches every fifteen years, at a height of seven feet from the ground, for the purpose of fuel. Deer, and cattle too, have been guilty of browsing upon the lower branches, and robbing them of their leaves. Nevertheless the Hornbeam continues to flourish in spite of all these obstacles; indeed, it is a most patient tree, for no soil, however wet or dry, comes amiss to it.

B

Both kinds of flowers are borne on the same tree, and somewhat resemble each other. The male Catkin grows from the axil of the leaf, and has a series of overlapping scales which hide and protect the stamens and their precious load of pollen. The female Catkin is usually found at the end of a young twig, and sometimes measures four inches

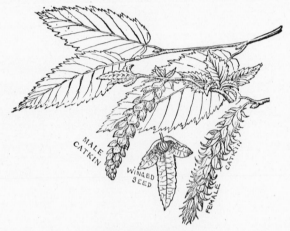

Fig. 4. Hornbeam.

by the time the seeds are ripe. Each seed is protected by what appears to be a three-lobed leaf; this is really a cup or " cupule," similar in function to that of the Acorn and Beech-nut.

How the Hornbeam came by its name is a very doubtful point, but some people assure us that the wood is so hard and tough as almost to resemble horn; hence it was called by the ancients the Hornbeam. Other botanists, however, are equally sure of their theories, so we will let the matter rest there.

Listen to those noisy Rooks which are making such a hubbub! Do you think that they, too, are arguing as to how the Hornbeam obtained its name? It is more likely they are discussing plans for a food-hunting expedition. Can you see their nests almost at the top of those tall trees?

Yes, that is an easy task, but how many of you can guess the name of those trees without first seeing their leaves? Each straight trunk seems to reach almost to the highest twig, and forms a back-bone unlike that of any other tree.

They are Elms or, to be more exact, Small-leaved or Common Elms. In all parts of England, especially in the southern half, their gaunt, sentinel-like frames are a familiar feature of the landscape. Even in Winter they have an appearance entirely their own. It is then that one can see the net-like arrangement of their terminal twigs, which cross and re-cross each other, as

Fig. 5. Common Elm.

though anxious to weave a fairy fringe to crown the head of the ancient tree.

But let us get nearer to these Elms and learn something more of their build and habits. The bark is very rough and has a tendency to become corky. The leaves have a rough, harsh surface, and somewhat remind us of those of the Stinging Nettle; usually the edges are doubly serrated, that is to say, the larger " teeth " into which the edges are cut are themselves sub-divided into smaller " teeth." An almost unique feature of these leaves is their lop-sidedness, the lower rim of each half being joined to the mid-rib at different points. Look at the illustration and you will then see what is meant by this.

Towards the end of March, even before the leaves have ventured out to greet the Spring, one may notice a purple tinge—at times dark brown—spreading through the upper branches of the Elm. The tree is then in flower; the countless blossoms are produced in small bunches, from which the purple-headed stamens—the pollen bearers— peep like pins out of a cushion.

Tucked away in the *same* blossom is the ovary, and when the seeds are ripe they are borne on the wind by means of a thin flat envelope, green in colour and about an inch in length; this may be described as a wing, and when seeds are constructed in this way the whole is known as a Samara or winged fruit. Similar growths are the " Keys " of the Ash and the " Dicky birds " of the Sycamore.

Unfortunately the seeds of the Common Elm rarely, if ever, germinate; the tree, therefore, has to produce its kind by means of suckers, which spring up not only near the parent tree, but from the root branches at a consider- able distance away. Thus the Common Elm makes a good tree for a hedge, and may often be found there.

The seeds of the Wych Elm, however, have a more useful career, and many a healthy sapling has been reared from them; thus it happens that the Wych Elm has no need to throw up suckers. It may also be distinguished from its cousin by its larger leaves, and by having branches of a more spreading nature.

In our wood we may possibly chance upon the Wild Cherry, of which there are three kinds. The one that most of us are familiar with is the Gean, since it is so largely

WOOD LOOSESTRIFE.

WOOD ANEMONES.

BUGLE.

used for ornamental purposes in many of our parks and gardens.

This elegant tree has been called by Meredith " The Vestal of the Forest," a name well deserved, especially in early Spring, when its young, bronzy leaves are almost hidden beneath a glorious mantle of countless white blossoms.

These leaves lose their brownish tinge as Spring advances, and assume a green colour until Autumn changes them to a bright crimson; they are oval in shape with sharply toothed edges, and are downy on the under surface. Their long stalks cause them to have a drooping appearance.

Although the fruit is bitter to the taste, it is greedily devoured by birds.

Winter is, of course, the best time to obtain a general idea of the shape of this tree, for then the short, sturdy branches, with their tendency to grow upwards, can be clearly seen. Many of the buds are grouped together and give one an idea of a bouquet of buds.

The bark is fairly smooth, but is scarred by a succession of horizontal lines, which almost encircle the trunk; this peculiarity is a considerable aid in identifying the tree.

IV.—CONIFERS

SCOTCH PINE—SPRUCE FIR—LARCH

How many of you, in your walks, trouble to distinguish between a Pine and a Fir? Perhaps you imagine these are but two names for the same tree. Let us search for a sprig of each and settle the question for ourselves.

Notice that the leaves or needles of the Pine are arranged in pairs, and unite before entering the branch; those of the Fir, however, seem more independent, and remain separate and distinct. Then, again, the cones are so different; a Pine cone is egg-shaped and has scales with thickened ends, whereas a Fir Cone is more cylindrical in shape and has scales which are thin and papery by comparison.

Fig. 6. Scotch Pine. A, Female flower; B, Cone of first year; C, Male flowers; D, Adult cone.

But look! Those gaunt, flat-topped Scottish Pines on yonder hill seem to beckon us. Let us accept the invitation since the climb is only a slight one. The soft sandy soil gives beneath our feet, and very soon the scent-laden air tells us we are near our destination.

What a forest of masts seem to spring up around us! Indeed, it is a peculiarity of the Scots Pine that the lower branches die early, and make the tree appear as though it had weathered many a storm. This idea is strengthened by its red, scaly bark, which boys have been heard to declare reminded them of a Crocodile's skin.

Have you ever stood upon a finer carpet than the one on which we are now treading? Millions of Pine needles have been shed to make it; in course of years these fallen leaves will enrich the soil, and thus provide food for plants which otherwise could not exist here.

Pick up a handful of these needles and you will see that the perfect ones are arranged in bundles of two. Try to break those which have recently fallen and you will learn how tough they are. In shape and in texture they are fitted to combat not only the cold and the storms of the Winter, but those seasons of drought when Transpiration should almost cease to exist.

When the bud at the end of a Pine branch develops in Spring, it produces, in some cases, a group of tiny yellow cones, each of which is plentifully supplied with stamens bearing the pollen. You have but to strike the branch with your stick to understand what is meant by " a shower of sulphur," so often touched upon by our poets.

The female flowers first show up as very small greenish-brown cones, close to the end of a branch. About June, the protective scales, which overlap like tiles, bend back to allow the pollen to enter, but do not open again until the *second* Spring after this act of pollination, and then the seeds are scattered. Each of these is attached to a wing, something like that of the Elm. It may be noted here that the seeds of the Fir ripen in *one* season.

An interesting collection can be made of these cones to show the various stages of their growth:—

1. The newly-formed cone near the end of the branch.

2. The one-year-old cone, green in colour, larger in size, and from two to three inches from the end.

3. The fully-grown cone, brown, dry, and woody, and probably with its seeds scattered.

From the Pine we get, among other things, Resin and Turpentine; the famous " Yellow Deal," so hard and durable, is also the product of the Scots Pine.

Shall we go back to our Fir tree, from which we secured a sprig just a few minutes ago? But while we examine it let us not forget that there are many kinds of Fir; the one we are now approaching is the Spruce.

What does it put you in mind of? " A giant Christmas tree," did you say? Yes, you are right, for a Christmas tree is nothing more than a baby Spruce. Its tall, tapering trunk, and its regular horizontal branches, decreasing in length as the summit is reached, all tend to give it that conical appearance by means of which we can distinguish it even at a distance.

Both the Scots Pine and the Spruce are evergreens.

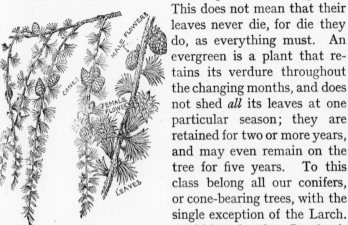

This does not mean that their leaves never die, for die they do, as everything must. An evergreen is a plant that retains its verdure throughout the changing months, and does not shed *all* its leaves at one particular season; they are retained for two or more years, and may even remain on the tree for five years. To this class belong all our conifers, or cone-bearing trees, with the single exception of the Larch.

Fig. 7. Larch.

Although the Larch is essentially a mountain tree, loving the clear, dry atmosphere, yet we may find a sturdy specimen on the outskirts of our wood, where there is plenty of light and air. Its lofty tapering trunk reminds us of the Spruce, but its leaves, which are put forth in early Spring, are arranged in bundles of thirty or forty, and are quickly followed by the tassel-like female flowers, so charmingly described by Tennyson as " rosy plumelets."

The male flowers are grouped together in clusters, and somewhat resemble those of the Pine. Here again there is a lavish output of pollen, as will always be the case where the wind is the carrying agent. The cones are rarely more than an inch long, and are usually the shape of an egg.

Does not Allan Quatermain express our idea of a tree when he says: "I do love a good tree. There it stands so strong and sturdy, and yet so beautiful—a very type of the best sort of man. How proudly it lifts its bare head to the Winter storms, and with what a full heart it rejoices when the Spring has come again! How grand its voice too, when it talks with the wind; a thousand Æolian harps cannot equal the beauty of the sighing of a great tree in leaf. All day it points to the sunshine and all night to the stars, and thus passionless, and yet full of life, it endures through the centuries—come storm, come shine —drawing its sustenance from the cool bosom of its mother Earth, and, as the slow years roll by, learning the great mysteries of growth and of decay."

V.—WILD PLANTS IN THE WOOD

PRIMROSE—WILD HYACINTH—DOG'S MERCURY—EARLY
PURPLE ORCHIS—WOODRUFF—WOOD SORREL

ALTHOUGH the trees reign supreme in the wood, and tower above the smaller things of earth, we must not overlook those frail and dainty plants which, as though grateful for the shade afforded, send forth so delicate and rich a perfume.

Perhaps the best known of these is the Primrose, which, arranged in cheap, tiny bundles, so often gladdens the heart of many a city dweller. But if you would see it at its best, you must seek for this flower down some leafy glade where, in the company of countless brothers and sisters, it forms one of the most beautiful floral pictures of Spring.

When quite a baby, the Primrose possesses a rosette of spear-shaped leaves capable of pushing their way un-noticed between the neighbouring plants. This fighting power can easily be accounted for by remembering that the Primrose belongs to that class of flowers which store up food in their roots during the ample times of Summer, to provide for their wants during the scanty days of early Spring.

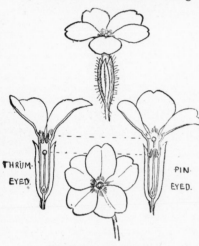

Eventually, when the little stranger has estab-lished itself, it throws out larger leaves; these are oblong and egg-shaped, and have a crinkled or crumpled appearance, due to the presence of a strong net-work of veins.

Let us search among that bank of Primrose blossoms and see if all are alike. In every case we note the fine, sulphur-tinted petals joined to form a long tube, which fits so well the green calyx-cup; in every case we note the spot of deeper yellow which marks the base of each smooth petal, and we come to the conclusion that all *are* alike.

Fig. 8. Primrose Flowers.

But if we look carefully down each tube, it is there we shall find points of difference. Here, for example, the five stamens can be plainly seen, and country children call this kind " thrum-eyed "; in another specimen the stamens are lower down, and completely hidden by the pin-like head of the pistil—hence the name " pin-eyed."

Now puzzle out the reason of all this for yourselves. Turn to the two drawings on page 32 and imagine a bee visiting first one flower and then the other in search of the nectar to be found around the ovary. What part of its body will be dusted by the pollen, and what will become of this golden dust? If you can answer these two questions you have solved the one-time mystery of thrum-eyed and pin-eyed.

Let us leave this riddle for awhile, and continue our ramble among the trees, for unless bad luck be with us we may soon hope to feast our eyes upon a woodland carpet of Wild Hyacinths. No words can do justice to this marvellous " sea of blue "; it must be seen to be fully appreciated.

The delicious perfume of the flowers, the clusters of dainty, nodding blossoms which hang like fairy ear-rings from a graceful wand, the blue mist " that seem the heavens upbreaking through the earth," all go to form an impression never to be forgotten.

" But whence come these bells? " you may ask, " and where are the calyx and corolla? " Here we have an example of these two parts of the flower becoming so united that to distinguish one from the other is impossible—and the six-pointed bell, with its tips curled back, is the result.

In the Autumn, should you happen to revisit these scenes, you will find all the leaves dead, and the flower stalks brown with age. But even then fresh wonders may be had for the seeking. At the tip of the stalk is the seed box; cut it off and shake it, and the little black seeds will rattle loudly enough to arouse an artful Squirrel, and send him scampering up a tree in less time than it takes to tell the story.

Whenever we speak of flowers we naturally think of

colours; but here, growing in hundreds of thousands along
this path, is a strong, upright, bushy plant, green in every
respect.   The Dog's Mercury—for such is its name—pushes
through the ground in February, the blossoms being beautifully tucked up among the unopened leaves.   Under favourable conditions it will reach a height of eighteen inches,
and spread so rapidly
that many regard it as
a harmful weed.

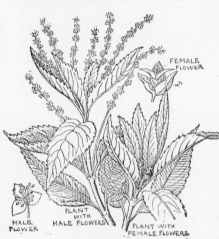

The   lance - shaped
leaves,   with   their
sharply toothed edges,
are   closely   arranged
in pairs along the stout,
four-sided stem, which
is slightly hairy; these
points may perhaps re-
mind you of the Sting-
ing Nettle, to which
indeed Dog's Mercury
is related.

Fig. 9. Dog's Mercury.

It is where the leaf-
stalk meets the stem
that we must look for the blossoms; these will probably dis-
appoint you, for there is ne'er a sign of a petal to give a splash
of colour, or to attract bees and other insect visitors.   But
what they lack in beauty, they partly make up for in interest.

Here, for example, the blossoms are arranged in tiny
clusters around a fairly long stalk, each with its three green
sepals and bunch of yellow-headed stamens; these are the
male flowers and produce the pollen.   If we wish to discover the other kind, we must search for quite a separate
plant; then, on a shorter spike, three similar sepals will

WILD STRAWBERRY.

SQUIRREL.

FOX CUBS.

appear, but in the centre, like two small peas joined together, will be found the ovaries.

Some of you, while wandering among the Wild Hyacinths, have come across the Early Purple Orchis; indeed these two flowers seem to love the same places and the same seasons, for wherever and whenever one appears, there and then you are likely to find the other.

The Early Purple Orchis is an intensely interesting flower from its root upwards. The latter somewhat resembles two small egg-shaped potatoes, one of which supplies food for the current year, whilst the other is busy storing up food for future occasions.

The strong juicy stem often rises to a height of one foot, and is clasped by strap-shaped leaves stained with dark purple spots. Every Orchis is a curious plant, and seems to delight in bearing flowers of

Fig. 10. Early Purple Orchis.

peculiar shapes. The petals and sepals cannot be separated from each other, and may be regarded as one structure.

Two of the petals bound the sides of the flower as it grows, whilst the third is different from them in size and shape and is known as the lip. It is usually larger and is continued back as a spur. This lip, by the way, makes an excellent landing stage for the Bee when visiting the flowers.

Probably you will never learn to love these blossoms, for very often they possess a strong and offensive odour. In this respect they are totally unlike the Woodruff—cousin of the Goosegrass—and one of our sweet-scented woodland treasures, whose slender weak stems may often be found in tangled masses wherever the soil is light and the shadows abound.

The firm shiny leaves are usually arranged in circles of eight around the stem, which is crowned by clusters of snow-white flowers, suggestive of clear-cut stars; these are succeeded by tiny black seeds, hooked to assist them in their dispersal. It may be said of this flower that it reserves its greatest charm until Death lays it low, for then it is that a sweet odour—like the scent of new-mown hay—arises from the plant and gladdens the heart of the farmer's wife, who values it next to Lavender.

Find a shady nook among these trees where the ground is always moist, and you have hit upon an ideal home for the Wood Sorrel. This frail-looking plant is a typical inhabitant of the woods, and will quickly perish if left to battle for itself against the heat of the sun and the vigour of the wind.

Each leaf, yellowish-green on top and purple beneath, is supported on a frail pink stem springing direct from the root, and is divided into three heart-shaped leaflets, which droop at the approach of night or at the first sign of a storm. These are acid to the taste; indeed the word Sorrel is said to mean sour.

A single blossom, provided with five white petals, tops each flower stalk, and is delicately streaked with purple-pink veins—guides to the honey, as some people assert. Each blossom is supported by a tiny green calyx formed by five green sepals.

Most authorities agree that the flower, beloved by St. Patrick and long since dignified by becoming the emblem of Old Ireland, is none other than the Wood Sorrel, so let us treat it with due respect.

VI.—MORE WILD PLANTS IN THE WOOD

WOOD LOOSESTRIFE — ENCHANTER'S NIGHTSHADE — WOOD ANEMONE—BUGLE—WILD STRAWBERRY—NECTAR AND ITS USES

WHO among you is not familiar with Creeping Jenny? Even a city urchin must have grown or seen this humble plant, and can tell you where to find it. Now when you speak of the Yellow Pimpernel—or Wood Loosestrife as it is sometimes called—you are dealing with Creeping Jenny's cousin, and the knowledge of the one will help you in discovering the other.

Look for it in the moist places of the wood, and then compare it with our city friend. The stems are weak and slender, and must need recline upon the ground; running off in pairs are the smooth, glossy leaves, oval in shape, but pointed at the tip.

The cup-shaped blossoms, each with its five bright petals, are of a brilliant yellow and backed by the thin green segments of the calyx.

It is said that Creeping Jenny does not bear seed in our country, probably because it has adopted other methods of producing its kind, such as sending down roots from the joints of its prostrate stems. In this respect it differs from the Wood Loosestrife, as you can prove for yourselves by gathering the ball-like seed vessels of the latter, when Autumn rules the land.

Probably while you are thus engaged you will also chance upon the seeds of the Enchanter's Nightshade, a plant which has similar tastes to the one just described.

The name at once suggests all kinds of awful poisons, so it would be as well if the Enchanter's Nightshade put out a

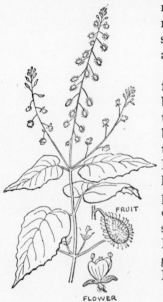

notice to the effect that it had *no* connection with any other flower of the same name — Deadly Nightshade and Woody Nightshade to wit.

The rounded stem, smooth but for a few silky hairs, divides into branches near the top, and from these depend the small white blossoms. It would almost seem that these had fallen in love with Figure Two, for they possess a two-lobed calyx, two heart-shaped petals, two pink stamens, two divisions to the seed box, and two seeds to be cast upon the bosom of Mother Earth. Yes, even the leaves grow in pairs, so what more can Figure Two ask than that?

You must not imagine that such occurrences are rare; on the contrary, flowers are most orderly in their build, the majority being dominated by some small number or its multiple.

Fig. 11. Enchanter's Nightshade.

When the winds of March and the showers of April are preparing the way for May flowers, then beneath the trees you will not look in vain for the Wood Anemone, the frail companion of the Primrose and the Violet.

Poets have also christened it the Wind Flower, and

many are the tales told to explain this name; some declare that it arose from the flower's preference for March, but others solve the riddle by pointing to the blossoms themselves, which are so hung as to be capable of turning their backs to the slightest breeze.

When first the bud peeps above the ground, it is protected by *false* leaves—false, because *true* leaves never appear on a flower stalk, but always on an ordinary stem. These false leaves, or bracts as you should call them, are wedge-shaped when full grown, and are divided into three leaflets, which are again split up into several parts, something after the pattern of the Meadow Buttercup; the ordinary leaves of this plant are very much the same.

You have already been told in *The Hedge I Know* that flower buds have a snug, warm coat, known as the calyx or cup, to protect them during their babyhood. This is nearly always green, and usually consists of a series of sepals. Now in the case of the Wood Anemone these take the place of the petals and give the colour to the blossom, being white, tinged with pink or purple. Another peculiarity to be met with here is that you can never depend upon the number of sepals, anything from four to nine being possible, although six is the favourite.

A delicate fragrance pervades each blossom and attracts insect visitors; these guests are probably disappointed when they find that their " host " provides no store of honey, and they have therefore to be content with sucking the sweet juices of the sepals.

Bugle is much more obliging in this respect, if a flower *can* be obliging. Each of its purple-blue blossoms consists of a slender tube, which is folded over at the mouth into a three-lobed lip, an admirable landing place for insects in search of nectar. There is also an upper lip, which stands

C

erect, and doubtless assists in the protection of the pistil and stamens.

These blossoms are arranged in rings around the square, hollow stem, and they and the leaves are so closely packed together as to form one compact spike. The leaves are oval in shape, those springing from the roots having long stalks, whilst those on the stem are stalkless.

You must not imagine that the flowers described in this book refuse to be seen outside a wood, and would die if they had to take up their residence elsewhere. It is quite true that they have a preference for shady and sheltered places, but many of them thrive and multiply on hedge banks and even in open fields. Of course all plants flourish best in those spots they specially love, but they, like ourselves, have often to struggle along under adverse circumstances.

What better example of this can you have than the Wild Strawberry? Although a lover of the woods, it may be found in all kinds of unexpected corners.

Even beginners feel confident that they can recognise a Strawberry plant when they see it, but they should take care lest they confuse it with the Barren Strawberry. The true species can be distinguished from the barren variety by its *erect* flower stalk, and by its habit of sending out runners, which take root, thus producing many sons and daughters.

The leaves, like the stem, are covered with soft silky hairs; they are oval in shape, bright green in colour, and arranged in threes with their edges coarsely toothed.

The blossom is sometimes described as a little White Rose; the arrangement of the five pure white petals, with a bright golden centre of clustered stamens, does certainly suggest this idea.

Possibly it will be difficult to persuade you that the fruit is a growth of an unusual kind, for who will dare hint that a delicious Strawberry is anything else but perfect? Nevertheless we must speak the truth even in Botany, so let us inquire into the matter. Can you find the receptacle of the blossom? It is that part on which all the others rest, and sometimes behaves itself in an extremely funny way, growing into all shapes and sizes. Something like this happens in the case of the Strawberry; the receptacle becomes large and spongy, and the tiny seeds, instead of being crowded together as in the Barren Strawberry, are spread over its surface; a sweet, juicy fluid is secreted, and, hey presto! we have our much-sought-after fruit.

If only flowers could reason and speak, they would surely explain that nectar is only a bribe held out to attract insects; their aim is not to supply food for these creatures, but to provide them with a stimulus for visiting blossom after blossom. Thus the precious pollen is carried from one flower to another, and fertilisation is made possible.

There is no better way of understanding flowers than by studying them in connection with their insect visitors. Blossoms, which are shallow and have an unpleasant smell, like those of the Buttercup, possess a special charm for Flies; those that are red or blue, with a cup-like corolla and a pleasing odour, are associated with the Bee; whereas those which are tubular and send forth a greater fragrance at eventide—the Honeysuckle and Evening Primrose, for example—are claimed by the Moths.

Everywhere signs are evident of the interdependence of the animal and vegetable worlds, and if we would understand Nature aright, we must bear this constantly in mind.

VII.—TWO MAMMALS OF THE WOOD

SQUIRREL—FOX

If you are fond of hide-and-seek then you cannot do better than pay a visit to a wood and keep your eyes well open for a Squirrel. This favourite animal is a wonderful acrobat, and the scampering noise we heard just now was made by a Squirrel we had disturbed. Directly he heard us he sprang to the nearest tree and scampered round it, peeping as he went, to see if we were looking.

FORE FOOT.

HIND FOOT

Fig. 12. Feet of Squirrel.

The noise he made was caused by his claws coming into contact with the bark, for the Squirrel must of necessity cling close to the tree or he would surely fall. Look! There the artful creature is, poking his head round the opposite side of that Oak. His ears are raised to their fullest extent, his bright eyes are glistening like black diamonds, and his whole body is agitated.

By a series of scrambles the animal at last reaches the upper branches; here he rests for a minute or two from his exertions. You can now see his bright reddish-brown attire and fine bushy tail. Of the latter he is very proud, and when sitting on the branch of a tree, the tail is brought right over the top of the head.

Quick as thought, the little rodent has started on his journey again. Now he is threading his way among the topmost branches with great cleverness, until at last he

NEST AND EGGS OF SONG THRUSH.

TURTLE DOVE.

YOUNG TURTLE DOVES.

reaches a clearing in the wood, and must spring to the nearest tree across the way. This is a small matter to the Squirrel, for see, there he goes, happy and excitable creature, darting through the air without the slightest hesitation or fear.

We lose sight of him now, and our eyes are really tired with watching his rapid movements.

Whither has he gone? Probably to his nest, or "drey," as it is called, and this is usually placed in a Fir tree, where, among the tangled branches, it is well hidden. The nest is built of roots, moss, grass, leaves, and other materials, and if you could peep inside one of them

Fig. 13. Squirrels and Nest.

about Midsummer three or four baby Squirrels would be seen.

This animal partakes of a large variety of food, and whilst perhaps fond of Hazel-nuts and the seeds of the Fir tree, it will also eat Beech-mast, buds, bark, haws, mushrooms, and even birds and their eggs.

The active creature, remembering the hard Winter days to come, lays up a store of food in the Autumn to which he can go during the severe weather. At this season he is much less active, and more rarely seen, than in the Spring, Summer, and Autumn.

Steady! What was that which bolted across the " ride " in the wood, allowing us to catch only a glimpse of its gliding form? It was a Fox. What brings Master Reynard here, for his " earth " is in a favourite bank in yonder field?

The wood is one of his chief hunting grounds, for here the Pheasants and other birds and animals are congregated. The Fox is one of those carnivorous mammals difficult to understand, for he kills far more food than he and his family can eat, and often seems to kill for killing sake. Fowls, Wild Birds, Rabbits, Hedgehogs, Rats, Mice, and Beetles are a few of the many creatures upon which this animal preys, and in game-preserving districts he does considerable damage. He hunts chiefly during the night, although sometimes the crafty creature may be stalked in broad daylight.

If we could have examined the specimen we just saw, we should have found that it was almost uniform reddish in colour varied with grey, with a fine white frill on the chest, and, as is so well known, a splendid bushy tail. The male is called a Dog Fox and the female a Vixen, whilst the young are known as Cubs. In the picture two of these may be seen at the entrance to their home, placed at the base of an old oak tree. Here the youngsters are waiting for their father to return with some food. Although the Fox often has its " earth " underground, such as the burrow of a Rabbit, and even shares the same " earth " as the Badger, yet it will also rear the young above ground in the hole of a tree and elsewhere. So far as experience teaches us, it rarely, if ever, digs out a home of its own.

If an earth be found, the untidiness of the place will at once be seen, for it is littered with various half-eaten animals, and the smell is abominable. If inhabiting the same earth as a Badger, it will be found that the latter is much cleaner in its habits, and far more particular about its home life.

A wary animal at all times, the Fox is largely preserved for the purposes of hunting. It has a wonderful way of escaping when kept in captivity, and seems to have at its command unlimited means for making good its escape. When being hunted by hounds, the latter follow on what is called " the scent," the Fox having a gland beneath the tail from which a strong scent is given off. We were really fortunate in catching even a passing glimpse of Mr. Reynard, for the reason of his speed is now quite evident. See! the wood is now tenanted by the hunt! Here come the hounds, and listen, the huntsman is sounding the " Tally-ho! "

VIII.—LARGE BIRDS OF THE WOOD

GREEN AND LESSER SPOTTED WOODPECKERS—SONG THRUSH—
RING DOVE — TURTLE DOVE — BLACKBIRD — KESTREL —
SPARROW HAWK

ONE meets in a wood several kinds of birds which are rarely seen elsewhere, and in this connection we may mention two of the Woodpeckers. The most handsome British species is the Green Woodpecker. In his green and yellow dress and crimson crown the male is a beautiful bird, and when he utters his laughter-like notes then, so the country people say, rain may be expected. That is why they have christened him Rain Bird and Wet-Ile.

The Squirrel loves the glossy-white eggs of this bird, and the Starling also tries to take possession of the Woodpecker's nesting hole. Battles, therefore, often rage fast and furious between these woodland rovers and are most interesting to watch.

A smaller bird, the Lesser Spotted Woodpecker, is a most delightful species, and when he is making the peculiar drumming noise with his beak and uttering his " chee, chee, chee, chee " notes, one may often listen to him but try to find him in vain! The drumming seems to be made by the bird tapping vigorously with his beak against a tree, but there is a difference of opinion as to exactly why this noise is made. Some say it is simply caused by the bird's constant search for insect food; others state that it is a sort of call, or love-song. Whatever it is due to, the fact remains that it is most curious, and it is not too much to say that the Lesser Spotted Woodpecker can drum out notes such as would do credit to a drummer boy in the King's army.

Although acorns, nuts, and seeds are also eaten, Wood-peckers live chiefly upon insects. In procuring the latter the long tongue aids the bird considerably, for by means of it insects can be licked from their hiding-places among the bark, etc. And where do you think the long tongue is put when not in use? It is wound round inside the head some-thing like the spring of a watch.

Woodpeckers may be called our Carpenter birds, for their nest is made in the hole of a tree hewn out by means of their strong beaks. They fly jerkily in the open, but when in their natural position, running nimbly up the trunk of a tree, or among the branches, they are well adapted for the life they lead.

Wherever there is a wood or coppice, there sure enough the Song Thrush will be found. Whilst this splendid songster also resorts to lanes, hedgerows, gardens, and other places, it dearly delights to build in a secluded wood where all is peace and quietude. Where Hornbeam, Laurels, or

Privet abound, there one may search for the first early nest
of either Blackbird or Thrush.

The nest is a well-built structure, and is composed of
grass, twigs, and occasionally moss, etc. The deep interior
is lined with rotten wood and mud moulded in a very clever
way. When first plastered, it is, of course, soft and wet,
but after a time it dries and hardens, and is well
calculated to form a compact home, first for the
beautiful blue eggs, marked with black
and dark brown, and afterwards for the
spotted chicks.

The Song
Thrush is one of
our sweetest and
most varied song-
birds, and has
long legs, lustrous
eyes, an olive-
brown back, with
a spotted throat
and breast. It
is specially fond

Fig. 14. Head of Green Woodpecker.

of snails, but also feeds upon earthworms, insects, berries,
and fruit.

What was that large bird which rose from the Fir tree
and set up such a commotion as it made its way into the
open? Was it a Ring Dove or a Turtle Dove? But what
is the difference by which we may know one from the other?
The Ring Dove, or Wood Pigeon, is a much larger bird, is
more highly coloured and far noisier than its relative. The
Turtle Dove is a Summer visitor only, the Ring Dove is a
resident. In Autumn the Turtle Dove flies away to Africa,
there to spend the cold months, whilst a large increase in

the number of our Ring Doves takes place, because of the Winter visitors from other climes. Both birds build a frail nest of sticks and twigs, but that of the Ring Dove is bulkier and placed higher in a tree. Only two eggs are laid, and those of the Ring Dove are larger and not so milky-white as those of the Turtle Dove.

A male Ring Dove in his best Spring livery is a very handsome bird, and may be recognised by his slate-grey plumage, glossed on the head, neck, and breast with green, blue, and purple. When he flies, carefully note the white bars on the wings and white patches on the sides of the neck, for in this way the bird may soon become familiar.

The Turtle Dove, on the other hand, is brownish above and white on the belly; there are black and white patches on the neck and, when flying, the fan-like dusky tail is spread out and displays white edges. The Turtle Dove has a soft flight, and an agreeable " croo-o-o " sort of note, whereas the Ring Dove has, as we have seen, a noisy, flapping flight, and sings loudly to his mate: " Don't scold so, Sukey, don't scold so, Sukey, don't! "

Where we find the Thrush, there, too, we may expect to see the Blackbird. This is another fine singer, and has a mellower song than the Thrush, but has not the variety of notes at his command. A shrill alarm note is also uttered. He is, too, a very solitary bird as compared with the Thrush. The latter goes about in flocks during Winter, but the Blackbird never flocks.

The Blackbird's family nursery is built in places similar to those of its relative, and somewhat resembles it in general structure. It is, however, not so deep; the inside is lined with fine grass, and the eggs are more green and more boldly marked with light brown.

The female is not black like her mate, but is something like a very dark-coloured Thrush.

Now we have reached an open part of the wood. Let us rest on this tree stump and look and listen. We have not long to wait before noticing something of interest, for did you not observe a large bird go darting through the trees? It was a Kestrel, and as both this bird and the Sparrow Hawk inhabit the wood, let us consider briefly the chief features concerning them.

Both birds are about the same size, but the Kestrel may be easily distinguished by means of the long pointed wings and rounded tail. The male is grey and chestnut on the upper parts, with pale buff below. It is streaked and spotted with darker colours. The female is larger

Fig. 15. Kestrel.

than her mate, and the whole of her upper parts are chestnut.

The male Sparrow Hawk is dark bluish-grey above and reddish-white below; the beak is blue and the feet are yellow. The female is brown above and greyish-white below, barred with dark grey.

Now both these birds belong to that class known as Birds of Prey. They live upon other animals and hover, soar, and sweep through the air with amazing skill, possessing remarkable powers of flight and vision.

Moles, mice, rats, birds, frogs, slugs, and beetles, such are some of the creatures upon which these birds prey, and whilst the Kestrel is a most useful bird, there seems some doubt as to the character of the Sparrow Hawk so far as concerns its value to mankind. It may be, however, that in one way or another it performs good and useful work.

Both birds often resort to the disused nests of other species, repairing and enlarging the old home rather than building nests of their own. They lay handsome eggs, that of each kind being shown on the coloured plate.

IX.—SMALL BIRDS OF THE WOOD

WRYNECK—NUTHATCH—GREAT TIT—BLUE TIT—COAL TIT—
TREE CREEPER — BLACKCAP — NIGHTINGALE — CHIFF
CHAFF—WILLOW WREN

THERE are small as well as large birds in the wood, from the modest Golden-crested Wren—the smallest bird in Europe—to the large Ring Dove. We will now have a peep at some of the smaller kinds.

There is a brownish-looking bird, which haunts trees, and is very noisy in the early Spring. It is then that he calls in a shrill voice, " Pee, pee, pee, pee, pee, pee, pee," repeating the note several times. Can you tell what bird this is? It has the habit of thrusting out its long tongue like a Woodpecker and also turns its head rapidly about, so much so that it has been named the Wryneck.

It is a Summer migrant, arriving just before the Cuckoo, hence it is often called the Cuckoo's Mate, or Messenger. A somewhat shy bird, it is not often seen; when the nest is molested, the Wryneck hisses in a very vehement way, and throws its body into many curious positions. The nest is

FEMALE BLACKBIRD ON NEST.

YOUNG BLACKBIRDS IN NEST.

GREAT TIT

YOUNG KESTRELS.

made in the hole of a tree, and the six to eight oval-shaped eggs are glossy white.

Listen! Do you not hear a note uttered by some bird which sounds like "twit-wit-wit?" Let us go in the direction from which the sound comes and see if we can find the bird. There he is, at the top of that stalwart oak, running along the branches like a mouse rather than a bird.

Fig. 16. Nuthatch.

Notice the short tail, but otherwise plump appearance, and strong beak. It is a Nuthatch or, as some country people call it, Nut-Jobber, Mud - Dabber, or Mud-Stopper. They call it Nut-Jobber because the bird is very fond of nuts; these it is in the habit of placing in the crevices of bark, and then hammering the shell with its beak so as to extract the kernel. You may see several trees bearing quite a large number of nuts, both full and empty, and may also catch the bird having his breakfast in this way.

Now the sunlight is resting upon the bird we have in view, and the plumage can well be seen. You will thus see that it is blue-grey above, with dark wings and tail, the latter marked with white. Carefully observe the white eye stripe, the black band on each side of the head, the white throat, and the chestnut belly.

In its nesting habits the Nuthatch is very interesting, and these explain how it has acquired the names of Mud-

Dabber and Mud-Stopper. The birds hew out a hole in a tree, and then build a nest of dry leaves, pieces of bark, etc.; the interesting point is that at first the hole made is too large, but the owners take the precaution to plaster it up with mud until at last it is only just large enough to admit the parent birds. The six or seven eggs are white, spotted or blotched with red-brown.

The loud piercing note of another bird—the Great Tit— reminds us that the eggs of these two species are almost identical. Listen to its shrill Spring song, a sort of " tinkle, tinkle, tinkle." It is called Saw Sharpener in some districts, because the note is supposed to resemble the noise made when a saw is being sharpened.

As its name implies, this is the largest of the Tits; it is a handsome bird, as the coloured plate shows. In the Winter it is a good plan to feed the birds in the garden and elsewhere, and if a piece of suet is hung up a Tit of some kind is sure to pay a visit to it.

The Great Tit, Blue Tit, and Coal Tit are woodland representatives of this useful and engaging family. The Blue Tit is another regular visitor to the garden, and it is remarkable to notice how well the bird knows when it is breakfast, dinner, and tea-time. The male bird is a bright little fellow and sings a cheery, trilling song, besides which it has a number of other notes well worth listening for. He is smaller than the Great Tit; has a blue crown, an olive-green back, bluish wings and tail, and yellow breast and belly. One of the distinguishing features of the Great Tit is his fine black waistcoat.

The Coal Tit is not nearly such a pretty bird, and may be known by the black crown and white cheeks.

All the Tits live very largely upon insects; they are most active birds and may be seen searching almost continuously for food; they hang head downwards and in many other positions when hunting for food, and are to be numbered amongst the most interesting birds found in the woodland.

Another modest bird, which needs looking for carefully, is the Tree Creeper. A strictly arboreal species, it is a tireless food-hunter, like the Tits. When flying from one tree to another the little brown-clad bird starts at the base and works upwards. It is remarkable to notice how firmly it grasps the trunk it is traversing, and how it is aided considerably by the sharp-pointed tail feathers which are placed close to the tree. It has a long beak, which helps it to secure the insects upon which it feeds, and is usually a very silent bird.

Fig. 17. Tree Creeper.

Listen! what beautiful songster is that in the briar bush? Is it the Nightingale? No, it is his first cousin, and if we could see the singer, we should find that he has a black head. That is why he is called the Blackcap. It is a matter of opinion which is the better songster, the Garden Warbler, whose nest we discovered in the hedgerow, or the Blackcap. There may be more harsh, thin, and White-throat-like notes in the song of the Blackcap, but the rich, bubbling, rippling song cannot fail to arrest the ear of all those who appreciate bird music.

The male has a black cap, the female being brown instead of black. A frail nest of dead grass and fibrous roots is built in a bush of some kind, and from four to six eggs are laid, which are dirty white or yellow in ground colour, blotched, spotted, and streaked with dark brown.

What feathered musician is this just above our head? It is Philomel himself, England's sweet-voiced Nightingale. He has not been here long, having spent the Winter in Africa. Most of our finest song birds of Spring and Summer are only with us at such times, bidding us adieu in the Autumn for sunnier climes.

Few people seem to know that the Nightingale sings by day as well as night. During the day its voice, mingled with the notes of other birds, is, however, not so entrancing as when listened to at night, when nearly all others are silent. The deep, long-drawn-out notes, the "jug, jug, jug" beloved by bird lovers, and the remarkable richness of the wonderful song are not readily forgotten.

Year after year the bird returns to the same haunt, and rears its young in almost the same spot. A thick bush is a favourite resort, and here, almost upon the ground, the deep nest is made. It is composed of dead grasses, oak leaves, roots, and similar materials, and in this cosy nursery four or five olive-brown eggs are laid.

The bird itself is plain-looking, a dress of reddish-brown and grey being all it has; but it is the rule that sober-plumaged birds possess fine voices, and that handsome birds like the Kingfisher, the Peacock, and the Parrot do not aspire to be song birds.

When the nesting season is on the decline, the voice of the Nightingale commences to lose its crispness and beauty; indeed, the bird then begins to utter two plaintive notes and a harsh "krrrrrrrrr" which are most difficult to reconcile with the sweetest songster of the woods.

There are two small birds in the wood which must be mentioned before we have a peep at some other animals;

these are the Chiff Chaff and the Willow Wren. They both haunt tall trees, but may be distinguished more by their notes than by their plumage. The Chiff Chaff cries in a shrill voice " chif-chaf, chif-chaf " or " chivy-chavy, chivy-chavy," but the Willow Wren utters a pleasing little warble, sweet, plaintive, and mellow. It has been called the piccolo soloist in the feathered orchestra.

Both birds are much alike, being clothed in grey, brown, and yellow, but the Chiff Chaff has black legs, whilst those of the Willow Wren are bright reddish-brown.

Although arboreal in their habits, the nests of

Fig. 18. Chiff Chaff.

both species are built on, or close to, the ground. The homesteads are dome-shaped, and are lined with a profusion of feathers. The six or seven eggs are white, marked with brown or brownish-red, the markings in those of the Chiff Chaff being much the stronger.

X.—INSECTS OF THE WOOD

GIANT-TAILED WASP—HORNET—RINGLET BUTTERFLY— STAG BEETLE

THE wood is populated by countless numbers of insects, many of which are so small as to be almost invisible to the naked eye. There are also a number of fairly large insects in the wood — especially at nightfall, when the Moths appear—but one cannot hope to do more than direct attention to a few of these.

D

Among them there are a few kinds of Wood Wasps, some of which, unlike the common kind, are solitary in their habits. Many people seem to imagine that Wasps are uninteresting and useless insects, but if inquiry be made, it will be found that their life-history is a very remarkable one, and that they have a useful career.

It is interesting to notice that the extensive order of insects to which the Wasps belong is split up into two large divisions. In the one section the females have an ovipositor, which is used as a saw or an auger, and in the second section this wonderful little instrument is modified into a sting.

The Giant-tailed Wasp belongs to the division possessing stout ovipositors, but the true Wasps, Ants, and Bees claim relationship with the section having a sting. One section of the " Borers," as we may call them, includes the Saw-flies, in which the boring apparatus is modified into a pair of toothed saws, and a highly magnified photograph of one of these saws will be seen facing page 74.

The prominent ovipositor of the female Giant-tailed Wasp is often mistaken for a sting, but it should be pointed out that this is a harmless species, so far as its stinging powers are concerned. The female, by means of her strong boring apparatus, makes a hole in a tree, and if there be any Silver Firs in the wood, there one may expect to find this handsome species.

The eggs, having been deposited in a suitable place, are in due course hatched, and then the young larvæ commence to bore galleries in the solid wood. These larvæ are fleshy and cylinder-shaped; they have strong mandibles but no eyes; they are also practically without legs. As the larva pursues its excavations, it fills up the gallery through which it has passed with the rejected particles of wood, and these are squeezed very tightly together so as to close the tunnel efficiently.

The creature feeds upon the solid wood, and when full-fed and the time has arrived for it to change into a pupa, it pupates in a cell in the wood. There it remains until it eventually comes forth as the perfect insect, boring its way out of the tree through a clean-cut tunnel.

Some authorities state that the female does not deposit her eggs in a healthy tree, show-ing a preference for one exhibit-ing signs of decay. The Silver Fir is a special favourite with this species, but several other conifers are also liable to attack. The female Giant-tailed Wasp is yellow in colour, with two black bands. The stout ovipositor is half as long as the abdomen, but

Fig. 19. Hornet.

the male may be distinguished by having a black-tipped abdomen which ends in a rectangular point.

Another woodland Wasp is known as the Hornet, which is the largest species of true Wasp found in Britain. It is a fine insect and, unlike the Giant-tailed Wasp, possesses a powerful sting.

The Hornet is a handsome yellow and red-brown Wasp, but its habits are very different to the species last mentioned. It builds a remarkable nest made up of a kind of paper manufactured from bark, and this is placed by preference in a hollow tree, in a bush, or under the eaves of a house.

A single female or Queen at first commences the nest unaided, she alone having lived throughout the Winter. Then she sets to work and constructs a series of cells inside the structure, and in each of these an egg is deposited. When the first brood is fully grown, they at once commence to assist the mother in building more cells; the Queen is then relieved of much of the hard work she had previously performed on her own account, for her children willingly assist in enlarging the home and various other ways. The female and worker both possess powerful stings, but the Drone, or male, is stingless.

Wasps feed upon various kinds of food, such as the nectar of flowers, honey-dew, the juices of sweet fruits, and also insects and their larvæ, Spiders, and the dead bodies of larger animals.

If possible the nest of a Hornet should be examined, for it is only by personal acquaintance with it that the wonderful industry of a common insect can be properly appreciated and understood.

Can you tell the name of that dark-coloured Butterfly which tenants the wood, especially that part of it where various grasses flourish in their damp bed? Where the shadows are falling, the Ringlet—for such it is—seems very much at home, and there it should mostly be sought for.

The yellow-white egg soon changes to pale brown, and may be looked for among grass in July and August. At that season the adult insects are upon the wing. The egg hatches in August, the larva feeds upon various grasses until chill October, and then, curious to relate, it hibernates until the following Spring, instead of pupating like most other British Butterflies. But when the March Violets are in flower, the Ringlet larva commences to feed again, and continues until June. The larva is pale brown in colour, with a darker line along the back. Search should be made among tufts of grass for the pupa, and this will be found to be brown, sprinkled with reddish-brown.

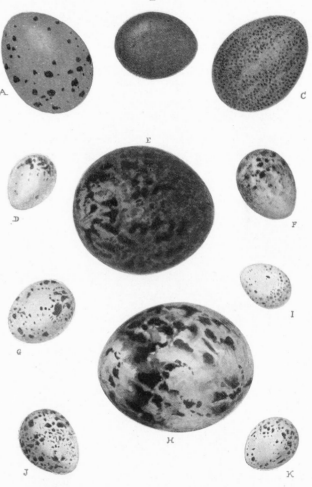

EGGS OF BRITISH BIRDS.

A. SONG THRUSH.   B. NIGHTINGALE   C. BLACKBIRD.
D. TREE CREEPER.   E. KESTREL.   F. BLACKCAP.
G. NUTHATCH.   H. SPARROW HAWK.   I. BLUE TIT.
J. GREAT TIT.   K. CHIFF CHAFF.

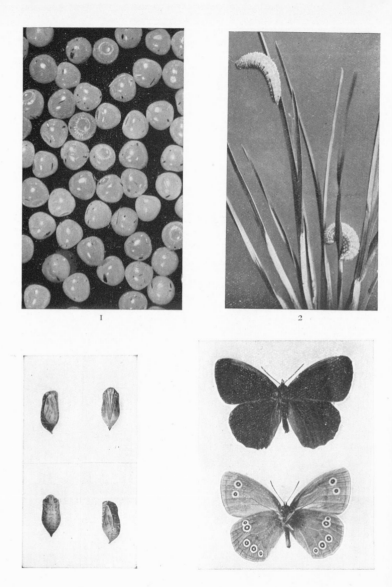

1

2

3

4

LIFE HISTORY OF RINGLET BUTTERFLY.

1. EGGS GREATLY ENLARGED.   2. LARVÆ.   3. PUPÆ.   4. MALE, Upper and Under Side.

The male Ringlet is sooty-brown to black; there are one or more black spots with pale rings on the fore-wings. The under sides of the fore-wings have two and sometimes three spots, whilst the under sides of the hind wings have five. The female is lighter in colour.

But now another creature claims attention, for see, crawling along the path we are traversing there is a large dark chocolate-coloured Beetle clothed in a horny coat of mail. It is a Stag Beetle, so-called because of the fine pair of "horns" possessed by the male we have under observation. The female does not have these prominent "antlers," although she has more powerful jaws.

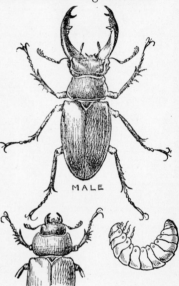

Fig. 20. Stag Beetle.

There goes the Stag Beetle crawling gently along, and who would imagine that this slow-moving insect had wings with which it can fly tucked away under a horny covering? It sometimes rises to a great height, and has been known to fight with a large Bat.

What is the Stag Beetle doing in the wood? The female makes a hole in a tree with her small "antlers," and then lays her eggs. When hatched, the larva feeds upon the solid wood, but, unlike that of the Giant - tailed Wasp, does not pupate there. At such time it comes from its hiding-place, and buries its body in the earth. It then builds a cocoon, or shroud, and sleeps.

Some time late in the Autumn, the perfect Beetle emerges, but it is loath to leave the old home, remaining attached to the cocoon all through the Winter and until the following Summer.

XI.—MORE INSECTS OF THE WOOD

BRIMSTONE BUTTERFLY—WOOD ANT—BURYING BEETLE—COCKCHAFER

EARLY in the Spring many creatures are tempted to come from their Winter hiding-places, and the sight of a Brimstone Butterfly flitting through the wood, like a dainty yellow fairy, is very pretty.

The trees and bushes being still leafless, for Fairy Sap has not yet risen from her underground home, the bright sulphur-yellow colour of the Brimstone's wings sheds a ray of light upon the surrounding bareness. Is it not remarkable that the insect should, after storing itself away for the whole Winter, come out in the early Spring looking so trim and neat?

Wherever there is Buckthorn growing, there one may expect to find the Brimstone Butterfly, this being the favourite food plant. The eggs are laid on the under side of the leaves during the Summer; they are quite small, but the enlarged picture shown in the coloured plate will give an idea of their shape and colour. They are slightly green when first laid, but change to yellow and later to dull purple-grey. This should be carefully noted.

The green larva has a bluish tinge with a pale line upon the sides of its body, and also specks of black. The pupa is also bluish-green. The male insect is brighter coloured than his mate, the female being a lighter greenish-yellow. There is an orange spot in the centre of each wing; the veining is very distinct; the antennæ, or feelers, are red, and the thorax will be found to be covered with long silky hair.

Now we are in luck's way, for we have suddenly stumbled across a mound of earth and twigs underneath a Fir tree; as we approach we disturb a Green Woodpecker

which was engaged feeding upon something on or near the mound. Let us get nearer and solve this woodland secret.

Here is a busy scene indeed, an insect fortress and city owned by the Wood Ant. See how the inhabitants of the citadel are all busily employed carrying pieces of stick to improve their stronghold, or morsels of food wherewith to feed the young.

They are indeed industrious and intelligent

Fig. 21. Wood Ants and Section of Nest.

creatures; Cicero ascribed to them mind, memory, and reason, and Aristotle praised their sagacity.

This large hillock, then, has been constructed by these small insects, and you will observe how well the Fir needles and pieces of twigs aid them in building the Ant City. Where Fir trees flourish, the ground around is soft and spongy, and it is here that the Wood Ants make their home.

If we could see beneath the citadel some such scene as that shown in Fig. 21 would be seen, the galleries, chambers, pathways, main streets, highways and byways, being of a most interesting description.

There are three classes of Ants in the City, known as males, females, and workers. It will be observed that the male and female both possess wings, but the worker Ant is wingless.

Let us catch a male and examine him. It is easier said than done perhaps. Now we have proved successful!

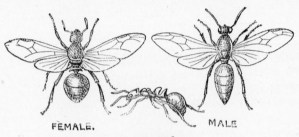

FEMALE.   MALE

WORKER
Fig. 22. Wood Ants.

Place him in this small glass-covered box until we catch a female. She may be destitute of wings, for at certain seasons they are shed and she becomes wingless like the worker. One has to be very quick in catching hold of these industrious creatures, for they have no time for gossiping with human kind, even if they do have their own sports and pastimes as some naturalists would have us believe. "All work and no play," it is said, "makes Jack a dull boy," and who can contradict the statement that some of these persevering folk try to carry out the same motto?

There, we have secured a female now. Place her also in the box with the male, for, by comparing the two, identification can be made doubly sure. Notice that the abdomen of the male is more lengthened than that of the female, the latter being more rounded.

Strong in comparison with their size, active beyond measure, tireless to a degree, useful in feeding upon smaller insects of an injurious nature and of eating refuse which is well cleared out of the way, highly intelligent and persevering, such are a few of the many interesting points concerning them.

All, however, are not so industrious. Some kinds have their slaves, others invite guests into the Ant City. Yet again there are those which have for so long led an idle life that they are actually dependent upon the labours of others.

Many are sociable, a few are solitary. Generally speaking, however, these tenants of the wood may be regarded among the most remarkable insects we possess, and in building their home, procuring food, such as honey and the sweet juices of plants, they display keen energy and perseverance deserving of notice.

"Of what use are the workers?" you may ask. These take care of the pupæ, which are carried from one part of the nest to another so as to be placed in a suitable temperature; they also help the mature pupæ to escape from their cocoons. The so-called Ants' eggs sold in bird shops are not eggs at all; they are pupæ enclosed in cocoons. The eggs are really very small objects, white or pale yellow in colour.

Much more might be written concerning these Wood Ants, but sufficient has been told to invite the reader's attention to their interesting ways; but be careful how the citadel is approached, for strangers are not permitted within the City, and sentinels are posted at the gates to warn off those who have no proper business there.

Let us move on, but we need not go far before finding something more of interest. Very rarely one meets with the dead body of a bird or other animal; this is partly explained by the presence of what are called Burying Beetles, which are of great service in digging the grave, interring the body, and thus disposing of the deceased animal.

Here we are fortunate in discovering the body of a small bird upon which some Burying Beetles are busily

Fig. 23. Burying Beetles.

engaged. These Beetles are also called Sextons, and the commonest are brownish-black in colour, spotted and banded with deep orange-yellow. The head is large and powerful, for by means of it the Sexton digs out a little grave in which to bury the dead body.

Having accomplished this, the insects cover it with earth, but before finally closing the grave, Mrs. Beetle lays some eggs in the body of the dead animal. There she leaves them, and the carcase is at last given a decent burial.

What happens afterwards may perhaps be guessed, for, when the eggs hatch, the larvæ find a good food supply close at hand. They feed upon the flesh still left upon the body, and clean it so well that only the skeleton remains. After this the larvæ pupate, performing their change underground, and eventually appearing as the perfect insects.

Another Beetle that may be looked for during May and June is the Cockchafer. It is brown in colour, with a hairy thorax, and the antennæ are like little fans when examined through a powerful glass.

In June the female Cockchafer lays her eggs in the ground. Towards the end of Summer these eggs hatch, and the grey larvæ have the head and legs covered with a brown shell. They are big feeders, living upon the roots of farm-crops, and the damage thus done is often very great, especially as they live as larvæ for three years.

At night the adult insects are upon the wing, feeding upon the leaves of trees. The Nightjar and the Bat are two creatures that help to reduce their numbers, whilst Rooks, Jackdaws, Starlings, and other birds unearth the fat larvæ from the ground and thus help the farmer to get rid of some of his worst enemies.

XII.—MISCELLANEOUS ANIMALS OF THE WOOD

WOOD LOUSE—CENTIPEDE—MILLIPEDE

An old tree has been blown down and has probably fallen with a crash across the ditch in our wood. Pull a piece of the loose bark off and see whether there are any creatures underneath.

Yes, there are several. One is a small grey animal

about the size of a pea, fond of rolling itself into a little round ball when disturbed; another is a flat reddish-coloured creature, which can travel very quickly; and a third is dark brown, long and worm-like, and much slower in its movements.

What then are these? Evidently they are not insects, as is shown by their structure. The first is a Wood Louse, a creature not very distantly related to the Armadillo; in fact it is also a cousin of the Crab and the Lobster.

It resorts to dark places and delights in hiding under bark and stones. As you see, it is well protected with a

Fig. 24. Wood Lice.

grey coat of horny mail; the body is jointed so that it can easily roll into a ball for protective purposes, and its legs are many. In fact the whole body seems to be made up of a series of joints which are of distinct service. It feeds for the most part upon decaying plants, and is a land representative of a number of similar creatures found in both fresh and salt waters.

The flat animal that travelled so quickly was a Centipede. It is of an active disposition, with a long flat body, and possesses a great number of legs. Indeed, it is sometimes called Hundred-legs. Like the Wood Louse it is a lover of dark places, hiding under stones and other situations.

The Centipede may at once be distinguished by its red colour, flat body, with one pair of legs on each segment, its hurried movements, and in other ways.

Our third specimen was a Millipede. It is about one and a half inches long, dark brown in colour, with yellow

HORNET.

COCKCHAFER.

GIANT-
TAILED
WASP.

"SAW" OF SAW-FLY MAGNIFIED 200 TIMES.

LIFE HISTORY OF BRIMSTONE BUTTERFLY.

1. EGGS GREATLY ENLARGED.   2. LARVA ON BUCKTHORN.
3. PUPA SUSPENDED BY SILKEN GIRDLE.   4. MALE BUTTERFLY RESTING.

rings and numerous pairs of short white legs. When
disturbed, the round body of the Millipede rolls into a
spiral something like a very small Catherine wheel beloved
by boys on the fifth of November.

Neither of the three creatures we discovered goes
through the changes so common to insects, for, like the
Spider, the young Wood Louse, Centipede, and Millipede

Fig. 25. Centipede.

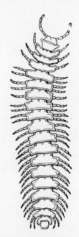

Fig. 26. Millipede.

come direct from the egg, and have no larval stage. True,
the young ones are either without legs, or only possess a
few pairs, but, as the creatures grow, the number of legs
increases, until at last the adult animal appears.

When our wood is shrouded in the sombre garb of Night,
many are the creatures which steal from their hiding-
places and lurk among the shadows. The Fox, the Bats, a
few birds like the Nightjar and the Owls, together with
hosts of Moths and other insects, hold high revel, and it is

impossible for us to follow them. Sufficient, however, has been seen by us during our tour through the wood to excite interest and to show the abundance of life to be met with there. Now follow up the story for yourselves, and take a pride in unravelling further secrets, which the wood can so well supply.

PRINTED BY THE TEMPLE PRESS AT LETCHWORTH IN GREAT BRITAIN

CALENDAR AND NOTES

OF

ANIMALS AND PLANTS

COMPILED BY C. S. COOPER, F.R.H.S.

I. BIRDS

BLACKBIRD.—In England all the year round. *Male bird :* general colour black; bill orange-yellow; length 10½ inches. *Female :* general colour blackish-brown; throat and chest rufous, mottled with black. *Nest :* March–September; in bushes, trees, shrubs, and hedges; coarse grasses woven together, plastered inside with mud, lined with fine grasses and leaves; *eggs* 4–6, greenish-blue with reddish-brown spots or blotches. *Food :* Insects, Worms, and Snails. *Song :* solemn, mellow, and powerful.

BLACKCAP.—A Summer visitor, arriving about middle of April; winters in N.E. Africa. *Male bird :* general colour greyish; crown of head glossy black; length 5¾ inches. *Female :* cap reddish-brown; length 5½ inches. *Nest :* May–June; in brambles, bushes, and small trees in hedges, shrubberies, and gardens; dry grasses, lined with roots and hair; *eggs* 4–6, dull white tinted with olive-brown, smudged with dark brown. *Food :* insects. *Song :* a rich, full, and sweet warble, not very loud.

BLUE TIT.—In England all the year round. *Male bird :* general colour above light green; wings and tail blue; crown blue, encircled with white; breast and abdomen yellow; length 4½ inches. *Female :* slightly duller in colour. *Nest :* April–June; in holes of trees, banks, or walls; dry grass and moss, lined with feathers; *eggs* usually 5–8, sometimes up to 12; white, with faint red-brown spots. *Food :* insects, especially those in fruit-buds. *Song :* mostly of one note, short and sharp, but a pretty trill is also uttered.

CHIFFCHAFF. — Mostly a Summer visitor, only a few birds being resident; arrives in middle of March, leaves for the South in September and October. *Male bird:* general colour above olive-green; under surface olive-yellow; feet dark brown, almost black; length 4½ inches. *Female:* similar. *Nest:* April–June; in banks, half-domed, of dry grass, lined with feathers; *eggs* 6 or 7, white spotted and speckled with reddish-brown or purplish-brown. *Food:* insects and larvæ. *Song:* two notes resembling its name and a complaining double note when it has young.

COAL TIT.—In England all the year round. *Male bird:* general colour above olive-brown; crown and throat black; breast and abdomen greyish-white; length 4¼ inches. *Female:* similar to male, length 3¾ inches. *Nest:* April–June; in holes of trees, walls, or banks; grasses and moss, lined with feathers; *eggs* 5–9, white, spotted and speckled with pale red. *Food:* insects. *Song:* mostly two notes, sharp and shrill.

GREAT TIT.—A constant resident. *Male bird:* general colour above green; crown, throat, and sides of neck black; under surface yellow; centre of breast and abdomen blue-black; length 5½ inches. *Female:* abdominal black streak narrow; length 5 inches. *Nest:* April–June; in a hole of a wall or tree; moss and grass, lined with feathers; *eggs* 5–12, generally 7 or 8, white, with pale red spots. *Food:* insects, seeds, fruits, and buds. *Song:* a strong, bell-like note, often repeated, and a " pink " like that of the male Chaffinch.

GREEN WOODPECKER.—Common in woods in the south and middle of England. *Male bird:* general colour above yellowish-olive; crown crimson; moustachial stripe crimson; under surface yellowish; length 12½ inches. *Female:* moustachial stripe black; length 12 inches. *Nest:* a hole in a tree, hewn by the birds; *eggs* 5–7, white and glossy, laid on the chips of wood at bottom of hole; end of April or beginning of May. *Food:* insects, acorns, and nuts; fond of visiting Ant-hills. *Call:* a noisy laughing note which, country people say, foretells rain.

KESTREL.—In England all the year, descending from highlands to lower ground in Winter. *Male bird:* general colour above rufous fawn or pale chestnut; head and neck slaty-blue; bill bluish, black at tip, yellowish at base; feet yellow; length 12½ inches. *Female:*

rufous above; head rufous; length 12½ inches. *Nest:* April and May; usually that of a Crow, Raven, Magpie, or Pigeon; *eggs* usually 3–5, reddish-brown, mottled with darker tint. *Food:* Mice, Moles, Rats, Birds, Frogs, Lizards, Cockchafers, and other Beetles. *Call:* a sharp, ringing, half-laughing cry.

LESSER SPOTTED WOODPECKER.—A constant resident in England. *Male bird:* general colour black and white; crown crimson; bill, legs, and feet dark slaty-grey; length 5¼ inches. *Female:* similar, but without any red on the crown; length 5 inches. *Nest:* none except rotten wood in hole of a tree; *eggs* 5–8, ivory-white; about middle of May. *Food:* insects, fruit, and berries. *Call-note:* said to be the drumming of the beak against a tree, and also cries in a shrill voice, " Chee, chee, chee, chee, chee."

NIGHTINGALE.—A Summer visitor, arriving in middle of April, and spending Winter in N.E. Africa. *Male bird:* general colour above russet-brown; under surface greyish-white; length 6½ inches. *Female:* similar; length 6 inches. *Nest:* May and June; on ground or low in a bush; dead leaves and grass, lined with rootlets; *eggs* 4 or 5, olive-brown or olive-green, occasionally dull bluish-green. *Food:* grubs and insects. *Song:* loud, rich, mellow, silvery, and clear, although a few notes are harsh and the bird utters also a grating k-r-r-r-r.

NUTHATCH.—A resident. *Male bird:* bluish-grey above; cheeks and throat ashy-white; flanks chestnut-red, under surface light fawn; length 5¾ inches. *Female:* similar; length 5½ inches. *Nest:* April-July; a hole in a tree or wall, plastered with clay, bed of dry grasses or dead leaves; *eggs* 5–7, white, spotted with red-brown. *Food:* insects, acorns, nuts, and berries. *Song:* a clear ringing note, oft repeated but often very deceptive.

RING DOVE OR WOOD PIGEON.—A resident; numbers largely increased in Winter. *Male bird:* general colour above slaty-drab, head bluish-grey; sides and back of neck green and lilac, with white patch on each side; under surface bluish-grey; bill orange-red and yellow; length 16 inches. *Female:* similar; length 15½ inches. *Nest:* March–July; in trees or bushes; a platform of crossed twigs; *eggs* 2, white. *Food:* peas, grain, young Turnip-tops, Charlock seeds, Beech-mast. *Call:* a " coo," oft repeated.

SONG THRUSH.—A constant resident; many from North come South in Winter. *Male bird:* olive-brown above; throat white, tinged with buff; fore-neck, chest, and sides of body golden-buff, spotted with black; feet yellowish; length 9 inches. *Female:* similar; length 8½ inches. *Nest:* February–September; in the lower limb of a tree, thick bushes, shrubs, ivy, or a rough bank; grass, moss, and twigs, thickly coated inside with mud or clay, lined with a smooth layer of rotten wood; *eggs* 4–6, blue, spotted with purplish-brown or black. *Food:* Snails, Insects, Worms, and fruit. *Song:* a great variety of clear rich notes, often repeated.

SPARROW HAWK.—A resident. *Male bird:* bluish-grey above, reddish-white below; bill blue; feet yellow; length 13 inches. *Female:* lighter grey above; whitish below; length 15½ inches. *Nest:* April–June; high in a tree or bush, or ledge of rock; twigs; *eggs* 3–5, whitish, blotched or marbled with dark reddish-brown. *Food:* Birds of many kinds, Mice, Rats, and Beetles. *Cry:* a harsh and screaming "mew."

TREE CREEPER.—A resident. *Male bird:* brown above, with a tinge of golden-buff; under surface silky-white; a streak of same colour above the eye; length 5½ inches. *Female:* similar; length 5 inches. *Nest:* April onwards; a hole in a tree, a crevice in the bark, or in a building; moss, small roots, chips of wood and bark, lined with feathers; *eggs* 4–9, white, spotted with pale red. *Food:* Insects and Spiders. *Song:* three or four shrill notes, resembling "treè, treè, treè."

TURTLE DOVE.—A Summer visitor, coming from N. Africa at end of April or beginning of May. *Male bird:* general colour above brown; head bluish-grey; sides of neck with patch of mottled feathers, black with bluish-white margins; abdomen white; bill brown; feet red; length 11 inches. *Female:* very similar; length 10½ inches. *Nest:* May–July; in a large bush or dense hedge, or in a tree; twigs and sticks; *eggs* 2, creamy white. *Food:* grain and small seeds, Snails. *Cry:* a soft, rich, low "coor-r-r, coor-r-r."

WILLOW WREN OR WILLOW WARBLER.—A Summer visitor, arriving at beginning of April, and leaving for Africa in September. *Male bird:* olive-green above, with tinge of sulphur-yellow; streak of dull sulphur-yellow above the eye; throat and fore-neck ashy-white, streaked with sulphur-yellow; breast and abdomen white; feet brown; length 4¾ inches. *Female :* similar; length 4½ inches. *Nest :* April onwards; on a bank, at bottom of a bush; half-domed, moss, grass, feathers, and leaves; *eggs* 5–7, white, speckled with light red. *Food :* insects. *Song :* a delicious warble.

WRYNECK.—A Summer visitor, arriving early in April, leaving for Africa in September; commonly called Cuckoo's Mate or Messenger. *Male bird :* reddish-grey above, with black and brown markings; under-parts creamy-white, with black arrow-head markings; bill and feet greyish-brown; length 6½ inches. *Female :* similar; length 6½ inches. *Nest :* a hole in a tree; *eggs* 6–8, or even 10, white; laid in May and June on chips of decayed wood. *Food :* Insects, Ants and their eggs. *Cry :* a shrill, musical " pee-pee," repeated several times.

II. INSECTS

BRIMSTONE BUTTERFLY. — February – May and August–October, hybernating through Winter. *Male :* bright sulphur-yellow, a small orange spot near centre of each wing; expanding 2½ inches. *Female :* greenish-yellow, similar orange spots. *Eggs :* May and June; on Buckthorn. *Larva :* June and July; dark green, with a pale line on each side; feeds on Buckthorn.

BURYING BEETLE.—Common in carrion in the Summer; smells strongly of musk; length 1 inch; elytra black, with two orange bands connected by a narrow band on the margin; a line of golden down on thorax; hind legs curved. *Eggs :* laid in carrion. *Larva :* long and narrow; legs very small; upper surface of each body segment has a horny plate, with toothed edges. *Pupa :* in cocoon underground; two sharp spines at end of body.

COCKCHAFER.—April–June. *Male :* 1⅓ inch long; elytra brown; abdomen produced to a point; fan of antennæ seven-lobed. *Female :* fan six-lobed. *Eggs :* laid in ground in June. *Larva :* body curved; yellowish-white; head and legs covered with brown shell; lives three or four years; feeds on roots of plants. *Pupa:* in cocoon in the earth.

GIANT-TAILED WASP.—*Male:* Length 1 inch, expanding 1¾ inch; body yellow and black. *Female:* length 1½ inch, expanding 2¾ inches; head black, with patch of yellow behind eyes; thorax black; abdomen yellow, with a black band; ovipositor reddish-brown. *Eggs:* laid in Fir tree. *Larva:* excavates tunnels, and feeds on solid wood. *Pupa:* in a cell in the wood.

HORNET.—May–September. *Queen:* length 1⅜ inch, expanding 2⅛ inches; body yellow, with red-brown markings. *Worker:* length 1 inch, expanding 1⅞ inch; feeds on insects. *Eggs:* placed one in each cell. *Larva:* fed by Queen. *Pupa:* passes through stage in its own cell.

RINGLET BUTTERFLY.—June and July. *Male:* wings expanding 1½ inch; smoky brown, fore wings with 1–3 indistinct white-centred black spots, each in a tawny ring, hind wings 2 such spots; under sides with 2 or 3 spots on fore wings, 5 on hind wings. *Female:* spots more distinct; expanding 1¾ inch. *Eggs:* July and August. *Larva:* August–June; greenish grey, darker line on back, two paler lines on each side; feeds on Millet and Annual Meadow Grass on to October, hybernating till March. *Pupa:* brown; among tufts of grass.

STAG BEETLE.—June–August. *Male:* Very variable in size, body measuring 2 inches or more; elytra deep chestnut, black on margins; armed with stag-like antlers (jaws). *Female:* smaller; no antlers; jaws small, curved. *Eggs:* laid in rotten wood, especially Oaks and Elms. *Larva:* white, soft, lives in tree for 5 years. *Pupa:* in the ground; Beetle emerges from cocoon in Autumn, remains attached to cocoon till following Summer.

WOOD ANT.—*Male:* length ⅓ inch; yellowish-black; legs red; four wings. *Female:* slightly larger; head and thorax rusty-red, abdomen black; four wings. *Worker:* darker than female and slightly smaller; there are large and small workers; no wings. *Eggs:* laid in cells of ant-hill. *Larva:* fed by nurse workers. *Pupa:* in a cocoon—the so-called " Ant's-egg " used for feeding fish.

III. MAMMALS

FOX.—A native of Britain. *General colour* of upper parts reddish-brown; under parts white; tail reddish, extremity white. *Length* of head and body 27–34 inches; tail 12–15 inches. *Home:* a burrow in sandy or gravelly soil; remains concealed during day, comes out towards evening. *Food:* the flesh of mammals, birds, and reptiles; its favourites are Partridges, Grouse, Rabbits, and Leverets.

SQUIRREL.—A native of Britain. *General colour* brownish-red on upper parts, white beneath; tail very bushy. *Length* of head and body 8¼ inches, tail 7–8 inches. *Nest:* in a hole in a tree, or in the fork between branches; roots, grass, twigs, and leaves. *Food:* nuts, acorns, buds, bark, fungi, and even young birds and eggs. *Habits:* passes most of its time among the branches; lays up store of food for Winter; during cold weather dozes for days at a time.

IV. MISCELLANEOUS

CENTIPEDE.—*Body:* red, flat, ¾ inch long; thorax and abdomen of similar segments; 15 pairs of legs, one pair to each segment; antennæ long. *Food:* chiefly worms. *Habits:* hides under stones and in loose mould; runs quickly.

MILLIPEDE.—*Body:* cylindrical, dark brown, almost black; legs white, very short, very numerous, one pair to each of the first three segments, two pairs to all other segments; antennæ short. *Food:* vegetable matter. *Habits:* subterranean, found among roots of grasses and other plants; rolls itself into a spiral.

WOOD LOUSE.—*Body:* grey, ½ inch long, oval, convex above, flattened below; seven segments, each with a pair of legs. *Food:* decaying vegetable matter. *Habits:* usually nocturnal; lives under loose bark, pieces of wood, and in cellars; rolls itself into a ball.

V. TREES AND FLOWERING PLANTS

Name.	Time of Flowering.	Colour.	Height.
Dog's Mercury	Feb.—May	Green	6–18 ins.
Oak	April, ,,	Greenish	Tree
Beech	,, ,,	,,	,,
Elm	,, ,,	Brownish	,,
Primrose	,, ,,	Yellow	3–6 ins.
Hyacinth	,, —June	Purplish Blue	6–18 ins.
Early Purple Orchis	,, ,,	Purple	6–12 ins.
Wood Sorrel	,, ,,	White	3–6 ins.
Wood Anemone	,, ,,	,,	4–8 ins.
Wood Strawberry	,, —July	,,	6 ins.
Gean	May, June	,,	Tree
Hornbeam	,, ,,	Greenish	,,
Scots Fir	,, ,,	{ Males Yellow { Females Greenish	{ ,,
Spruce Fir	,, ,,	{ Males Yellow { Females Reddish	{ ,,
Larch	,, ,,	{ Males Yellow { Females Rosy	{ ,,
Woodruff	,, ,,	White	9 ins.
Bugle	,, ,,	Purple	6–12 ins.
Wood Loosestrife	,, —Oct.	Yellow	3–12 ins.
Enchanter's Nightshade	July—Sept.	Pinkish White	12–18 ins.

THE
MEADOW I KNOW

EDITED BY

W. PERCIVAL WESTELL, F.L.S.
& HENRY E. TURNER

General Secretary of the School
Nature Study Union

WITH

12 COLOURED

& MANY BLACK AND WHITE
ILLUSTRATIONS

J. M. DENT AND SONS LTD.
BEDFORD ST. LONDON W.C.2
TORONTO VANCOUVER
MELBOURNE WELLINGTON

" Every blade of grass, each leaf, each separate floret and petal, is an inscription speaking of *hope*. Consider the grasses and the oaks, the swallows, the sweet blue butterfly—they are one and all a sign and token shewing before our eyes earth made into life. So that my hope becomes as broad as the horizon afar, reiterated by every leaf, sung on every bough, reflected in the gleam of every flower."—RICHARD JEFFERIES.

PRINTED IN GREAT BRITAIN

CONTENTS

7

LIST OF ILLUSTRATIONS

COLOURED PLATES AND HALF-TONES

ILLUSTRATIONS IN THE TEXT

9

THE MEADOW I KNOW

I.—GENERAL INTRODUCTION

FIRST VIEW—THINGS THAT PASS—USES OF A MEADOW—
THE ASH

Can any of you suggest a more delightful occupation than sitting on a wooden stile some bright Summer's morning, gazing across the sunlit meadows, that seem to stretch themselves lazily and contentedly before one's half-closed eyes? Perhaps the glistening dewdrops are still in evidence, and crown the rich green blades of grass, which nod without ceasing in their restless but friendly way to every passing breeze.

What better way than this can we have of making the acquaintance of our meadow? For as the day marches on, things have a tendency to grow stale, and to lose that sweet freshness which was their portion at early morn.

Then, as we sit and dream, we are borne on the wings of fancy to the realms of the past, and we wonder how many other folk have climbed the stile and wandered—maybe in search of pleasure, maybe on business bent—across this self-same meadow. But are we sure our meadow was always here? Has it had ever so many birthdays, and faced the storms of countless years? Was it always a field? And did it always look like this?

These are difficult questions to answer, for agricultural England has seen endless changes, and much has depended upon the farmers' wishes. Forests have given place to ploughed lands, ploughed lands to green pastures, and green pastures to waving fields of corn; thus our meadow may have passed through many phases. But it is with the present we would deal, so let us not concern ourselves too much with the past.

If we visit our meadow again and again, at all times and at all seasons, does it not convey to us the idea of "Things that pass"? For either the flowers die out each Autumn to be reproduced the following Spring by means of their seed, or they are perennials, which are renewed each year from buds in the underground stems. This is so unlike the wood, where the ever-present trees persist, almost in spite of time and weather.

But although the flowers of our field pass to come again, yet how wonderfully they are adapted to their surroundings. They are dependent upon bright light for their well-being, and here they can enjoy it to the full. Are they not also prepared to battle against the wind, which so often sweeps across these unprotected spots? Some, like the Thistle, have woolly or bristly leaves, and stems that do not easily break; others, such as the Tormentil, are stumpy and grow close to the ground, thus avoiding all conflict with the wind; a third class, in which may be included the Buttercup, have stems that bend before the storm, and are therefore unharmed by its violence.

But what *is* this meadow of which we have been speaking? What gives it the right to bear the name? Few of us love definitions, but surely we ought to know exactly what we are talking about. Does the absence of trees or the presence of grass make a meadow? Must there be a hedge to mark the boundary? Or is the hedge only a matter of convenience?

In America the word meadow is applied to any low land on the banks of rivers consisting of rich mould or an alluvial soil, whether grass land, pasture, tillage, or wood land. In England the term is more restricted, for it only includes a level tract producing grass to be mown down, or a rich pasture land. The hedge really plays no part in the matter, and only serves to separate one field from another.

What a variety of ideas are associated with our meadow! To the very young, perhaps, it is the land of Buttercups and Daisies, the magic world in which they roll and romp. Visions of cricket, football, and tennis are conjured up before the minds of others; and yet again, to the tired mothers and fathers, it is the scene of the quiet evening stroll.

But he who owns the land, what of him? What has the farmer to say upon the matter? To him the meadow is a piece of land where his cattle may feed and thrive. The rich, juicy grass, the sunny situation, the babbling brook which drains the land and slakes the thirst of his many sheep, these are the details he considers, not from a poetic point of view, but for their commercial value. He has his living to get, and knows full well that dreams will neither provide him with bread nor pay his rent.

How few meadows there are, which can claim to be absolutely treeless! Certainly ours cannot, for almost in the centre there stands a sturdy Ash, which must have watched over the varying fortunes of the surrounding fields for many a long year.

No one tree can claim to belong to the meadow, but few there are which will not flourish there, even more so than in a wood. The greater freedom to stretch out their long limbs, the more abundant supply of air and light, the absence of rivals in the struggle for existence and in the matter of obtaining a sufficient supply of food, these are most important factors to be considered, and tend to produce a perfect tree.

Our Ash is no exception to this rule, for it has made the most of its isolated position, and now lords it over the surrounding vegetation.

Should you visit this tree in Winter, you could not help being struck by the sturdy appearance of its boughs and blunt branches; indeed there is an entire absence of that delicate network of terminal twigs so noticeable in the Elm. The dark olive-green buds—black to all appearance—are special features of this tree, and distinguish it from every other.

Fig. 1. Ash.

In its early youth, it possessed a smooth, pale grey bark, which, as the years rolled on, became rough and showed signs of many vertical cracks, although the colour remained; indeed some people ascribe the name of the tree to its ash grey appearance.

About April or May the flowers appear—poor things, by the way, for they contain neither sepals nor petals; clusters of purpled-headed stamens surround each seed box, and make up in quantity what they lack in quality.

Later on, the leaves burst forth, and give to the tree that graceful feathery appearance, which has earned for it the title of " Venus of the Woods." These leaves are compound, and consist of from four to seven pairs of leaflets with an odd one at the end, the edges being distinctly toothed.

In spite of its beauty, the farmer is not over pleased to have an Ash on his land, for its dense roots keep near the surface, and thus deprive the upper soil of much of its richness. The wood is tougher and more flexible than that of any other European tree; indeed, before the reign of iron and steel, it was of great commercial importance. Even the Romans and Greeks valued it, and used it in the manufacture of their spears.

One word must be said about the fruits of the Ash, those narrow oblong scales with the seed at one end. Look for them during the Autumn, and when once you have found a bunch, you will easily understand why they are usually described as keys.

II.—GRASSES

WHAT THEY ARE—THEIR STRUCTURE—AND USES

How many of you, if sent into a meadow to gather a nosegay, would dream of including Grasses? Most of you would scorn the suggestion, and treat it with contempt. " Fancy a bouquet made of grass! The idea is absurd! " you would exclaim. And yet our Grasses are very beautiful plants, although they are so common; perhaps it is because they are so plentiful, that few people take the trouble to study and appreciate them in the way they deserve.

Although, for the present, we are only concerned with those which grow in our meadow, we ought to bear in mind that they form an enormous family, and include Wheat, Oats, Barley, Rye, Maize, Rice, Bamboo, and Sugar Cane. It is difficult to believe that all these plants are related to each other, but such is the case, and a most useful and necessary family they are. Not only do they provide human beings with a wholesome and endless supply of food, but the humbler animals enjoy and appreciate their excellent qualities.

The question may now arise, " What then is a Grass? "
The answer is thus given by Marshall Ward: " There are
two or three easily discoverable marks for distinguishing all
our Grasses from other plants. The first is their leaves are

Fig. 2.
A. Sweet Vernal Grass.
B. Smooth Meadow Grass.
C. Dog's-Tail Grass.

arranged in *two rows*, alternately,
up the stems; and the second
that their stems are circular or
flattened in section, or if of some
other shape they are never *triangular and solid*. Moreover, the
leaves are always of some elongated shape, and without leaf-
stalks, but pass below into a
sheath, which runs some way
down the stem and is nearly
always perceptibly split. Further,
the stems themselves are usually
long and cylindrical, and distinctly hollow except at the
swollen nodes (joints), and only
branch low down at the surface
of the ground or beneath it."

When we look around our
meadow, Grass seems everywhere,
and the blades are countless in
their numbers. How healthy they

appear! How easily they hold their own against other
plants! The secret of this activity and success partly lies
in their roots, which are so well developed, and branch in so
many directions, that they are capable, not only of keeping
the Grasses thoroughly well supplied with food, but of
robbing the less fortunate plants of their share.

Then again, the blades look as though they had been

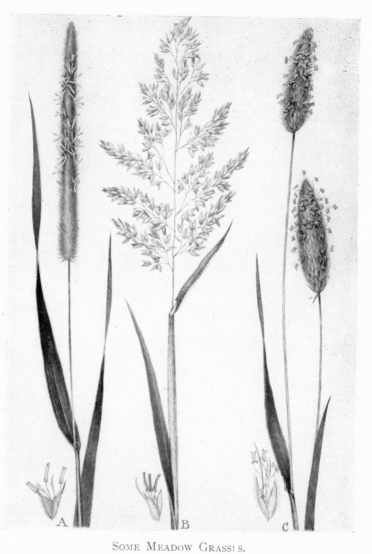

SOME MEADOW GRASSES.

A. COMMON CAT'S TAIL GRASS.   B. MEADOW SOFT GRASS.
C COMMON FOX TAIL GRASS.

DANDELION.

SEED-HEAD OF DANDELION.

coated with varnish; this appearance is due to the presence of a material called silica, which gives to the plant its hardness and polish. This peculiarity is specially marked in the Bamboo, which has this " coat of mail " so hard, as to resist the blow of a hatchet. What a splendid protection such armour must be!

When the fierce heat of noon is beating down upon the meadow, many of the blades, which were quite flat a few hours before, fold themselves up like a cigarette paper, one edge over the other, and form a kind of tube. What purpose does this serve?

Do you remember reading about Transpiration in *The Wood I Know*? There you were told that plants only give off the water they do not need—the surplus stock, in fact; but if they expose their surfaces to the full glare of the sun, they stand in danger of losing all their moisture and probably their lives. Thus Grasses, in common with many other plants, have resorted to various devices for preventing excessive Transpiration.

Where the sheath and blade meet, a small scale may be observed, which varies in size and shape for different species of Grass. The exact function of this scale is not clearly understood, but it has been suggested that it may prevent water from making a way between the sheath and the stem, where it would stagnate.

" The flowering stem of Grasses, usually spoken of as the culm, but better known to us as straw, is quite distinctive of this order of plants, being hollow except at the knots, which are a solid mass of fibres dividing the culm into a series of chambers." These are solid in a young state, but as they grow in length they become hollow, as previously stated.

It has been proved beyond doubt that a hollow tube is

stronger than a solid one *of the same weight*. Here, then, we have the reason why Grass has adopted this form—strength and lightness combined. One has only to think of a quill to realise the full truth of this.

The flowers of Grasses are arranged in clusters or spike-lets, and cannot be described as attractive, for they depend upon the wind to carry their pollen, and therefore have no need to put on gaudy apparel in order to attract the insects. The tiny bags of pollen ripen within the flowers, protected from unfavourable weather by waterproof scales. As soon as the pollen is ready for dispersal, the stamens lengthen and lift their precious burdens quite clear of the flowers, where they dance on their slender stalks in the slightest breeze.

There is no better way of studying Grasses than by making a collection of them for yourselves; differences small and large can then be noted, and the specimens compared with the drawings given in this book. Perhaps the most unfortunate point respecting them is their *true* names, usually so long and difficult as to frighten beginners. The sham English ones are often unsatisfactory, since many of them have come into use owing to the resemblance—more or less fanciful—of the Grasses to some well-known object.

However, do not let this concern you overmuch. Make your collection from the meadow, and later on you will not be content until you have gone farther afield. Gradually you will learn something of the habits of your new friends, and then it will not be a difficult matter to commit their names to memory.

Remember, too, that knowledge is power. In the West of France, for instance, enormous tracts of land and large sums of money have been saved by the planting of shifting sand-dunes with a particular type of Grass, which not only fixed the sand, but prepared it for gradual afforestation, first with bushes and eventually with trees.

III.—MUSHROOMS AND TOADSTOOLS

THE TOADSTOOL SEASON—THEIR STRUCTURE—AND SHAPE

WHEN the evening mists of early Autumn gloomily hint of Winter's approach, how strange and ghostly our meadow appears! To the old and feeble, perhaps, these sights and signs spell nothing less than coughs and rheumatism; to others, younger in years and stronger in limb, they signal the approach of the Mushroom season.

Doubtless most of you have tasted and enjoyed these breakfast luxuries; however, it is one thing to see them dished up with eggs and bacon, or even in a grocer's shop, but it is quite another thing to see them growing in their own beloved native place.

Mushrooms are cousins to the Toadstools, and both belong to the great family of plants known as Fungi. Will it not therefore be advisable if we make quite

Fig. 3. Mushrooms.

sure what a Fungus is? " Mushrooms, Toadstools, the mildew on walls, the mould on bread, the rust on wheat, the potato disease, the yeast with which bread is made and beer fermented, the vinegar plant which is used to turn sugar and water into vinegar, and the disagreeable skin-disease called ringworm, all belong to the large and varied group of plants comprised under the name of Fungi."

B

Such a list is enough to frighten any boy or girl, so let us hasten back to our meadow, and content ourselves with the Fungi we can find there. Search should first of all be made for tiny white threads—a kind of " down " in fact—which branch in all directions beneath the surface of the ground; these are not the roots, but form the true plant, known to florists as spawn.

No green leaves aid it in obtaining carbon from the air, and no roots bring it moisture absorbed from Mother Earth. How then does it live, cut off as it is from the air and sun? It is in reality a scavenger, having lost the power of pre-paring food for itself, and feeds upon dead and decompos-ing vegetable matter, giving them, so to speak, a decent burial.

When the delicate threads, which go to make up the plant, become strong and numerous, they often assume a kind of tuft at a point just below the surface of the ground. From this tuft there springs up the object with which we are all so familiar, the worthy Toadstool itself, the *fruit* of the plant.

What a host of fairy stories are associated with the Toadstool! Has it not been for centuries past a shelter for the tiny elves, who hold high revel beneath its spreading cap? Is it not the throne whereon sits the Toad whose eyes are jewels of priceless worth? And when we come to consider the quaint shapes so often assumed by Toadstools, their unusual colours, and the lonely places they love to frequent, we no longer wonder why goblins, fairies, and other strange creatures are regarded as their friends and associates.

Although Mushrooms and Toadstools have a preference for the misty days of October, yet many specimens may be found at all times of the year. It must not be thought

that their home is limited to a field; on the contrary, that
is the least of their abiding places, for hundreds may be met
with on the ground under trees, on decaying stumps and
leaves, in damp, clayey woods, among the Beeches and
Pines, and on many a mossy bank.

Would you like to pick a few, and learn for yourselves
something of their nature?   Here,
for example, is quite an ordinary
specimen of the Mushroom type.
" It consists of a stalk supporting a
sort of cap.   Forming the lining of
the cap are a number of folds called

Fig. 4. Toadstools.

gills from their resemblance to the gills of a fish.   When
the Mushroom was young, the gills were concealed by a
kind of veil; as the cap expanded this veil was rent, but
the more central portion remained attached to the stem in
the form of a ring." [1]

Cut away the stalk from the cap, and place the latter
 with the folds downwards upon a piece
of paper, and leave it there for some
hours.   Use dark paper if the gills look
light, and *vice versa ;* by this means
you will get a more definite result.
It is also convenient to stick a pin
into the cap by way of a handle.

Fig. 5. Puff-ball Fungus.

When the cap is *carefully* lifted from the paper, a beautiful
pattern usually presents itself, formed by very fine dust.

What is this dust, whose tiny particles curl away like
smoke at the least breath of wind?   These are the spores,
those minute cells from which Fungi, like other flowerless
plants—Ferns and Mosses to wit—are reproduced;   they
differ from seeds in that they do not contain a miniature

[1] *Toadstools at Home,* by Somerville Hastings.

plant in their interior. It is therefore evident that the gills are the spore-producing layer.

Another simple experiment, which may interest you, is to " tease " out a Toadstool by means of a pin or some such instrument; it will be seen that the whole structure consists of threads, there being neither veins nor hard parts.

You have already been told that there is no better method of studying Grasses than by collecting them. The same plan should be adopted in the case of Fungi. Do not gather them thoughtlessly, but endeavour to make your collection as varied as possible. To do this you must not be content with remaining in the meadow, but must continue your search among the trees and along by the hedges.

Before long you will discover that, although many Toadstools have neither cap nor stem, every one has a spore-producing layer. This is, of course, the most important part of the " fruit," and upon its position and arrangement depends the group to which a Toadstool belongs. Do not rest satisfied until you have seen and handled a specimen of each of the following:—

1. An ordinary type of Toadstool with the spore-producing layer under the cap.

2. A specimen with this layer outside the cap.

3. One which looks like a bracket fastened to the trunk of a tree.

4. A coral or club-shaped Fungus.

5. An Elf-cup, which reminds one of a button depressed in the middle.

6. A Puff-ball, which opens at the top to let out the spores.

7. An Earth-ball, which has no definite method of open-

MEADOW CROWFOOT.

Oxeye Daisies.

ing, but retains its spores until decay or the foot of an animal sets them free.

When all these treasures have been yours—for most of them have a brief life—you will have commenced to understand something of what a Toadstool is.

IV.—COMMON COMPOSITE PLANTS

DANDELION—DAISY—OX-EYE DAISY—SOW THISTLE—
HAWKWEEDS AND HAWKSBEARD

IF we visit our meadow in early Spring, we may practically rely upon seeing the ever-present Dandelion. This is a flower of three seasons, for from March to October its yellow head is a feature of almost every field.

Its smooth, glossy leaves all spring direct from the long, thick root, and are deeply cut into sharply-pointed lobes; the latter are said to resemble the teeth of a Lion, and thus give the flower its name. Down the centre of the leaf runs a thin white line.

Each flower-head stands at the end of a hollow stalk, which gives out a milky juice if bruised or broken. It is when we come to the blossom itself that our real difficulties begin. The sepals and petals, that we have grown so familiar with during our walks along the hedge and among the trees, here seem to have undergone some change. The truth is, we have before us one of the "composite or compound group," each of whose flower-heads consists of numerous small flowers called florets; the latter are enclosed within a case something like a calyx, but which consists of bracts or modified leaves, modified in so far as they are not growing on an ordinary *leaf* stalk.

Let us gather a few Dandelions, now that we know something of the family to which they belong. Pick out one of the tiny florets! You will require a microscope to examine it thoroughly, but with your naked eye you can see that it is tube-like at the base, widening out at the mouth into a long yellow strap. It is these yellow straps that give to the blossom its well-known appearance.

Fig. 6. Leaf of Dandelion.

The floral envelope—the calyx-like case to which reference has just been made—consists of a double row of bracts, which remind one of overlapping scales. The inner row stands erect, but those outside bend back and appear to clasp the stalk.

Each sharply-pointed seed is crowned with a tiny parachute, to enable the wind to bear it away. Before dispersal the seeds are arranged like pins in a pincushion, and these can easily be dislodged by the mere act of blowing. Have not we all, at one time or other, pretended we could tell the hour of day by this simple method? Country children, at least, are familiar with this practice.

Another occupation in which they love to indulge is the plaiting of a Daisy chain, all unconscious, perhaps, of the beauty of the flowers they are so skilfully arranging.

Here in our meadow the Daisies are most plentiful, and the wonder is that they have the strength to blossom so early. Are you puzzled by the expression? Does it sound strange to suggest that a flower must have strength before it can bloom? Let us look into the matter for awhile.

" Just as animals do not live and grow upon the food they take into their mouths, but rather upon that food very much changed in the stomach and intestines, so plants cannot, and do not, live and grow upon the food taken from the soil and air, but from various substances that the leaves manufacture from that food. Bear in mind, also, the fact that flowering is a very exhaustive process, so much so, indeed, that many plants, *e.g.*, Mignonette, Sweet Peas, Stocks, etc., die after producing the flowers and fruit.

" Such plants do not bloom early, because it is some time before they can form and store sufficient food to supply the needs of the flowers, which, not being green, are unable to obtain food from the air for themselves. What ought we to expect to find, then, with plants that bloom very early? That they are not true annuals, but that, like Snowdrop, Crocus, Primrose, and Hazel, some part, at least, lives from season to season,

Fig. 7. Common Daisy.

and has a store of food laid up, as in bulbs, roots, and woody stems." [1]

These are called perennials, and to this group the Daisies belong. Shall we add a few to our bouquet, and thus get a close view of them? Take this one, for instance! Has it not some sort of resemblance to the Dandelion? Yes, for it too is a member of the composite family.

Look at the yellow centre, for there we shall find the perfect florets, each capable of shedding pollen and producing seed. These are tube-like and crowded together in unsuspected numbers. Count them, and you will be surprised at the total.

But the outside ones, the white strap-shaped florets,

[1] *Observation Lessons in Plant Life,* by F. H. Shoosmith, B.Sc.

what of them? They, poor things, are not perfect, and are more for show than anything else. They advertise the plant, so to speak, and attract the insects. More than this, they curl over at night to protect the important parts of the flower; many a small beetle has cause to be grateful for this habit, when cold, wet nights make it necessary to seek shelter.

The spoon-shaped leaves are arranged in the form of a rosette, and spring direct from the root; from their shape and arrangement one could believe that they had been specially designed to conduct the raindrops towards their roots.

Is there any difference between the flower we have just discussed and the Ox-eye Daisy? Put the two side by side and then draw your own conclusions.

The flower-heads of the Ox-eye are certainly much larger, and are surrounded by several rows of scales or bracts tipped with brown or purple; in the case of the smaller flower, only one row of green bracts is to be seen; then again, the former has a main stem for its leaves, the latter being deeply toothed, both of which points mark it out from its cousin.

To see the Ox-eyes at their best, we must wait until we find a field all a-bloom with them; the flowers are so large and the leaves so comparatively small, that they form a pure sheet of white. But however delightful they may appear to us, the farmer has a different opinion, for he sees in them nothing but harmful weeds, difficult to be got rid of.

Another plant, which the farmer would willingly destroy, is the Thistle, and all things that are like unto it. This would form a most difficult task, for they are many and numerous. The one which now claims our attention is the

Sow Thistle, so called, it is said, because of the liking displayed by pigs for its leaves and stems. Although it is dignified by the name of Thistle, yet in reality it has no connection with Scotland's beloved flower.

The Sow Thistle is not particular as to where it grows— meadows, waste places, and corn-fields all coming alike to it. The thick, juicy stem often rises to a height of four feet, and supports a number of large, brilliant yellow flower-heads. These consist of ray florets only, similar in shape to those of the Daisy.

The upper leaves clasp the stem, but those lower down possess stalks; they are fairly long and are divided into numerous lobes with sharply-toothed edges.

It would almost seem that our fields and waste places have a special love for big yellow flowers. So numerous are they, and in some cases so similar, that even botanists have a great difficulty in placing them in their correct groups.

Fig. 8. Sow Thistle.

The ordinary passer-by, however, is content to label them all Dandelions, and in this way the claims of our countless Hawkweeds, and even the Hawksbeard itself, are often overlooked.

It would take more space than this book can spare to put the matter right; but be warned in time, and when next you see a field decked in a cloth of gold, do not jump to the conclusion that you are gazing upon the handiwork of the Dandelion.

V.—MORE COMMON PLANTS OF THE MEADOW

BUTTERCUP—FIELD SCABIOUS—FIELD CONVOLVULUS—
COWSLIP—SHEPHERD'S PURSE—YELLOW RATTLE

AT the mere mention of a meadow one's thoughts naturally turn to Buttercups and Daisies; the latter we have already gathered, so let us pay our respects to the former. The five bright golden petals, placed in the form of a cup, at once explain the name. Many people, however, prefer to speak of the plant as Crowfoot, from the fanciful resemblance of the leaves to the foot of a Crow. Each leaf is divided into three parts, and these again are deeply cut.

Will it surprise you to hear that there are three distinct species of Buttercup, all of which may be found in this meadow? Doubtless our best plan will be to search for a specimen of each, in which case the following notes should prove of some use.

The Meadow Crowfoot has a *smooth*, upright stalk, rounded in shape, and often rising to a height of three feet. The broad petals are more or less flattened out, and the sepals grow close up to the blossom.

The Bulbous Crowfoot, so called from its bulb-like root, has a *furrowed* stalk, and sepals that bend away from the blossom as if anxious to clasp the stalk. The cup-like shape of the blossom is most pronounced in this species, and it seems to cradle the cluster of yellow-headed stamens and the knot of tiny green seed vessels.

The Creeping Crowfoot is a most troublesome weed, for it sends out many runners, which take root and impoverish the soil. Here, again, the flower stalks are furrowed, but the sepals are not folded back.

THE MEADOW I KNOW 33

In spite of their beauty, Buttercups are useless, nay, even harmful to the farmer. They exact their toll of the richness of his land, and give him nothing in return, since their bitter acrid flavour makes them unacceptable to his cattle.

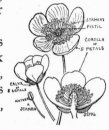

However, we must leave the Buttercups to fight their own battles, whilst we seek for new treasures. There, for instance, among the tangled vegetation that borders our meadow, is a tall lilac-coloured flower, the Field Scabious.

The hairy stem, rounded in shape and almost three feet in height, is crowned with

Fig. 9. Meadow Crowfoot.

a flower-head consisting of from forty to fifty florets, beautifully arranged into a dainty bouquet, and surrounded by two rows of pointed floral leaves or bracts. The inner florets are tinged with red, and are smaller than their outer companions, which are usually pale blue or lilac in colour.

Although the tiny corollas vary in length, they all have, comparatively speaking, wide, funnel-like mouths; thus their honey can be reached by long-tongued and short-tongued insects alike, and among the numerous visitors may be seen Bees, Flies, Moths, Butterflies, and Beetles.

Fig. 10. Field Scabious.

The leaves behave somewhat strangely, and vary not only on the same flower, but in different specimens; those near the root are generally lance-shaped with toothed edges, but farther up the stem they are divided something after the fashion of a feather.

In deep contrast with the Field Scabious is the Field

Convolvulus. Nothing is there about it to suggest sturdiness; on the contrary, it seems to be a weakly plant, apparently dependent on others for support.

And yet, to a certain extent, its appearance belies its powers, for few flowers can claim greater strength of purpose in pushing their way and increasing their numbers. Once it takes possession of the land, nothing short of vigorous measures can thrust it out; the roots creep and branch for many feet underground, sending up several stems clothed with leaves shaped like the head of a spear.

Convolvulus is a Latin word meaning to twine and twist about. Its other name, Bindweed, is equally suitable, as you will readily agree if you endeavour to set free some unfortunate herb from its "spiral embrace."

The five green sepals form a small case into which the petals fit; the latter have united to form the funnel-shaped corolla, dainty to look at, but so frail that the advent of night or the approach of a storm causes it to fold up.

Only long-tongued insects can gather its honey; this is situated beneath the base of the stamens, against which the tongue of the insect must come into contact when the nectar is being collected. Thus you can understand how the pollen is borne from flower to flower.

What a feast the Bees must have in our meadow; but, perhaps, few flowers are more intimately associated with those busy insects than yonder Cowslip.

You have all heard of Shakespeare's charming song which begins—

" Where the bee sucks, there lurk I,
In a cowslip's bell I lie."

What a delightful cradle for a fairy the pure yellow flower would make, strengthened as it is by an unusually long calyx of a pale green tint.

Marsh Marigold.

Meadow Sweet.

FIELD CONVOLVULUS.

The drooping blossoms are borne on little stalks, that hang from one point; and if you look down the tubes of varying specimens, you will see that, which will remind you of the story of pin-eyed and thrum-eyed Primroses described in *The Wood I Know.*

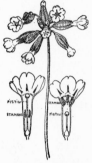

Fig. 11. Cowslip.

The crinkled egg-shaped leaves will also revive memories of the Primrose, to which, indeed, the Cowslip is closely related.

Again and again as we have wandered among the flowers, the fact has been brought home to us that pollen is carried from one blossom to another by an outside agency, maybe the wind, maybe an insect. This act is spoken of as " cross-fertilisation," but it must not be inferred that all other methods can only end in failure.

" What cross-fertilisation does is to produce more brilliant individuals, and to keep up large flowers of bright hue. In fact, it produces a kind of floral aristocracy; whilst the principal work of the vegetable kingdom—the abstraction of carbon from the atmosphere, the setting free of oxygen, the production of food for the entire animal races — is done mainly by the less brilliant weeds and grasses and trees — the working classes." [1]

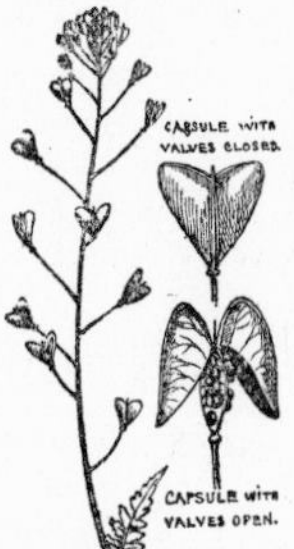

Fig. 12. Shepherd's Purse.

Among the latter may be numbered the Shepherd's Purse, a most interesting weed in its way. It seems to disapprove of virgin soil, and confines its attention principally to those spots which have been tilled by man, or disturbed by the animals which

[1] Edward Step in *The Romance of Wild Flowers.*

he keeps. In other words, it is a " mere hanger-on of industry," and probably this fact has gained for it the alternative name of Pickpocket.

This hairy plant ranges in height from a few inches to a couple of feet, according to the suitability of its surroundings. The lowest leaves are large, deeply cut, and arranged in the form of a rosette. They are stalkless farther up the stem, and this they clasp, giving one the idea of arrow-heads robbed of their shafts.

Fig. 13. Yellow Rattle.

The four small white petals are arranged in the form of a cross, after the manner of those of the Wall-flower, to whose family the Shepherd's Purse belongs.

Each of the numerous seed-boxes is placed at the end of a small stalk, and somewhat resembles those heart-shaped leather purses worn by our forefathers. It is this peculiarity that gives the plant its name. Such an abundance of seed is produced, that the seedlings take possession of all cultivated ground as soon as the husbandman's back is turned.

Another frequenter of the meadow, and one which often causes the farmer annoyance, is the Yellow Rattle. This plant has the habit of preying upon the roots of its neighbours, to which it attaches itself by means of small suckers; thus it is often described as a parasite. The smooth, square stem is sometimes one foot in height, and bears narrow, deeply-toothed leaves, having no stalk.

The light green calyx resembles a bladder with flattened sides, and from this peeps out the yellow tube-like corolla. This consists of two lips, the upper of which arches over and reminds one of a helmet; the lower is flatter, and affords an excellent alighting place for a Bee in search of honey.

The seed vessel contains several rather large and flat seeds, which rattle in their case when shaken; hence the name of Yellow Rattle.

VI.—MOISTURE-LOVING PLANTS

MEADOW SWEET—LADY'S SMOCK—MARSH MARIGOLD—
RAGGED ROBIN—RIBWORT PLANTAIN

IT has already been pointed out in these books, that most plants have a preference for some particular spot, and that their structure is specially adapted to fit them for their beloved haunts. This is admirably shown when we come to visit the moist parts of our meadow, those parts, for example, which border the rippling brook or the more frequent ditch.

Here the leaves are usually smooth, and the stems thick and hollow; very often, too, the roots are short and do not burrow deep down into the ground.

Shall we search for some of these, and, all regardless of the mud, hunt for new specimens along the ditch? Maybe we shall find the ground fairly dry, but it is always as well to go prepared for the worst; thin shoes and Sunday clothes are best left at home, when country rambles are to the fore.

Probably the queen of moist lands is the Meadow Sweet, a tall graceful plant, which often measures four feet in height. The stem may be tinged with red or purple, and is usually furrowed, though smooth to the touch.

The leaves are very prominent, and consist of large and small leaflets arranged alternately, with a large single one at the end; all of these are deeply serrated. The upper surfaces are dull green in colour, but if the underside be exposed, we shall find it covered with white, silky hairs.

But the joy of the plant is the head of small creamy-white blossoms, which give forth such a delightful scent, very suggestive of almonds. Separately the blossoms are insignificant—five small petals and a crowd of stamens; but when they are grouped together in dense clusters, the effect is magical, and few insects there be that can resist their united beauty.

In spite of their delicate odour, no honey is secreted, but Bees may find their reward in the abundant supply of pollen for which Meadow Sweet is famous.

You are not surprised, are you, to hear that Bees collect pollen? One of the most entertaining sights imaginable is to stand near a hive and watch these busy insects land on the platform, which borders their " front door," and then waddle in, their hind legs laden with the golden dust destined to make Bee bread.

We shall not have far to hunt before finding " Lady's Smock all silver white." Silver white it is at times, although its colour is more often of a pale lilac.

This light and graceful plant, one of the earliest to flaunt its blossoms, is not satisfied with one kind of leaf, for whilst those which arise from the root have leaflets inclined to be round, those which spring from the stem have leaflets of a longer, narrower, and more strap-like form.

Another curious feature of these leaves is the habit they have, when lying prostrate on the ground, of taking root and sending up a fresh plant.

Lady's Smock—or, to give it another of its many titles,

the Cuckoo Flower — is related to the Wall-flower, as the arrangement of its four petals, and, at a later date, its long, thin seed pod will testify.

In striking contrast to the frail-looking Lady's Smock is the sturdy, highly-coloured Marsh Marigold or King Cup, which, to quote Tennyson, " shines like fire in a swamp."

The broad, kidney-shaped leaves are highly polished, and do not grow to their full size until after the blossoms have reached their prime; probably this is one of Nature's methods of keeping these blossoms in full view of the insects, until such times as their visits are no longer necessary for the cross-fertilisation of the plant.

We have already come across flowers without petals—the Wood Anemone to wit. In the King Cup we have a further example of this, for the five " burnished discs of gold," which go to form the well-known cup, are sepals.

Fig. 14. Leaf of Marsh Marigold.

A big bunch of yellow stamens and numerous seed vessels occupy the centre; indeed the whole blossom, often two inches in diameter, reminds one of an overgrown Buttercup.

Tradition says that many of the flowers that decorate our highways and byways have, at one time or the other, been dedicated to the Virgin Mary. Indications of this fact still linger in the names of these plants. Thus we have Marigold, Lady's Smock, and many others; but it must be confessed there are doubts as to the reliability of this somewhat ancient explanation.

However, we need not concern ourselves over much with this question, for after all, " A Rose by any other name

c

would smell as sweet." Still, it is interesting, and very often instructive, to trace the origin of names.

Look at that rosy flower, for instance, which stands by the side of the King Cup! Do not its colour and untidy appearance at once suggest the reason for its being called Ragged Robin? Here along the side of the ditch it grows in great abundance, for it delights in such places, but is rarely seen where the soil is hard and dry.

Fig. 15. Ragged Robin.

The leaves resemble those of the Stitchwort, being long and narrow, and usually clasp the stem; the latter varies in length from one to two feet, and is slightly sticky in its upper parts. Each of the five rose-coloured petals is cut into four narrow segments, which give to the blossom its ragged appearance.

Before saying good-bye to the flowers of our meadow, we must stop awhile to examine the despised Plantain. This type of weed is everywhere abundant, but the Ribwort species is seen at its best where the ground is moist.

Like the Primrose, its leaves are arranged in the form of a rosette. Is there any advantage in this? Leaves are as anxious to get light and air as

Fig. 16. Ribwort Plantain.

you are, and Nature is ever bringing to our notice numerous methods by means of which leaves are made to occupy the minimum of space yet obtain the maximum of light and air.

The bough of almost any tree at its prime will provide an excellent example of this.

But let us return to our Ribwort Plantain. The leaves, which have already been mentioned, are long and narrow, with veins prominent enough to suggest the presence of ribs. The stalks are so tough and wiry that country children use them as weapons of war, and challenge all comers to " cross swords " with them. This simple game is sometimes dignified by the name of Soldiers.

The erect flower stalk is crowned with a cone-shaped head, around which the tiny brown-tinted blossoms are clustered; the most conspicuous part of these is the stamens, and the abundant supply of pollen indicates that the wind is the carrying agent.

VII.—SOME MAMMALS OF THE MEADOW

HARE—MOLE—SHORT-TAILED FIELD VOLE—
COMMON SHREW

AMONG the wealth of grasses and wild flowers growing in the meadow, there are a number of animals which find a snug hiding-place, and with some of these we may now strike up an acquaintance.

Let us take a saunter round the border of the meadow, keeping as close to the hedge as we can, so as not to injure the hay-crop that will soon be gathered in. If we keep our eyes open, we shall then see some of the animal tenants which make their home in the meadow we are visiting.

Should we be fortunate, we may perhaps disturb a Hare, or better still, find some young ones—called Leverets

—squatting in the " nest." It is really a poor apology for a nest, as this interesting animal, unlike the Rabbit, does not make a burrow in the ground. The Hare squats in a favourite spot, known as a " form," and it is here that the three to five young ones may be looked for.

Are you aware of the chief differences between young Rabbits and young Hares? Should we be lucky enough to find both animals during their infancy, the question could soon be answered, for we should then see that whereas young Rabbits are born blind and do not open their eyes for some few days, young Hares are born with their eyes well open. And why is this?

Fig. 17. Foot of Hare.

You will remember that the Rabbit is, to a very great extent, a burrowing, or underground animal. We shall meet with a number of them upon the Common later on, and shall then have more to tell concerning them. It is important to point out here, however, that young Rabbits, being born in a nest usually built underground, are more protected from enemies than the young Hares; hence it is only natural that the latter should have some means whereby they are able to protect themselves from numerous foes. Thus, when born, their eyes are open, and the little creatures are soon able to run about and take care of themselves, a proceeding that would be impossible if their eyes were closed.

Stop! what was that creature which so suddenly scampered almost from our feet? Watch the grasses move as the Hare—for such it was—makes its way across the meadow. Follow closely the movement of the herbage, for the animal may then come out into the open at the far corner. Wait and watch. Look! there it is, shuffling

CUCKOO FLOWERS AND DAISIES.

MOLE.

SHORT-TAILED FIELD VOLE.

along and turning its head to see if it is being watched. Use these field glasses, so that you may observe what it is like. Can you see its grey and red fur, the white under parts, the long legs and ears, and prominent eyes? It is a fine runner over open country, and a splendid swimmer. Unlike the rabbit, it lives a solitary life, and is at all times well worth watching.

Yet another visitor, the Mole, ran quickly across the path just now. Did you notice it? It was black in colour, and moved rapidly as we spoke. Let us follow upon the track of this meadow lover, starting at the spot where the grass under the trees is short and firm. A little hole is all that is left to denote the place where it entered the earth. A wonderful little underground creature this! He is able, by means of a pointed head and soft, silky fur, that may be brushed either way, to force his barrel-shaped body through

Fig. 18. Forefoot of Mole.

the earth; his strong, flesh-coloured fore-feet, armed with sharp claws, assist him to dig and tunnel with alarming rapidity. These fore-feet are more like strong little hands, and are quite different from those behind.

See, here is a tunnel just below the surface, and running right across the path, and under the trees yonder there are many large hillocks of soil that have been thrown up by this interesting creature. Are these all nests? No, they are not, for, although so many Mole-hills are thrown up, each family has a central citadel, as it were, and from this numerous galleries and chambers lead to various parts of the underground runs. Along these pathways the Mole travels for the purpose of securing food, and this consists of earthworms, various kinds of caterpillars, and even mice, shrews, small reptiles, and frogs.

It is a lover of water, too, and has the habit of sinking a shaft in the earth so as to quench its thirst. It is also a good swimmer, but, unless necessity demands it, rarely takes to the water of its own accord. Its greatest enemy —next to man—is the Weasel, and this animal steals from the hedgerow yonder, and waits a favourable opportunity for stalking the velvet-clad little gentleman.

Is it not wonderful how clean the Mole keeps its coat when it is remembered that it dwells in the earth? This remark may be applied equally well to a number of burrow-

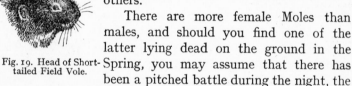 ing animals, such as Ground Beetles and others.

There are more female Moles than males, and should you find one of the latter lying dead on the ground in the
Fig. 19. Head of Short-tailed Field Vole. Spring, you may assume that there has been a pitched battle during the night, the males fighting during the breeding season for possession of a wife.

Beneath one of the hillocks of earth, the nest should be sought for about July, and here from five to seven young ones may be found. At first they are pale brown or grey, with a light pink snout. When the baby Moles are able to leave the nest, it is forsaken altogether, the main citadel then forming their meeting place and chief resort. Accused of doing damage to lawns, gardens, and fields, the Mole is in some districts killed in large quantities, but it has been stated that its runs help to make natural waterways and so drain the land. That the animal does more good than harm seems agreed, but this cannot be said of the next species we may find in our meadow, namely, the Short-tailed Field Vole.

The Long-tailed Field Mouse, that we found in the

hedge, is first cousin to the Short-tailed Vole, but the latter is a smaller animal, and can at once be distinguished by its shorter tail. It is dull grey-brown or greyish-white in colour, and in some seasons is found in such large numbers that the farmer is at his wits' end to know how to keep them down. Almost any kind of vegetable food is eaten, such as grass, clover, seeds, roots, corn, turnips, potatoes, fruit, berries, Beech-mast. If there were not certain animals like the Fox, Weasel, Stoat, Owls, Kestrel, and others which prey upon Voles, we should soon be over-run with these harmful pests.

The Short-tailed Field Vole burrows underground, riddling the land and destroying almost every living vegetable with which it comes into contact.
Search should be made about twelve to twenty-four inches below ground for the nest. This consists of hay, or grass and moss; from four to eight young ones may be found snugly tucked up in their cosy home.

Fig. 20. Head of Common Shrew.

Look here, we have discovered a tiny animal, brown and red in colour, with a pointed snout and prominent whiskers. What little creature is this that tenants the meadow? It is a Common Shrew, and a near relative of the Mole. It belongs to the insect-eating tribe, and not to the Rodents as does the Vole.

For some reason at present unknown, one finds dead Shrews upon a pathway; they appear to suffer from some mortality, which cannot be explained. Notice the Mouse-like form of the specimen we have found, the long, pointed head and nose, the slender jaw, which contains sharp, red-tipped teeth, the close, rounded ears, the whiskered snout, and the musky smell. Examine also the short, bristly, four-sided tail which is a sure method of identification.

This is a quick, engaging little creature, possessed of keen powers of hearing, and bold and courageous in disposition. Yet, when kept in captivity, so timid is this wee beastie that it is easily frightened to death!

It measures about three inches in length, and brings forth from five to eight young ones in late Summer. The nest is usually made in some slight depression in the ground. Like the Mole, it is mostly a lover of the night hours, stealing forth on its feeding expeditions under the cover of darkness, and procuring its food above and not below ground.

In the Winter the Shrew enters into sleep; cold does not affect the little slumberer, and all through the short days and long nights it slumbers soundly, until Fairy Spring raises her wondrous wand and awakens all things to life again.

VIII.—SOME BIRDS OF THE MEADOW

LAPWING—CORNCRAKE—SKYLARK—TREE PIPIT— RED-LEGGED PARTRIDGE

THERE are some birds that are nearly always resident in the meadow, others only visit it during the Summer for nesting purposes, and others again make a pilgrimage there as a feeding ground. Three of the five birds we have set out to observe will be easily seen, the Lapwing, Skylark, and Tree Pipit, but the remaining two, the Corncrake and Red-legged Partridge are much more difficult to find.

Wheeling adroitly over the meadow there may be observed a large dark green and white bird. Listen to its plaintive cry of " pee-wit, pee-wit, pee-wit," and watch the lapping motion of the wings, the twisting and turning, rising and falling. This is the Lapwing, or Green Plover, and in the early Spring, before the meadow is a blaze of colour, it lays four pear-shaped and olive-green eggs in a slight depression in the ground. If any materials be used, they will be a few straws, bents, and dry grasses; perhaps a little moss may be added.

The eggs, which are somewhat large, are handsomely blotched with black, and they are placed in the " nest " with the small end pointing towards the centre, so that they occupy a small space, thus permitting the bird to cover them securely.

When the young Plover is hatched, it is well protected by its colour, and is soon able to run about and take care of itself.

The parent birds detest interference, and if one approaches too close, they wheel round and utter loud cries of

Fig. 21. Head of Male Lapwing.

dissent. They swoop through the air with amazing speed, dart and fall with remarkable control, and will even feign a broken wing, so desirous are they of enticing the onlooker from where the eggs or young are secreted.

Closely examined, the Lapwing is a beautiful bird, for it has a crest upon the head somewhat like that possessed by the Cockatoo. It is a useful as well as a beautiful species, and is one of the farmer's best friends, feeding upon various kinds of harmful insects as well as upon earthworms and slugs.

In the Winter these birds congregate in large flocks, and at such times many are seen feeding in the meadow. At that season they are not so shy and wary, permitting a fairly close approach; they look very pretty with their heads all turned one way, standing at attention like a regiment of green and white soldiers. Then, as they take to flight, and the sunlight plays upon them, they rise slowly in the air, until by easy stages they mount upwards, and are finally lost to view.

Hark! what curious note is that which comes from the far end of the field? Now it seems nearer, now far away! What bold ventriloquist is this plying his art in our meadow? What is the note like? Does it not remind you of a couple of stones rapidly knocked together, or the noise made by running the fingers along the edge of a comb?

You would like to see the bird? More easily said than done,

Fig. 22. Head of Corncrake.

for it is the Corncrake, or Landrail, we have been listening to, and this is a difficult bird to stalk. It is a Summer visitor to our country, spending the Winter in foreign climes, and reaching our shores some time in late April. Although undertaking such a perilous journey over land and sea, the bird is rarely seen to take flight when here, and among the grasses, or the corn, it spends the whole of its sojourn.

Could we see the Corncrake, we should find that it is about the size of a large Thrush; it is a plump bird with long legs and a short tail. The head is carried well forward, and in colour the bird is reddish-yellow with a white throat. It runs swiftly, and has the habit, when uttering its " crex, crex, crex," of rapidly turning its head, which results in the impression that the bird is near one moment and far away the next.

Among the hay in the full glow of Summer, this bird passes its time, feeding upon snails, slugs, worms, beetles, weed-seeds, and other things. There also it makes its nest, and this is composed of dry grass and leaves with finer grass as a lining. The seven to twelve or more eggs are reddish-white, blotched or spotted with a darker colour. For such a comparatively small bird the egg is large, but there is reason for this, it being essential that the young should be well advanced when hatched, so as to run about without causing their father and mother any untoward alarm, because of the many enemies to whom a young bird is so acceptable.

There, towering above us like a feathered chorister suspended in mid-air, carols a Skylark. What a splendid songster this favourite bird is! A lover of the air, a typical bird of the meadowland, a scorner of the ground, the Lark sings and soars in all weathers, and always with its head to the breeze. The poets have written lovingly of the Skylark's beautiful song. Sit down upon this inviting bank, and listen to a few verses written by a well-known admirer of the Lark, and then learn to repeat the verses by heart. Here they are:—

> Hark! to the joyous lark!
>   On buoyant wing,
> Voicing his raptured lays—
>   Pæans of Spring.
>
> Pearl of the feathered race;
>   Prince of the air;
> Full-throated Alauda;
>   Songster so fair.
>
> Cleaving the ether blue,
>   I hear thee sing
> Love-songs of welcome
>   For Earth's blossoming.
>
> Bird of the meadowland;
>   Speck of the sky;
> Earth's gay ambassador,
>   Soaring on high.

Snow, wind and rain may come,
  Naught dost thou care;
Still soar and sing aloud,
  Prince of the air.

Spirit of blithesomeness,
  Happy and gay!
Love-flights of gladsomeness,
  Day after day.

Why dost thou scorn the ground?
  Why mount the cloud?
Sending back lullabies,
  Rich, long and loud.

Joy-bird of early spring;
  Compass in feathers;
Head to the breeze thou soarest
  High in all weathers.

Bird-sprite of lilting lay;
  Laureate of glee;
Lone minstrel of the air,
  Happy and free.

Sing thou again to me,
  Through rain or shine,
Shimmering bridal-songs;
  Minstrel divine!

Brown bird of Happy-land,
  Sing, ever sing—
Call earth from her slumber,
  Thou Herald of Spring.

It is interesting to notice that, although such a lover of
the air, such " a scorner of the ground," as Shelley the poet
has so well described it, the Skylark should build its frail
nest upon the lowly earth. This is often merely a depression in the ground, in the footprint of a horse, or cow, for
example, but the four or five brownish freckled eggs match
the surroundings in a wonderful way, and thus make them
difficult to find.

1   2

3 and 4

5   6

SOME MEADOW BUTTERFLIES.

1 and 2. MEADOW BROWN, Upper and Underside.
3 and 4. SMALL WHITE, Male above, Female below.
5 and 6. GATEKEEPER, Upper and Underside.

YOUNG LEVERETS IN NEST.

Nesting, feeding, soaring, and singing, what a happy and active bird-sprite we have here! Except for a few weeks in the Autumn, the Lark sings all the year through, and although it will sometimes perch in bushes and small trees, the free, unfettered air is its chosen home.

For its beautiful song we must highly regard this British bird, but care should be taken during the Summer not to confuse it with another Lark-like bird, the Tree Pipit.

Those who live in the country should seek out some trees along a lane, or hedgerow, or in a meadow, especially where there is a nice thick grassy bank wherein the March violets hide their white and purple blossoms. Look up into a tall tree, and you will perhaps note a little brown and grey bird about the size of a Sparrow. He does not fly right away, for see, he is soaring in the air somewhat after the manner of a Skylark, but is in reality a Tree Pipit. Watch him carefully; there, having reached a certain height, the bird commences the descent. Notice that he comes down almost like a shaftless arrow; there is hardly any motion of the wings or body, but listen to the sweet sounds the bird is uttering.

As he nears the ground or the tree from which he rose, the song increases in volume and sweetness, until at last, the listener stands spellbound, captivated by the little mite in feathers whose song-flights, to those who know them, are one of the greatest joys of our English countryside. He, too, builds his nest upon the ground like the Lark, but the eggs are much smaller, and are marked in a different way.

We found the English Partridge in *The Hedge I Know*, and although we may find its French relative there also, the Red-legged or French Partridge is a great lover of fields and meadows. It is a larger and much handsomer bird than its English cousin, but more quarrelsome in disposition, and of a wandering nature.

It was introduced into England in the reign of Charles II., but did not then thrive to any extent. On being re-introduced some time afterwards, it quickly made itself at home, and is to-day a very common species.

Although it builds its nest in our meadow, or in the hedge surrounding it, the structure may also be found

Fig. 23. Head of French Partridge.

elsewhere, for, as has been mentioned, the bird wanders about a good deal; sportsmen despair of it, because of this habit, and also by reason of its love for keeping to the ground, and not rising to such an extent as does the English bird, which, from 1st September onwards, affords so much sport.

The twelve to eighteen eggs are laid in a nest built of dead leaves, grasses, or similar materials. These eggs are much larger than those of the Common Partridge, and are cream or yellow in colour, well marked with red or brown.

In the meadow, or its near vicinity, the French Partridge finds a congenial hunting and nesting ground, the food consisting of insects, grain, grass, weeds, and clover.

IX.—BIRD VISITORS TO THE MEADOW

ROOK—STARLING—JACKDAW—SWALLOW

THERE are many birds attracted to the meadow by reason of the abundance of insect life that there abounds, and among these the Rook, Starling, and Jackdaw take first place. During the Summer, too, it is one of the fairest sights in all England to watch the Swallows careering over the tops of the grasses and wild flowers, darting hither and thither after some winged denizen of the air.

Fig. 24. Head of Rook.

Rooks, Starlings, and Jackdaws all belong to the Crow family, but are of course easily distinguished one from the other. The Rook is glossy black in colour, with a bald patch of dry skin at the base of the beak which at once identifies him, and makes confusion with the Crow impossible.

All three kinds of birds are social in their habits, and frequently congregate together in large flocks. They also seem to delight in feeding in company, and then is a good time to carefully watch their habits. The Starling is much smaller than either of the other two, but few people seem to realise what a really handsome species it is. Whilst the young birds—called Stares—are of a brown tint, the adult bird, in its best Spring livery, is a veritable picture; the green, bronze, and copper reflections upon its dark, shiny plumage, together with its speckled markings, are very beautiful indeed.

The Jackdaw is black in colour, and, it must be admitted partly black by nature; it is a smaller bird than the Rook, has an easier flight, a saucy gait, bright twinkling eyes, and a grey patch on the back of the head. This is a bird that in some districts is increasing by leaps and bounds; indeed, there are various parts of the coast where it nests in the cliff sides to such an extent that it has become, as it were, the chief inhabitant of that inaccessible retreat.

Fig. 25. Starling.

It is interesting to observe the different habits of birds *when upon the ground,* for each in its way possesses some curious trait worthy of notice. You may, for instance, watch a crafty old Rook waddling sedately in the meadow, or a Starling progressing in springy fashion as if to the manner born, or a Jackdaw busily engaged unearthing some tasty tit-bit, his head held on one side, and with a saucy twinkle in his eye!

But what food do these bird visitors to our meadow find? What is harboured there which so attracts them? Without doubt the several kinds of insect larvæ, which feed upon the grass and the wild plants, are the tempting bait. The destructive larva of the Crane Fly is there, as we shall presently hope to prove; many kinds of Beetles find the meadow a desirable abode, whilst the Earthworm and countless other creatures, which a bird can find although we cannot, are located in a meadow, and all tend to show *the reason why* our feathered friends are so fond of paying it a visit.

They are to be seen hunting for food soon after it is light, and sometimes it is very late in the day before they retire to bed. What real good work they must perform in ridding the land of many harmful pests! In spite of this, however, some people still persecute them without reason. That all three kinds do harm nobody can gainsay; the Rook loves corn, young turnips, and gamebirds' eggs in a dry season; the Starling visits orchards and gardens after ripe fruit; and in more ways than one the Jackdaw is undoubtedly a nuisance; but, judged all through the year, it is certain that our three friends are beneficial birds.

Fig. 26. Head of Jackdaw.

And there is, happily enough, not the shadow of doubt as to the welcome we accord the Swallow, for he gladdens our sense of sight, even as the wandering Cuckoo does our sense of hearing, and is a wholly useful bird, feeding exclusively upon insects. Watch him now as he flashes across the meadow on unerring wings, chattering as he goes, or uttering two sharp notes something like those of the Pied Wagtail, which we met at the Pond.

The Swallow's powers upon the wing and its really pretty song, its constant hunt for insects and its marvellous migratory movements, are features worthy of interest, whilst its great usefulness as a destroyer of pests makes it a general favourite, and a welcome bird visitor to our meadow.

Yet there are many people who do not know the difference between a Swallow, a Swift, and a Martin. Are you among the number? Briefly stated, the differences may thus be given. The Swallow is black above, with a bright red throat, and reddish-white on the breast. Particularly

D

note it is a longer bird than the House Martin or the Swift, and that it has a long forked tail.

The Swift does not belong to the Swallow family at all, but is so often referred to as such, that it is essential to point this out. This species is wholly black, and may be distinguished by its large, clean-cut wings, short tail, rushing flight, and loud squealing note.

Fig. 27. Swallow.

The House Martin is blue-black above, and pure snowy white below. There is a prominent white patch on the rump, which is well displayed when the bird is in flight, and the legs are feathered right down to the toes. The tail is more catapult-shaped, and it is this bird that builds under the eaves of houses, the Swallow rarely constructing *an exposed nest*, but usually choosing the inside of a barn, an old chimney, or some such situation.

One more bird may be mentioned for comparison, and that is the Sand Martin. This little species is at once identified by the distinct *mouse colour* on the back. Sometimes it visits the meadow for insects, but it dearly loves a pool of water where insect life is abundant; its tunnel-like home is made in a sand-pit, or on high banks or cliffs.

X.—SOME MEADOW BUTTERFLIES

MEADOW BROWN—SMALL WHITE—GATEKEEPER—
SMALL COPPER—COMMON BLUE

You will soon begin to think that our meadow is a really wonderful place, and so it is! All through the year it is well worth your while to pay a visit to it. Especially is this the case when the beautiful grasses and countless legions of wild flowers deck the ground as with a living garment. Then is the time that the lover of the outdoor world hardly knows which way to turn for fear of missing some hidden treasure.

Birds, insects, mammals, flowers, trees, creatures above and below ground, all, all are busy when the Summer sun is high in the heavens, for then it is their family affairs cause so much excitement and attention.

When the meadow is really bright with wild flowers, then is a good time to watch for various kinds of Butter-flies, from the tiny Small Copper to the larger Meadow Brown, and several others that cannot now be detailed. Let us visit the meadow on a typical Summer's day and see if we can manage to find a few of these bright or sombre-clad insects, which give to the countryside so much of its gaiety and joy.

It is the Meadow Brown Butterfly season; the hottest days of the year are here, and as we walk through the tall grasses, we disturb a Meadow Brown at almost every step we take. The insects refuse to move very far away, and we put to flight the same specimen several times over. Theirs is a flickering and not a very prolonged flight, but among the bright coloured flowers, the dark hue of both the male and female presents a pleasing contrast.

If we examine a male closely, we shall find that he is blackish-brown upon both pairs of wings, and that there is a black spot near the tip of the fore wings. The female is more orange colour on the fore wings, and is not so dark as her mate. But why is she here? Ah! that is the secret, for, besides sipping juices from the flowers, she also finds the grasses a suitable spot in which to lay her eggs.

Flying strongly over the meadow are a number of white Butterflies somewhat small in size, and it will be noticed that whereas some have three spots of black, others have only one; these belong to the Small White Butterfly tribe; the male, hatched from the Summer brood, has one spot, but the female three. The male, too, has black tips to the fore wings.

Both are very common inhabitants of the meadow, although, generally speaking, they are lovers of country places of almost all descriptions. They visit gardens, and are very fond of laying eggs on cabbage plants, which the larvæ, when hatched, greedily devour, and they cause the gardener much trouble because of their ravages. There is, however, a useful insect that comes along and lays her eggs in the body of the living larva of the Small White Butterfly. Her name is the Ichneumon Fly. When the eggs of the latter hatch, the Ichneumon larvæ feed upon the body of their host, and actually use the old skin on which to pupate or form a chrysalis; thus, in this curious way, good work is carried out by the Ichneumon in preying upon an injurious pest.

It seems hard to write thus of a pretty Butterfly, but the truth must be told; indeed, there are many things in Nature which are as yet unexplained. But what is that

LAPWING AT NEST.

NEST AND EGGS OF LAPWING.

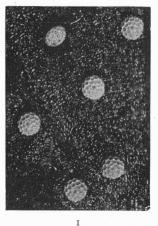

1   2

3

4   5

LIFE HISTORY OF SMALL COPPER BUTTERFLY.

1. EGGS GREATLY ENLARGED.   2. LARVÆ ON SORREL.   3. PUPÆ.
4 and 5. FEMALE (on left), MALE (on right), showing Upper and Undersides.

dark-coloured Butterfly we are continually disturbing among the grasses? It looks like a small edition of the Meadow Brown! And such it is in reality, being known as the Gatekeeper, or Small Meadow Brown.

Wherever there are tall grasses, one may search with hopes of success for this species; beyond being smaller in size than its larger relative, it should be observed that the Gatekeeper is not so dark in colour. It has more orange on the wings, and the black spots usually have two white dots instead of one.

Now keep your eyes well open for a little Butterfly, coppery in colour and a perfect jewel in the Summer sunshine. We shall probably be successful in our hunt, for a specimen of the Small Copper is easy to capture. There is no need to catch it, however, for it will remain fairly still whilst we are watching.

You will notice that the fore wings are bright copper-red spotted with black. On the hind wings there is a notched black band along the margin, with a band of copper inside. If we could see the under sides of the wings, the insect would appear much lighter in colour, being yellowish-orange, spotted with black on the fore wings and greyish-brown on the hind wings.

There are some Dock plants in the meadow as well as in the hedge, and upon these the Small Copper lays her eggs. These are yellow-white at first, but they eventually turn to grey. The larva is dotted with pink, whilst the pupa is pale white-brown, marked with a darker colour.

We have left until last the fairest insect treasure of the meadow; let us search without delay for this dainty creature. It is known as the Common Blue Butterfly, and its beautiful blue adds a bright touch of colour to the scene before us. Peep cautiously among the herbage, for we may find one of these Butterflies resting with the wings closed. Pay special attention to the Bird's Foot Trefoil beloved by this species, and the hunt may then be successful.

Come quickly, for here is a female at rest. She is distinguished from her mate by her brown underdress, the male being blue-grey below. There are, as you will see, a number of white-edged black spots on both the fore and hind wings. Now let us put her to flight. See, she is dark sepia brown above tinged with blue. Notice also the band of spots edged with red on both wings.

Now let us search for her partner. We have not long to wait, for here flies one attracted by the " young lady " we were recently watching. Is he not a gay little fellow in his bright blue attire? The blue you will observe is tinged with purple, and there is a narrow black line dividing the blue from the fine fringe of white.

However, our time is limited, so we must needs leave these many-coloured creatures to go their way undisturbed by our presence; other sights and sounds now claim our attention, and to these we will turn.

XI.—OTHER MEADOW INSECTS

COMMON GRASSHOPPER—MEADOW ANT—DADDY LONG LEGS
—FIELD CRICKET

ON a hot Summer's day, when there is hardly a breath of wind, then it is that the cheery song of the Common Grasshopper is heard among the grasses of our meadow.

Are you aware that this happy little insect is a near

relation of the destructive Locust which, in other lands, commits such havoc among every living plant with which it comes into contact? Locusts travel about in great battalions, thousands and even millions strong, and whilst we in England are rarely troubled by these insect hosts, in foreign lands a visitation of Locusts is something to be remembered.

Our gay little Grasshopper, however, does not appear to do any appreciable damage, so that we need not trouble further on this score. When you are in the meadow, or by the grassy wayside, listen to the chirping of the Grasshopper, and watch him tumbling and falling, jumping and climbing for all the world like one of the penny toys one sees in the street, a veritable monkey on a stick!

Fig. 28. Grasshopper.

All day long this typical inhabitant of our meadow will be found hopping and falling about in the grass, climbing a stem, feeding upon the herbage, or, if a female, depositing eggs. How and where are these laid? If Mrs. Grasshopper be examined, it will be found that she has a short, stout ovipositor at the extremity of the body, and by means of this she makes a hole in the ground. After laying the eggs, she takes the precaution to cover them with a fluid which becomes hard, and forms a sort of irregular capsule.

You will find Grasshoppers of various colours, light and dark brown, pale green, green and red; but in any case a specimen should be obtained for examination. You will then notice the large eyes at the top of the head, the beautiful pattern work on the thighs, the long hind legs, and other interesting features.

How do you think this meadow insect makes its chirping noise, for it is not a vocal effort? The right wing cover of the male bears a clear round membrane stretched on a ring; this is set in vibration by being rubbed by a toothed ridge on the under side of the opposite wing cover. In other words, the left wing cover is the bow, and the right is the fiddle of the Grasshopper's music.

If we examine the ground closely we shall find that the Common Meadow or Turf Ant inhabits the field in large

Fig. 29. Meadow Ant.
A. Male.
B. Female.
C. Worker.

numbers. This is a near relative of the large Wood Ant which we met in the wood; much that was said on that occasion applies equally well in this case. Here is a heap of loose earth, dome-shaped; every tiny particle of which this " dome " consists had to be carried here by the little creatures we are watching. Is not this evidence of their remarkable industry, and a testimony to the persevering labours of these tiny insects?

See, all are busy running hither and thither; near the nest there is a scene of great activity. Could we peep underneath the earthen dome, we should find various galleries and cells with attendants, courtiers, nurses, guests, slaves, workers, sentinels, the rank and file, eggs, pupæ, and last, but not least, the queen. But look! There now seems to be an unusual amount of excitement; the little creatures are hurrying through the grass back to the Ant citadel. Some are removing the eggs, which had been placed in the sun; others are busily engaged in carrying the helpless pupæ. What means this unusual activity?

The clouds above are the reply, for there a storm is threatening; but before the rain descends, the wise Ants are hastening to get within the city gates, so as to secure shelter until the storm has passed.

And we ourselves must lose no time if we would see a few more interesting things in the meadow before bidding it adieu, so let us use our eyes and ears diligently whilst the sun shines on. Bobbing up and down the tall grasses and among the flowers, have you not noticed for some time a curious-looking insect with very long legs?

There goes one; catch it quickly, but do not take hold of one of the long legs, or you will surely lose your prize. Now having secured a specimen, observe how difficult it is to hold the creature properly. What strange insect is this, and what is it doing in the meadow? It is the Crane Fly, or as it is more popularly known, Daddy or Harry Long Legs. There are two species in the meadow that may be sought for, one

Fig. 30. Daddy Long Legs.

having variegated brown wings, and the other yellow markings towards the end of the body.

The one we have under examination has a slender form, long thin legs, and is a female. How do we know this? Because there is a short, horny point on the tip of the abdomen. What purpose does this serve? It is the ovipositor, and by means of it the female is able to lay her eggs among the grasses. See, there are many hereabouts bobbing up and down, and threading their way among the herbage like tiny men walking on long stilts.

The larvæ are hard and leathery, and are very destructive to the roots of grass and other things. You remember the visit of the Rook, Starling, and Jackdaw to the

meadow? This was one of the insects the birds wer
attracted by, and in feeding upon these larvæ they perforr
useful work.

If a Daddy Long Legs be captured by the leg, the pro
bability is that you will soon find yourself possessed of th
leg only. for this is one of those creatures that surrender
part, or parts, of the body and so make good their escape
We find this curious means of escape adopted by othe
creatures, such as the Lizard—when held by the tail—an
the Brittle Starfish.

There is another chirping noise close by. Is this als
made by a Grasshopper? Does it not rather remind on
of the Cricket found in houses, and other dwellings? Tr
and catch the little musician. There he goes! Be quick
for he is a wonderful adept at leaping. Now we have him
You will observe that it is black in colour, and that it is a
stouter and bolder-looking species than the House Cricket.

It is the Field Cricket we have secured, and although i
possesses wings, it rarely uses them, jumping, burrowing
and leaping being its more usual methods of locomotion. I
is sharp of hearing, having perfect little ears, but how doe
it make the sibilous noise? It is akin to the Grasshopper
and has a " file " on the under part of each fore wing; wher
this is brought quickly over a sharp ridge, the friction
results in the cheery chirp known to almost every one.

XII.—TWO " WORMS," ONE REAL, AND ONE SO-CALLED

EARTHWORM—SLOW WORM

WHAT we owe to the common Earthworm is little appreciated. Through the ages these lowly animals have performed useful work in dragging into their holes leaves, straws, petals of flowers, and other vegetable matter. Upon these the Earthworm feeds, and then at night it comes to the surface and deposits its castings in the form of little pellets, which greatly aid in enriching the soil, and help to make our lawns, meadows, and fields rich and fertile.

Fig. 31. Common Earth worm.

When the grass is damp, the Earthworm delights in coming from its underground home and lying at full length on the surface, but usually with its tail end anchored in its burrow. It is a lover of moisture, and this may be proved by digging when the ground is dry, for at such time one has to go down fairly deep before an Earthworm can be turned up. There is a special reason for this, for these creatures breathe entirely through their skin; if this becomes dry, it ceases to act, and the worms are practically suffocated.

When the ground is being dug, they have often been noticed to come suddenly to the surface without any apparent reason; have you ever considered what caused them to do so?

The Mole, as we have already learned, feeds upon them very largely, and so also does our friend the Thrush.

When the ground is disturbed or even tapped, the worm probably mistakes the sound for the digging of a Mole or some other animal that preys upon it, and so he bolts to the surface in double quick time.   Have you also noticed how very clean the worm is even when it has newly come from below ground, and what a really beautiful colour some of the specimens are?

If you let one of these large Earthworms travel over your hand, you will find that it is bristly to the touch. These hook-like bristles, aided by powerful muscles, which run along the length of the body and surround it in circles, are the means by which the creatures travel from one place to another.

Whilst the Earthworm is *a real worm*, there is a make-believe specimen in our meadow, which must not be forgotten.   This is the Slow, or Blind, Worm.   It is not a worm at all, and it isn't slow, and it isn't blind!   What then is it?

It is Snake-like in general appearance, but is in reality a legless Lizard!   Catch hold of the tail of one, and you will find that, like the Lizard, the Slow Worm has the habit of bidding adieu to that appendage and so making good its escape.   Then again, you will find it has eyelids, which Snakes have not, and when these have been seen closed, doubtless the misleading name of Blind Worm has been applied to this species.

It should also be noticed that, unlike Snakes, it has rows of scales on the belly; the jaws are firmly united; it has a notched tongue, and, what is important, it is perfectly harmless.   Thus we see that the Slow Worm, as it is called, is neither a Worm nor a Snake!

It is grey or brownish in colour, or it may be bright copper or bluish.   There is a thin dark line running along

COMMON GRASSHOPPER.

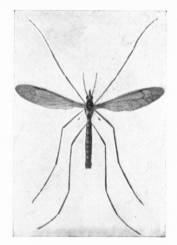

DADDY LONG-LEGS.

SLOW WORM.

LIFE HISTORY OF COMMON BLUE BUTTERFLY.

1. EGGS GREATLY ENLARGED. 2. LARVA. 3. PUPÆ.
4. FEMALE, Upper and Under Side. 5. MALE, Upper and Under Side.

the side, and a further one down the back. The young ones are silvery-white above, and black below.

The food largely consists of Slugs, but doubtless Earth-worms and insects are also partaken of. So fond is it of slugs that one specimen has been known to eat seventeen, one after the other. Thus you see that, although often killed because of the supposed harm it does, and in spite of the blunders that are made concerning its worm or snake-like appearance, this is really a useful animal, and not the least interesting inhabitant of the meadow.

MADE AT THE
TEMPLE PRESS
LETCHWORTH
GREAT BRITAIN

CALENDAR AND NOTES

OF

ANIMALS AND PLANTS

COMPILED BY C. S. COOPER, F.R.H.S.

I. BIRDS

GREENFINCH.—A resident in Britain; many migrate to the east coast in Autumn; also a regular migration on south coast in Spring and Autumn. *Male bird :* general colour above olive-yellow, shaded with ashy-grey, especially on the head; cheeks and under-surface of body bright yellow, with ashy tinge; lower abdomen white; tail-feathers yellow at base; bill fleshy pink; feet brown; length 6 inches. *Female :* duller in colour; tail-feathers not yellow at base. *Nest :* April onwards; in shrubberies, hedgerows, and evergreen trees; twigs and rootlets, with lining of horse-hair and a few feathers; *eggs,* 4–6; variable; white, suffused with bluish tinge, spotted and streaked with pinkish or purple. *Food :* seeds, grain, and insects; young largely fed upon caterpillars. *Song :* chiefly a long, plaintive note while on the wing; often improves considerably in captivity.

GREY WAGTAIL.—A somewhat local species; a partial migrant, many going northward in the Summer, and southward in the Winter. *Male bird :* back and head bluish-grey; throat black, with a white streak on each side; breast yellow; bill black; in Winter the throat is white; length 6⅜ inches. *Female :* similar, but less black on throat;

ruins, holes in cliffs, rabbit burrows, hollow trees; sticks, dry grass, straw, and feathers; *eggs* 3–6, bluish-green or bluish-white, spotted with grey and brown or greenish-brown. *Food :* offal, Mice, young birds, reptiles, Earthworms, grubs, and insects. *Call.* a mere " jack "; can be taught almost anything in captivity.

LAPWING or GREEN PLOVER.— A resident. *Male bird :* General colour above glossy olive-green with purple reflections; crown greenish-black with a crest of elongated plumes; throat and fore-neck greenish-black; under surface white; length 13 inches. *Female :* similar, but crest shorter; length 11 inches. *Winter plumage :* throat white, head brown. *Nest :* March–June; a natural hollow or other depression in the ground; lined with grass, straws, or heather; *eggs* usually 4, ground colour varying from olive or greenish-brown to clay-brown, blotched or mottled with black or dark brown. *Food :* grubs, slugs, Earthworms, etc. *Call :* " pee-wit, pee-wit, pee-wit."

RED-LEGGED PARTRIDGE.—A resident. *Male bird :* Reddish-ash above; throat white surrounded by a black band; feathers of the chest with wide black margins on sides; belly bright rufous-buff; bill and feet red; length 13½ inches. *Female :* similar; length 13 inches. *Nest :* April–June; a hollow scratched in the ground under a hedge, or in tall grass or growing crops; *eggs* 10–18, pale stone or buff, spotted and blotched with dark reddish-brown. *Food :* weeds, grain, grass, insects, etc. *Call :* a musical, piping cry.

ROOK.—A resident. *Male bird :* black, with purple gloss; bill and feet black; whitish patch at base of bill; length 17 inches. *Female :* similar; length 16 inches. *Nest :* March–May; in trees, often at a great height; twigs and sticks, plastered with clay and mud, lined with roots, grass, and straw; *eggs* 4 or 5, ground colour greenish, mottled with greenish-brown. *Food :* almost everything, grubs, fruit, eggs, etc. *Call :* a " caw," repeated several times.

SAND MARTIN.—A visitor, arriving in April, leaving for India and Africa in September. *Male bird :* mouse colour above; cheeks and under parts white; legs and feet naked; tail short and forked; length 4¾ inches. *Female:* similar; length 5 inches. *Nest:* May–July; holes in sand-pits, tunnels sometimes 3 ft. or more in length; dry grass and straw, with a lining of feathers; *eggs* 4–6, white. *Food:* insects. *Call:* a low monotonous note.

SKYLARK.—A resident. *Male bird:* brown above, feathers streaked with black centres; head crested; under surface white, washed with tawny-buff; length 7 inches. *Female:* similar, but slightly smaller. *Nest:* April–June; in a hollow or depression of the ground, nearly always hidden by long grass or herbage; dry grass, lined with fine roots and grasses; *eggs* 3–5, greyish-brown or brownish white, spotted and freckled with brown and grey. *Food:* seeds of weeds and insects, grubs, and worms. *Song:* a thrilling lay poured out when on the wing.

STARLING.—A resident. *Male bird:* black, with reflections of green, purple, and violet; bill yellow; feet reddish-brown; length 8 inches. *Female:* similar, but not so glossy. *Nest:* April–June; holes in trees or walls and under the eaves of houses; grass, straw, and sticks, lined with a few feathers and a little wool; *eggs* 4–7, pale blue or bluish-white. *Food:* grubs, insects, fruit. *Song:* a long drawn-out whistle and curious chattering.

SWALLOW.—A Summer visitor, arriving in April, leaving for Africa and India in September. *Male bird:* glossy purplish blue-black above; under surface pale rufous-buff; cheeks and throat deep rufous; bill and feet black; tail long and forked; length 7⅓ inches. *Female:* not so red on under surface, outer tail-feathers rather shorter; length 6½ inches. *Nest:* April–September; generally on a beam or rafter, in barns, outhouses, or under bridges; mud, mixed with grass and straw, lined with dry grass and feathers; *eggs* 4–6, white, spotted with reddish or purplish-brown. *Food:* insects. *Song:* a pleasing little twitter. *Call:* a short, sharp cry of two high notes.

TREE PIPIT.—A Summer visitor, arriving in April, leaving in September for Africa and India. *Male bird :* general colour above sandy-brown, streaked with black centres to the feathers; below sandy-buff, streaked with black, inclining to buffy-white on centre of breast and abdomen; bill and feet dark brown; length 6 inches. *Female :* similar, but with narrower streaks on under surface; length 6 inches. *Nest :* generally on a bank; dried grasses, moss, and rootlets, lined with finer grasses and hair; *eggs* 4–7, very variable, from purplish or pinkish-red to stone-grey, spotted nearly all over with greyish-brown. *Food :* caterpillars, beetles, flies, and seeds. *Song :* a delicious Lark-like trill, with a few deep notes, uttered both in flight and when perched.

II. INSECTS

COMMON BLUE BUTTERFLY.—May–September. *Male :* lilac-blue. *Female :* lilac-blue tinged with brown, with a marginal row of indistinct orange spots. *Wings* expand $\frac{2}{3}$–$1\frac{1}{2}$ inch; under sides of fore wings ashy-brown, 2 black spots in white rings; under sides of hind wings, a row of red spots towards hind margin; fringes white, unspotted. *Eggs :* May and September. *Larva :* June and August; green, with a darker dorsal line, and a row of white spots on each side; feeds on Clover, Bird's-foot Trefoil, and Rest Harrow. *Pupa :* May and August.

DADDY LONG LEGS or CRANE FLY.—August and September. *General colour* ochreous-yellow; thorax black, with ashen-grey down; abdomen with a short slate-coloured streak on each side; length of head and body 1 inch; legs very long. *Eggs :* in the ground among grass. *Larva :* known as Leather Jacket; skin very tough; dirty white in colour; $1\frac{1}{2}$ inch long; feeds on roots of grasses. *Pupa :* in the ground; head large.

FIELD CRICKET.—April–August. *Male :* black, with yellow patch at base of elytra. *Female :* dark brown. *Wings,* when folded, projecting beyond elytra. *Eggs :* laid in the ground in early Autumn. *Larva :* resembling adult in appearance, but without wings; appears at mouth of burrow in February. *Pupa :* resembling adult, with rudimentary wings; casts its skin in April. *Habits :* hides in burrows during the day, feeds on vegetable matter at night; begins to chirp in May.

GATEKEEPER BUTTERFLY.—Also called Small Meadow Brown and Large Heath. June–August. *Wings :* expand 1½ inch; brown, each with a large central tawny patch; fore wings with a black spot containing two white dots. *Male :* a clouded brown mark on fore wings. *Female :* a white centred black spot near the anal angle. *Eggs :* July. *Larva :* August–June; greenish or grey, with a dark line on back, and pale lines on each side; feeds on Annual Meadow Grass.

MEADOW ANT.—*Body :* yellow; one knob in waist; no sting. *Male :* winged. *Female or Queen :* winged, larger than male. *Worker or Neuter :* no wings. *Eggs :* yellowish, very tiny, laid in late Summer. *Larvæ :* some live through the winter. *Pupa*—the so-called " ant egg"; in a cocoon. *Habits :* seldom comes above ground; no regular openings to nest; keeps aphides on the roots of plants.

MEADOW BROWN BUTTERFLY.— June–August. *Wings :* expanding 1¾–2 inches; dull brown. *Male :* fore wings with a white-centred black spot in a tawny ring; hind wings greyish-brown beneath, with two black dots. *Female :* fore wings with a white-centred black spot in a tawny patch. *Eggs :* July. *Larva :* May; pale apple-green, with white stripe on each side; feeds on Meadow Grasses.

SMALL COPPER BUTTERFLY.—April to beginning of October. *Wings :* expanding 1–1⅓ inch; fore wings bright copper-red, spotted with black, hind margin blackish; hind wings blackish, with bright copper-red hind margin, under side ashy-brown. *Eggs :* June and

October. *Larva :* May–August and October–April; green, a red line on back, a red stripe on each side; feeds on Sorrel, Sheep Sorrel, Ragwort, and Dock.

SMALL WHITE BUTTERFLY.—April–June and middle of July–August. *Wings :* expanding 1¾–2⅛ inches; white, under side yellowish. *Male :* fore wings spotless or with one black spot; hind wings one spot. *Female :* two black spots and a clouded dash on margin of fore wings; hind wings one spot. *Eggs :* May and August. *Larva :* June and September; green, yellow stripe on back, yellow spots on sides; feeds on Cabbage, Mignonette, Water Cress, Hedge Mustard, etc.

III. MAMMALS

COMMON SHREW.—A native of Britain. Fur on upper parts usually a reddish mouse-colour; under parts greyish; muzzle slender and pointed; ears small, rounded; teeth 32, tips reddish-brown; tail four-sided, with short, stiff hairs; length of head and body, 2¾ inches, tail 1½ inch. *Habits :* hides during the day among grass, hunts for food at night; sleeps during Winter; smells of musk. *Food :* Earthworms, insects, grubs, slugs, and snails. *Natural enemies :* Mole and Owls.

HARE.—A native of Britain. General colour of upper parts tawny-grey, tinged with rufous; under-parts white; ears long and narrow, tipped with black; hind legs long; tail black above, white beneath; length of head and body 22 inches, tail 3⅜ inches; ears 3¾ inches; average weight 7–8 lbs. *Habits :* during day usually reposes in its " form "; searches for food during night; advances by leaps, running quickly uphill. *Food :* grass, clover, corn, turnips, bark of young trees.

MOLE.—A native of Britain. General colour usually some shade of black; body almost cylindrical; fur short, soft, and velvety, set vertically in the skin; no external ears; eyes very small, and hidden by fur; teeth usually 44; fore-feet turned outwards, broad and flat, claws large; tail short; length of head and body 5½ inches, tail 1½ inches. *Habits :* passes most of its time underground. *Food :* Earthworms, larvæ, and occasionally Frogs, Lizards, and even young birds.

SHORT-TAILED FIELD VOLE.—A native of Britain. Colour of upper parts dull greyish-brown; under surface greyish-white; head with a blunt, rounded muzzle; ears short, almost buried in fur; length of head and body 3¾–4¾ inches, tail 1¼ inch. *Habits :* very destructive, and at times very numerous, riddling the ground in all directions; stores up food in its burrow, and sleeps during coldest weather. *Food :* grass, clover, corn, roots, turnips, potatoes, seeds, fruit, berries, nuts, and acorns. *Natural enemies :* Fox, Weasel, Stoat, Kestrel, and Owls.

IV. MISCELLANEOUS

EARTHWORM.—All the year round. *Body :* cylindrical, pointed at both ends, slimy; eight rows of locomotive bristles; no teeth; no eyes. *Eggs :* laid underground in spring, covered with mucus which hardens. *Food :* decayed vegetable and animal matter. *Habits :* hides during the day; feeds at night, dragging food into burrow, 3–8 ft. deep.

SLOW WORM or BLIND WORM.—*Body :* cylindrical, 10–14 inches long; upper surface brownish-grey, with a silvery appearance; underneath bluish-black, with whitish network; rows of dark spots along sides, one down middle of back; covered with scales; eyes small, movable eye-lids; tongue broad, notched at tip; teeth minute, slightly hooked; skin cast in one piece, tail portion sometimes excepted; tail easily broken off. *Food :* Slugs, Earthworms. *Habits :* generally hides among herbage; sometimes basks in sunshine.

V. TREES AND FLOWERING PLANTS

Name.	Time of Flowering.	Colour.	Height.
Daisy . . .	Jan.—Dec.	White	2–5 ins.
Shepherd's Purse .	„ — „	„	6–16 ins.
Ash	Mar—May	Greenish Yellow	Tree
Marsh Marigold .	„ —June	Golden Yellow	1–2 ft.
Dandelion . .	„ —Oct.	Yellow	6–12 ins.
Cowslip . .	April—June	„	6–12 ins.
Lady's Smock .	„ — „	Lilac to Whitish	1–2 ft.
Yellow Rattle .	May—July	Yellow	12–18 ins.
Bulbous Crowfoot .	„ —Aug.	„	1–2 ft.
Creeping „ .	„ — „	„	6–12 ins.
Ragged Robin .	„ — „	Rose Pink	1–2 ft.
Ribwort Plantain .	June, July	Green	2–18 ins.
Meadow Crowfoot	„ „	Yellow	1–3 ft.
„ Sweet .	„ —Aug.	Creamy	1–3 ft.
Field Scabious .	„ — „	Lilac	2–5 ft.
Ox-eye Daisy .	„ — „	White	1–2 ft.
Sow Thistle .	„ — „	Yellow	2–4 ft.
Field Convolvulus .	„ —Sep.	White or Pink	Twining

THE STREAM I KNOW.

THE
STREAM I KNOW

W. PERCIVAL WESTELL, F.L.S.
& HENRY E. TURNER

*General Secretary of the School
Nature Study Union*

WITH

13 COLOURED

& MANY BLACK AND WHITE
ILLUSTRATIONS

LONDON
J. M. DENT & SONS LTD.

" Nature study is a means of obtaining knowledge which may rightly influence the conduct of the individual. Knowledge is still the object, but it is not the knowledge that lies, like the miser's hoard, unproductive while other heaps are accumulating; it is rather like the wealth which is continually current, and is ever ministering to the necessities and comforts of mankind."

JOHN RUSKIN.

CONTENTS

LIST OF ILLUSTRATIONS

COLOURED PLATES AND HALF-TONES

ILLUSTRATIONS IN THE TEXT

9

THE STREAM I KNOW

I.—INTRODUCTION

THE BABY BROOK—A SURFACE SPRING—WATER ACTION—
THE SPEED OF A STREAM—ITS CURVES—AND USES

WHEN we write the history of a famous man, is it not our usual custom to comment upon the days of his childhood and youth? Do we not love to discuss the character that he then displayed, and to describe the scenes amidst which he dwelt?

And those whom we call our friends—even though they be far removed from the ranks of the famous—what of them? Are they not at all times and under all conditions most interesting to us? Their habits, their sayings, their home, surely these form part of our most cherished recollections?

So let us deal fairly with the stream, for with the famous things of the earth it most certainly ought to rank, and among our friends it most certainly should be.

Come, then, and climb up yonder hill, for there must we seek the cradle of our stream! The baby brook is at first so frail, so feeble, that one can scarcely believe that one is witnessing the early struggles of a future warrior.

Perhaps you consider the word " warrior "a term scarcely suitable to be applied to a river; but withhold your decision until you have heard of its brave struggles against unfavourable conditions, of difficulties faced and overcome, of battles fought and victories won, all by the untiring patience and persistent plodding of its slow-moving waters. At last, having done its duty, the majestic river—for such it will become—enters, and is lost in, the great sea beyond.

Have you found the cradle of which we have just spoken? Yes, there it is, that small hollow in yonder rock! Out from this issues a tiny streamlet fed by a bubbling spring. Some of you may wonder how the spring came there, for although we can only see it as it bubbles from the ground, yet we are quite sure that bare rock cannot produce water from nothing; therefore let us trace the matter back a step further.

"When the rain-water falls upon a porous rock like Sandstone, or one like Limestone penetrated by joints or fissures, it continues to travel downward till stopped by some impervious and unfissured rock like Clay. It is then compelled to travel along the junction plane of the two rocks, and if it comes to the surface again by travelling steadily down-hill, it issues as a *surface spring*."[1] Here, then, we have the true origin of our stream, which is in very truth the child of the clouds.

Down the steep hill-side it scampers, singing on its way, jumping from ledge to ledge, and carving out a path where perhaps none existed before. Here and there it joins forces with other happy streamlets, all as eager and agile as itself; together they make their way ever downwards, until the hill-side merges into the plain beneath.

But in this hasty flight what a havoc is made among the surrounding hills! Gradually the would-be rivers deepen their channel, and sweep before them fragments of rock, which the rain and frost have split from off the neighbouring crags. What is the result of all this apparent waste?

"Suppose, for the sake of distinctness, that one special

---

[1] *Geology for Beginners*, by W. W. Watts.

crag could be singled out, the rock of which, from its colour or composition, might be distinguished, even in small fragments, from those of the crags round about it. Rising boldly from a steep hill-side, it looks perhaps down a long slope to the little stream, which in the distance seems a thread of silver winding through the green meadows far below. In the long course of time, rain and frost have carved the front of this crag into deep clefts and gullies, which, when wet weather sets in, become each the channel of a torrent, that pours down the slope and sweeps away every loose bit of stone or earth within its reach.

" The stones first fall or are swept from a hill-side into a brook as mere angular chips. But by the time they have travelled down the brook a little way, and have suffered from the grinding of a few floods, they lose their sharpness and become more or less rounded, until at last, after some miles of transport, continued, perhaps, during several years, they appear as well-worn Gravel. A rounded stone will travel farther and faster than an angular one, but may in the end be worn done into mere Sand.

" As the stones grow rounder, they necessarily at the same time become smaller. And as they not only wear away each other, but also grind out the sides and bottom of the channel of the brook, a good deal of stone must be consequently rubbed down into Sand and Mud.

" The finer particles, being more easily moved, travel farther than the coarser fragments. Hence, while Gravel and coarse Sand are pushed along the bottom, fine Sand and Mud are carried along, suspended in the moving water, which may transport them many miles before they can slowly sink to the bottom, there to form a deposit of Silt or Clay." [1]

[1] *Geology*, by Sir A. Geikie.

Would you like to discover the speed of our stream?
Well, then, spread yourselves out along its banks so that
between each of you there is a distance of ten yards. The
boy farthest up the stream must now launch a tiny boat—
a small piece of cork or even cardboard will serve the purpose. As soon as the frail messenger is on the move, be
careful to note the exact time; a similar record must be
taken at the very second the boat reaches the spot opposite
each boy, who should shout out loudly enough to warn the
time-keeper of its approach. Thus we obtain a series of
results, a series showing the various times taken by the
boat to travel ten yards. An average rate can then be
obtained, when a simple proportion sum is all that is
necessary to discover the speed of the water per hour.

All regardless of watches and such like, our stream
glides calmly on, winding first one way and then the
other; here it bends to the left, and there to the right,
seeking those places where the slope—so slight at times
as to be almost imperceptible—helps it on towards its
final goal.

Even in these bends there is something of interest.
Look at them closely! Can you see any difference between
the opposite banks? Does not the *outer* or *concave* curve of
the river, where the speed of the water is greater, wash a
steeper bank than the *inner* or *convex?* Why should this
be so?

The answer is partly suggested in the question, for the
bank which overlooks the swifter current is the more
likely one to be robbed of its soil.

One bank is being washed away, and is more or less
steep; the other is being built up, and is consequently
inclined to slope gently. This " laying waste " and " reclaiming " are, of course, much more apparent in large

rivers, but the result is the same in both cases—the course of the river is shifted.

But we must not forget that a river is something more than a thing of beauty, for its uses are great and manifold. Not only is it the chief source of our water supply, but it irrigates our fields and makes fertile the soil. Are not our boats borne upon its placid bosom, and do not its waters abound in fish? In our work and in our play it is our constant friend and helper, asking nothing for its services and claiming no reward.

Truly it is not a matter for wonder that, among the idolatrous nations, there be those who worship their river, regarding it as the gift of heaven, a special favour granted to mankind. The holy Ganges and the sacred Nile have brought blessings untold to countless human beings, who, in return, regard the river with reverence and awe, and in gratitude enshrine it among their gods.

II.—WATER-LOVING PLANTS

GREATER WILLOW HERB—HEMP AGRIMONY—COMFREY

If you had to spend all your life in a pond or in a stream, would you not take steps to ensure that you were prepared for your watery surroundings? Your first care, no doubt, would be to protect yourself in such a way that the stagnant pool or rippling brook should do you no harm; indeed, you would endeavour to derive the greatest possible benefit from their presence.

Thus it is with the water-loving plants; in the course of years, Nature has gradually adapted them to their environment. Usually we find that their stems are slender, since the buoyancy of the water affords them nearly all the support they need. When the stems are of a sturdier growth, we frequently find they are sword-shaped, and thus do not impede the flowing water to any appreciable extent.

Their submerged leaves are very often much divided, and do not possess stomata, those tiny mouths by means of which they breathe; the leaves which float *on* the water, however, have these stomata on the *upper* or exposed surface, so that they may come into contact with the air.

" Stomata " is the plural of " stoma," a term derived from a Greek word meaning a mouth. These stomata are special openings, microscopic in size, through the outer skin of the leaf or young stem, and are for the breathing and feeding of the plant; by their means, also, the aqueous vapour escapes in the process known as Transpiration.[1]

They are nearly always found on the *under* side of the leaf, away from the glare of the sun. But this rule, as has already been shown, varies in exceptional plants; thus the Iris has them on *both* sides, whilst the Water Lily has them on the *upper* surface. Usually the stomata are closed at night.

Now that we know the type of flower we are likely to meet with in our stream, had we not better walk along the bank and gather a few specimens? It is true that we shall find many plants that we have previously seen in, and gathered from, the pond, but these we can ignore for the present, and confine our attention to the things that are new.

Look at yonder tall plant, for instance! What do its long narrow leaves with their sharply - toothed edges remind you of? " Those of the Willow," did you say?

[1] See *The Wood I Know*, p. 13.

GREATER WILLOW HERB.

BROOKLIME.

Yes, that is true, and it is for this reason the plant is called the Willow Herb.

We have many species of Willow Herb in all parts of Great Britain, but the one which graces the edges of our stream is tall and very hairy; indeed, the whole plant is of a woolly nature, and is therefore spoken of as the Great Hairy Willow Herb.

July and August are the months in which we see it at its best, for then the large rosy-purple blossoms, each with its four notched petals, are greatly in evidence.

The sturdy stem, which branches in all directions, often reaches to man's height, and is clasped by the stalkless leaves. Should you try to pull it up by its roots, you will not have a very easy task, for these creep hither and thither, sending up shoots at frequent intervals.

Fig. 1. Seeds and Seed-vessels of Greater Willow Herb.

Perhaps the most interesting stage of the Willow Herb is the time when it casts its seeds. What was apparently the long stalk of the flower turns out to be the ovary or seed case; this splits up into four long strips, which curl back and reveal the seeds, each with a tuft of silken hairs of great length. These delicate filaments are buoyed up by the passing breeze, and thus the seed gets borne away to fields and pastures new.

Another tall plant, whose roots love to penetrate widely and deeply into the soft rich mud, is the Hemp Agrimony. Its rounded red-tinted stem gives one the idea of strength and solidity, but in this case appearances are somewhat deceptive, for the central part is full of white pith.

The dull green leaves are arranged in pairs, and may almost be described as stalkless; each leaf is slightly downy and is deeply cut into lance-shaped leaflets from three to five in number, all having serrated edges.

Towards the top of the stem are several branches, which are crowned by clusters of pale purple or lilac-coloured blossoms. The latter belong to the simplest of the composite group, each flower head having only five or six florets, the ray florets being entirely absent.

These blossoms, grouped together as they are in such  large numbers, and containing as they do such plentiful supplies of honey, form the happy hunting-ground of many a Butterfly and Moth; indeed, at certain seasons of the year, the Red Admiral and the Peacock may be seen there in joyful swarms, and by their aid the fertilisation of the plant is brought about.

Tall flowers are the rule rather than the exception in moist places, and a further illustration of this is the Common Comfrey.

Fig. 2. Comfrey.

This large and handsome plant has a stem from two to three feet in height, and angular in shape. It is covered with hard, rough hairs or bristles, and like many of its neighbours it is hollow.

Once the plant has established itself in the soil, it is a difficult matter to eradicate it, for the roots are extremely brittle, and the smallest portion will grow.

The coarse hairy leaves are narrow and pointed and " are all but stalkless, their bases running down the stem in such a manner as to give it a winged appearance;" those which spring direct from the root are broader and possess stalks.

Towards the end of April the blossoms begin to appear, and these may be seen until Autumn puts an end to their beauty. They vary in colour from a pale yellow to a rich purple. The five petals form a bell, the edges of which are deeply toothed. These bells are arranged in drooping clusters, and are hung from a very short stalk.

III.—MORE WATER-LOVING PLANTS

PURPLE LOOSESTRIFE—GREAT YELLOW LOOSESTRIFE— BROOKLIME—WATER-CRESS

PERHAPS one of the chief characteristics of the tangled mass of vegetation adorning the banks of our stream and other moist places is the intense green of the leaves. It is true that this colour prevails in almost every plant community, and surely there must be some reason for this.

The green colour of plants is *never* the result of coloured sap, but is a special substance called Leaf Green. Those of you who love hard words, and wish to call things by their exact name, may like to know that the correct term for this is Chlorophyll. It can be extracted from the leaves by soaking them in methylated spirit.

The presence of light is necessary for the manufacture of this colouring matter; thus the whiteness of such well-known foods as Celery and the heart of a Cabbage is explained by the fact that these vegetables have been grown in the dark, the former underground and the latter under cover of the large outside leaves.

A certain amount of warmth is also requisite, and the yellow tinge, which we find in our Spring bulbs, is probably the result of cold impeding the complete formation of Leaf Green.

But when it *has* been formed, of what use is it? Experiments have proved beyond all doubt that it is only by the aid of this colouring matter that plants, *in the presence of light*, can form the starch [1] upon which they feed, and give off the oxygen which purifies the air. Hence it is no longer surprising that green should be everywhere in evidence, since upon its presence the very life of a plant depends.

It is time, however, that we continued our walk by the side of the stream, for much remains for us to see and examine ere yet our task be complete.

Look among yonder Sedges and Rushes! Do you see

Fig. 3. Flowers of Purple Loosestrife.

that tall handsome plant with its tapering spikes of purple flowers, which, from this distance, we might almost mistake for a Foxglove? It is the Purple Loosestrife, and grows in great abundance in watery places. Let us get nearer to the plant, for it is well worth our attention.

This stem, as you can see, is square, but such is not always the rule, for you may often find a specimen with five or six sides. The lance-shaped leaves run in pairs, and, being stalkless, they clasp the stem.

The blossoms, often one inch in diameter, may be looked for from July to September; they are sometimes described as purple stars, for the six long and narrow petals radiate from the centre and stand out quite clearly from each other; these are supported in a tube-like calyx, the edges of which are cut into twelve teeth, six of them being large and six small.

Again, the blossoms are arranged in clusters around the

[1] See *The Hedge I Know*, p. 19.

stem, each cluster being separated from the one above and below by a pair of leaves.

Really the plant has no right to its name, for the true Loosestrife is yellow in colour, and belongs to quite a different family. " Both are equally common, both are found in the same localities, and both are called Loosestrife, and there the resemblance ends." Our forefathers made the blunder; they wrongly christened the plant, and the error has been allowed to remain.

Good luck seems to be with us, for there, sure enough, is the *true* species. Would you like to hear how it obtained its name?

Years ago it was commonly thought that the plant had the power of calming certain restive animals; for instance, when put beneath the yokes of the oxen at plough, it made them quiet. One does not require further information to understand how the name Loosestrife came into circulation. Although it is extremely interesting to trace back these matters to their beginnings, we are forced to admit that our ancestors were very rough and ready in their methods, and that their knowledge of Botany could scarcely be described as perfect.

However, let us leave the past and deal with the present! This Yellow Loosestrife, for instance, is cousin to Creeping Jenny, and also a distant connection of the Primrose. We met with another of its relatives when tramping through the wood, the Yellow Pimpernel to wit. Its size, and the brilliant yellow of its flowers, make it conspicuous even amongst its big neighbours.

Yellow Loosestrife is a perennial; therefore, as soon as it has taken up its residence in suitable quarters, it may be looked for year by year adorning the same spot.

The leaves taper to a point and grow in whorls clasping

the stem. This, perhaps, is a phrase you will not quite understand, until you have learnt that a whorl consists of three or more leaves—or at times blossoms—arranged in a circle around a stem.

From the axils of the upper leaves come the stalks which support the clusters of yellow blossoms; these are somewhat bell-shaped, dotted inside with orange. The calyx is deeply cut into five segments, each of which is daintily tipped with red.

In the study of flowers, one of the most interesting points to notice is the manner in which two specimens of the *same* group will vary one from the other, according to their environment.

An excellent illustration of this may be found among the Speedwells. Those which grow in dry places have to be protected from certain creeping insects, and consequently are often covered with hairs, especially at the entrance to the tube down which search must be made for the honey. Again, their seeds are sometimes dispersed by means of tiny hooks on the calyx; the latter gets attached to the coat of some animal, and the contents are thus carried away from the spot where they first saw light.

Fig. 4. Brooklime.

The Brooklime, however—the Speedwell that frequents our ponds and streams—is smooth, doubtless because the water not only affords sufficient protection from the inroads of Ants and such like, but can act as an excellent carrier of seeds.

You will not be surprised to find that the stem is round, hollow, and juicy. This has a tendency to trail, throwing out bunches of rootlets from its lower portion, and at intervals sending up flowering stems. Each of these stands

PURPLE LOOSESTRIFE.

WATER CRESS.

erect in its muddy bed, and has its smooth glossy leaves arranged in pairs; the latter are oval in shape with edges best described as wavy.

Many people confuse the Speedwell with the Forget-me-not, and at first glance there is some excuse for this; notice, therefore, that whereas the latter has five petals all of equal size, the former has four, one of which is smaller than the rest.

Shall you be surprised if you are asked to hunt for Water-cress? Can you believe that it is indeed a plant having roots, stem, leaves, and blossoms like any other flower? Or have you bought it so often for "tea" that you have gradually grown to believe that it can only be found in a greengrocer's shop?

Should you have any doubts on this point, come along to a quiet backwater that we shall find about ten minutes' walk up stream. There you can see a bed of Water-cress in blossom—a veritable sheet of white.

Fig. 5. Water-cress.

" This plant grows most luxuriantly in clear and gently moving streams having a gravelly bottom, and the plants have then a far finer development and a richer flavour than those that have sprung up either on mud or in almost or quite stationary water."[1]

The roots of Water-cress are long and creeping, and possess numerous tufts of slender white fibres. The plant is easily removed, and if cast upon the stream will probably find a quiet shallow spot wherein it may again take root.

Come and gather one of the pure white blossoms. What does it put you in mind of? " The Wallflower," did you say? Yes, it belongs to this great family, as the cross-

[1] *Familiar Wild Flowers*, by F. E. Hulme.

wise arrangement of the four petals clearly indicates. Later on the long seed pod will appear, a further proof that the plant is akin to the Wallflower.

Many years ago Water-cress was introduced into New Zealand, where it has flourished to such an extent as to become a nuisance. The huge stems formed a network across rivers and other water-ways, putting a stop to navigation; the local authorities have had to spend hundreds of pounds per annum to keep down the growth.

IV.—WATER-SIDE COMPANIONS

RUSHES—SEDGES—MOSSES—LIVERWORTS

You must not imagine that every plant growing by the water-side is worthy of a place in a bouquet, for such is not the case. All are interesting, even though they can scarcely be described as beautiful. Some, alas! seem to have fallen on evil days, and although they exactly suit their damp and often dismal surroundings, yet, judged from a botanical point of view, they are very low down in the scale of plant life.

Among these we must place the Rushes, which " may best be described as degenerate Lilies—plants that have turned their backs on the insect friends that have induced so many of the family to become brilliant, gaily-coloured, and often sweet scented."

" They appear to have argued that expensive petals richly coloured, with their adjuncts sweet perfumes and sweet liqueurs, made too heavy a demand on their resources; they must retrench. They have retrenched to such an extent that all-round degeneration has resulted—simple stems, leaves scarcely recognisable as such, and poor little brown or green flowers massed together and fertilised by the winds." [1]

Thus, in the course of ages, they seem to have resigned their right to a place in the richer soils, and have crowded together as a tribe of marsh or bog plants. Tufts of them may be seen dotted here and there in pasture lands, but then they are a sign of insufficient drainage.

Generally speaking, Rushes are perennials, with roots that creep and send up fresh plants. The stems are erect, usually unbranched, and filled with pith. The leaves are flat or cylindrical, but at times they are no more than a series of scales clasping the stem.

Fig. 6.
Heath Rush.

Nevertheless, they have proved of great use to man. With them he has repaired his chairs, woven his mats, and plaited his rope. Fresh Rushes, strewn over the floor, made an excellent substitute for the more modern carpet; indeed, a fresh supply in the castle hall was an ancient method of honouring a distinguished guest.

Gilbert White tells us how, by carefully dipping the Rushes in grease with a little wax added, the poor man might enjoy five and a half hours of light for a farthing. What economy is here, to be sure!

But even in the world of Nature they have their use, for just as Grasses will aid in reclaiming sandy wastes, so Rushes tend to " fix " the soil of many a marsh and bog.

Side by side with these you will find the Sedges—plants so often confused with Grasses. May we not as well learn

[1] *The Romance of Wild Flowers*, by Edward Step.

the differences between them at once? " The stem of a
Sedge is always solid and generally triangular; that of a
Grass is generally hollow, rounded, and never three-sided.
The leaves of a Sedge are in three ranks; those of the Grass
are alternate in two ranks.   In both, the leaves embrace
the stem with sheaths, but in Grasses
the sheaths are nearly always split,
while in Sedges they are not. Further,
where the leaf-blade joins the sheath
in Grasses, the inner side of the sheath
is more or less prolonged into a sort
of membranous edging known as the
ligule, whereas a Sedge has no ligule." [1]

Figs. 7 and 8.
A. Greater Pond Sedge.
B. Rough Cock's-foot Grass.

A few Sedges grow in dry places,
but the majority prefer moist soils;
indeed, they form the sole vegetation
of some swamps, which, in time, they
have been known to convert into dry
land.

Before we introduce ourselves to
other of our water-side companions,
let us make quite sure what parts
we are to look for in the highest type
of plant.

Firstly, there are the roots, which
anchor the plant firmly in the soil,
and absorb from the latter not only the moisture, but a
weak mineral solution necessary for the feeding of the plant.

Then there are the leaves, the organs by means of which
a plant breathes, absorbs carbon dioxide from the air, and
manufactures starch.   Remember, too, that the leaves are
the " headquarters " for Transpiration.

[1] *Manual of British Grasses*, by W. J. Gordon.

We must not forget the vessels which carry the food to all parts of the plant, and which can be seen so clearly in the leaves.

Lastly, there are the decorative and reproductive parts, viz., the blossoms and the seed. These bring no nourishment to the plant they ornament, but, on the contrary, they depend upon the other parts for their sustenance, and are often a great tax on the resources of the plant.

Judged from this standpoint, the Fungi that we discovered in our meadow must be numbered among the lowly; the Mosses, however, which we shall find on the stones and banks of our rippling stream, are of higher rank, for some of them possess leaves, stems, and roots of a kind, although no true Moss can boast of vessels.

Beginners are inclined to regard Mosses as being all alike in appearance and habitat, but " the tops of walls, the banks of lanes, the shady woods, the mountain passes, each inhabited by different classes of Mosses, are as distinct in their vegetation as the Oak, or Elm, or Beech counties of England, or the Pine-clad slopes or the Birch groves of the Alps."

Unfortunately we have not the time just now to prove the full truth of these remarks, but keep your eyes open, and you will be surprised at the number of different kinds of Mosses you may gather, even in one day's walk by the side of a stream.

Shall we clamber over these rocks? Here, sure enough, are specimens galore. Be careful how you go, for the path is slippery, and sprained ankles are more quickly obtained than got rid of.

Here is some Moss that seems to be growing into the stone itself. Pull it away from its hard rocky bed, and examine the tiny and finely pointed roots, for it is by means of these it can penetrate into, and find a footing upon, surfaces that other plants might despair of.

The leaves are usually of a clear green, shaded with golden brown or different tints of red and purple; they may be arranged spirally round a stem, but " they are never opposite, never whorled, never on leaf stalks, never truly veined, never compound, and never furnished with stomata.

" We must remember that the whole mode of life of a Moss Plant, especially as regards its water supply, is very

Fig. 9. Moss.

different from that of higher plants. Many Mosses often grow in places such as the tops of walls, or in sandy soil, where they are liable to be completely dried up in hot weather. Yet they are none the worse, and revive as soon as rain comes again. This rapid recovery is due to their power of absorbing water by their leaves—a power which is absent or which only exists to an insignificant

extent in most of the higher plants. Hence less work falls on the conducting tissues of the stem than in the latter, for only a small part of the water supply is taken up from below, though this part of the supply is important as it carries with it the necessary mineral food substance." [1]

Look again at the Moss which you have in your hand. Can you see those long thin stalks each bearing a nodding pear-shaped case? These are the fruits of the plant, and contain the spores. When the case opens, the spores are scattered by the wind, and if they be successful, something like this happens: the spores germinate and produce simple threads; these give rise to buds which, in their turn, produce the new plant.

[1] *Flowerless Plants*, by D. H. Scott.

Curiously enough, Mosses resort to other methods of reproducing themselves. In some species the roots and the leaves have the power of forming " buds "—somewhat similar to the bulbs of the higher orders—and from these the new plants spring.

A few words must be said with respect to their uses. They may be described as forerunners, for they precede and pave the way for their more important brethren. Bogs have been filled up by their agency; year in and year out their growth and decay have improved the soil by adding to it vegetable mould sufficient for the nourishment of plants of a higher organisation; even a bare mountain side may thus become the site of a flourishing forest, which could never have existed there, but for the patient work of the humble Moss.

Fig. 10. Liverwort.

Ruskin beautifully describes them as " The first mercy of the earth, visiting with hushed softness its dintless rocks. And, as the earth's first mercy, so they are its last gift to us: when all other service is vain from plant and tree, the soft Mosses and grey Lichen take up their watch by the head-stone. The woods, the blossoms, the gift-bearing Grasses, have done their parts for a time; but these do service for ever. Trees for the builder's yard, flowers for the bride's chamber, corn for the granary, Moss for the grave."

A little lower down in the scale of plant life are the Liverworts, many of which show no distinction of leaf and stem, but consist of bodies performing the function of both these organs. Usually they grow by the sides of brooks or in damp woods, sometimes actually living under water.

Like the Mosses, they do not possess true roots, but

such as they have fix them to the ground. When the plants begin their new growth in the Spring, a great number of small crowded branches are sent out, giving the growing edge a parsley-like appearance.

V.—TREES BY THE STREAM

OLD FRIENDS—THE ASPEN—LICHENS

As we journey along our stream, we cannot help being struck by the large variety of trees that shade its waters. Some seem out of place, as though they had taken up their abode there more by chance than by choice; one can fancy them longing for the more congenial soil and atmosphere of the meadow, the hedge, or the wood.

Others—and these are in the majority—are quite at home, and appear to caress the beloved water with their delicate leaves and branches.

Among this second class we shall surely find some, if not all, of our old pond friends, the Alder, the Willow, and the Poplar to wit. These are, indeed, the companions of the stream, and are never seen to better advantage than when growing in the neighbourhood of still or flowing water.

For grace and beauty it is difficult to find a rival to the Aspen, one of the children of the great Poplar family.

This soft-wooded tree will secure a foothold in almost any soil, but it is in the moist lands that it flourishes best and arrives at perfection.

In March or April the leafless grey boughs are covered with catkins—those long fluffy tails so characteristic of the Poplars. Those which bear the pollen have bunches of

LIVERWORT.

MOSS.

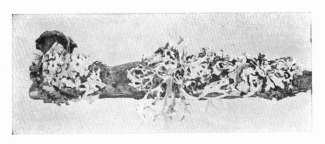

LICHEN ON TWIG.

A. COMMON RUSH.   A¹. SINGLE FLOWER.
B, GREAT SEDGE.   B¹. SINGLE MALE FLOWER.
B². SPIKELET, showing Male Flowers at top and Female Flowers at base.

purple-headed stamens arranged along their spikes, each
bunch being protected from wind and rain by a jagged
scale. The other catkins, though similar in appearance,
bear the seed, and search should be made for a seed vessel,
which resembles " a small green pea sitting in a tiny green
cup."

When the leaves appear, they are rounded in shape and
have toothed edges; their stalks are long and flat, and thus
it is, at the faintest breath of the wind, a quivering movement is set up among the leaves, producing that rustling
sound which harmonises so well with
the song of the brook.

Throughout the Summer and Autumn
the tree continues in this state of agita-
tion. Our forefathers have explained
this in their usual quaint fashion by
suggesting that the cross on which the
Saviour was crucified was hewn from the
Aspen, which, horror-stricken, has ever
since shown the signs of its terror and
grief.

Fig. 11. Leaf and Cat-
kins of Aspen.

Its roots have a tendency to keep
near the surface of the ground, and they impoverish the soil
to such an extent that few plants can flourish in its immediate vicinity. These roots send up young shoots or
suckers, and, strange to say, the leaves, which they bear,
differ from those on the main branches in so far as they
are heart-shaped and do not possess toothed edges.

Many an Aspen has come to an untimely end through
the excavations of the Goat Moth larvæ, that find in its
soft wood an excellent material in which to bore their
tunnel-like homes.

Growing upon the bark of the trees fringing our stream,

and also upon the rocks, that are for ever splashed with its waters, are curious growths, which, at first sight, we are inclined to regard as Fungi. These are the Lichens, and they, unlike the Fungi, neither live upon the dead nor attack the living.

A Lichen is a compound organism, consisting of a Fungus and numerous Algæ; it is thus described by Dr. Frank Cavers in *The Book of Nature Study :—*

" The Fungus, composed of branching and interlacing threads, has grown around the Algæ, and enclosed them in a sort of nest. The result is that the Lichen can grow in places which would be quite unsuitable for the independent existence of either the Fungus or the Algæ of which it is composed.

" Algæ grow in water or in moist places, and very few can live without a regular and abundant supply of water, while (apart from the leathery and cakey Bracket Fungi) Fungi are, beyond most other plants, sensitive to cold and drought. . . . Yet Lichens can thrive in the bleakest positions and in the most severe climates . . . or where they are exposed to the greatest extremes of heat and of cold."

Like the Mosses, the Lichens are the pioneers of vegetation; they are the first to appear on cooled lava or newly elevated coral reefs, and by their action the hard rock is slowly broken up, and a thin layer of soil produced.

VI.—BIRDS OF THE WATER-SIDE

REED BUNTING — MUTE SWAN — KINGFISHER — SEDGE
WARBLER — GREY WAGTAIL — HERON — BIRDS WHICH
COME TO DRINK

AMONG the birds that may be met with by the stream, the
Reed Bunting cannot fail to arrest attention. The male
may at once be distinguished by its black head and throat,
white breast and collar, and also by its scratchy little song.
This is a kind of harsh chatter, and as the bird is of a lively
disposition, its notes are sure to attract more than ordinary
notice, though they possess little variety.
The female has a reddish-brown head instead
of black.

Fig. 12. Head of
Reed Bunting.

Wherever Reeds and Sedges fringe the
stream-side, or where Osiers abound, there
search may be made for the nest; this is
composed of moss, dry grasses, reed-stems or
leaves, with a lining of fine grass, reed flowers,
and hair. The four or five eggs are ash-coloured, boldly
marked with jet black streaks in the manner so characteristic
of the Bunting family.

But there are large as well as small feathered folk which
inhabit our waters, and yonder Swan, swimming so majesti-
cally, is certainly entitled to some consideration. This is
the Mute Swan, and is the only species of Swan that nests
in a wild state in this country.

Most of these graceful birds are semi-domesticated,
although they are at all times somewhat ferocious looking,
and hate to be disturbed in their favourite haunts. Whatever spot they frequent they distinctly ornament, for their

snowy-white plumage and beautiful movements are such as to attract notice and comment. A pair of these Swans have tenanted our stream for many years, and early in each Spring a huge nest of Rushes and Reeds is built.

In this large flat structure, six or seven green eggs, about the size of a small Rugby football, are laid, and when the female is sitting, the male bird ably protects her by warning off intruders in a manner calculated to strike terror into the heart of the unwary and too venturesome. The young are known as Cygnets, and very pretty little Swan babies they are.

The stream is one of the favourite homes of this graceful bird, for here it procures its living, feeding upon water plants of various kinds, as well as upon insects; tiny shellfish also form part of its diet, but these are probably swallowed quite accidentally.

When rambling by the water-side, it is as well always to keep a sharp look-out for the most beautiful bird we have in Great Britain, to wit, the Kingfisher. Unless you are fortunate enough to catch this bird fishing, your quest may prove in vain, for it will dash by before you are aware of the fact. Sometimes, when the patient angler goes a-fishing, he has good opportunities of observing this lovely creature; it has been seen to fly rapidly down stream, hover suddenly in the air like a large green and orange-red butterfly, and then make a plunge at some fish, which were bathing their bodies in the sunlight. It is a splendid fisherman, and obtains far more sport than the keen disciple of old Izaak Walton sitting on the bank waiting for a bite!

With plump little body, short tail, large head, and dagger-like beak, the Kingfisher may sometimes be seen sitting on the bough of an overhanging tree, or on a neighbouring post or railing. He looks like a little old man as he

sits there without the slightest movement; but, all of a
sudden, he espies his prey in the water, dashes headlong
into the stream, procures a fish or two, and flies off to his
young ones further down the river.

To find the nest is not an easy task.   Search should be
made in holes along the bank, but sometimes the tunnel
made by a Water Vole or a Sand Martin is chosen.   In the
dark recesses of the home Mrs. Kingfisher deposits from
six to eight beautiful glossy-white
eggs, the nest itself consisting of
the bones of small fish!

The young ones are quite unlike
their handsome parents—for both
the father and mother are equally
beautiful—being curious-looking, stumpy birds.
When observed, they huddle together in an
extraordinary way, hating to be watched,
much less interfered with.

To describe the plumage at length is unnecessary; the remarkable mingling of azure-
blue and bluish-green on the back and head,
the white throat, the orange-red under parts, and the red
band under and behind the eye, being such that nothing
short of a long, detailed description would do justice
to it.   The bird measures about seven and a half inches in
length.

Fig. 13.
Sedge Warbler.

As we wander along the stream, peeping into the rushes
as we go, we suddenly disturb a small brown bird which at
once shows its resentment by uttering a passionate song,
that seems as if it is sung to the listener!   Throw a stone
gently into the herbage, and the little rascal will sing with
increased vigour.   Now and again the notes of other birds
may be distinguished in its song; in fact, it is something of

a small Mocking Bird that we are listening to.   What, then, is it?

It is a Sedge Warbler, a Summer migrant to our country, which arrives during late April, and at once sets up a chattering by the stream to let all his friends know that he has arrived after a safe journey.

Try and get a sight of the restless creature.   More easily said than done, for the bird manages to be close at hand and yet well hidden.   Could you see him—and you may do so if you wait long enough—it would be noticed that his whole body is agitated, and one wonders why the excitable Warbler should be so cross at our having quite unconsciously disturbed him.

Fig. 14.
Nest of Sedge Warbler.

You may know him by a prominent broad streak of yellowish-white over the eye; otherwise he is grey-brown above, with a white throat and pale buff underneath.

Among the Rushes, or in a thick low bush, the neat nest may be sought for; it is made up of the stems of plants, coarse grass, moss, hair, and fine grasses.   It is a somewhat deep home, and the five or six pale brown and pointed eggs occasionally have a thin dark streak upon them.

Some country people call this the Mock Bird, a name that is, for a wonder, not altogether misapplied.

You will remember when visiting the pond, we watched a black and white bird which flirted his tail so gracefully, that we identified him as the Pied Wagtail.   See, there by the old waterfall yonder is a bird of similar habits, but grey and yellow in colour.   That is the Grey Wagtail, which delights in placing its nest near water, for it finds abundant insect food there. If you see the bird in Summer, you will notice that it has a black throat, but in Winter this gives way to whitish-yellow. The eggs of this Wagtail are smaller than those of its relative we met at the pond, and are pale French-grey, mottled with faint creamy-brown.

The Kingfisher is not the only feathered fisherman that haunts the stream, for occasionally the Heron may be found there. And why does he come from his stick-like

Fig. 15. Grey Wagtail.

home in the tree tops? For the purpose of obtaining food for his young ones. Standing in the water with his long stilt-like legs, the Heron is able to wade into the shallows.

There he stands with shrugged shoulders, sometimes with his eyes half closed. But, should a Water Vole venture too near, or a Frog, or a shoal of fish, then the wary bird rouses from his lethargy, snatches at and secures his prey by means of a great strong beak as sharp as a bayonet, and rises slowly. Finally, the bird sails away on majestic wings well satisfied with the result of his labours; for has he not secured food for his ungainly little ones, which are eagerly anticipating the feathered fisherman's return?

On a hot Summer's day an interesting time may be

spent by a stream watching the various kinds of birds which visit the water for the purpose of quenching their thirst. Birds, it should be noted, are more fond of drinking than many people give them credit for, and it has been observed that in a dry season fruit is greatly relished by some feathered choristers which, during a rainy Summer, do not trouble the fruit-grower to any appreciable extent.

By quietly sitting down and carefully watching, it is possible to make a series of notes concerning some birds which come out into the open from their hiding places

in the trees, hedgerows, bushes, and woods, where the thick foliage largely shields them from view. The gay Chaffinch, for example, whose mossy cradle is secreted in a blossoming thorn-bush, pays the stream a visit, and with that happy gait for which it **is** so famous entertains the looker-on by its active manœuvres.

Fig 16 Head of Heron.

The Greenfinch—a voracious feeder at all times—also finds out the shallow part of the water, and very frequently quite a small collection of British birds gather together, which makes watching them a pleasure. Sometimes they bathe their bodies in the stream, and ragged-looking mites some of them are after partaking of a bath, especially if they happen to finish off the performance by dusting themselves in the road! In this way they dry their bodies!

Our friend the Common Sparrow, and also the Skylark, are very fond of thus attending to their toilets.

The handsome Song Thrush and the sober Blackbird will also come to the stream to drink, and very often the speckled Starling ceases hunting for grubs in the meadow bordering the water and slakes its thirst,

FEMALE REED BUNTING AT NEST.

NEST AND EGGS OF REED BUNTING.

MUTE SWAN.

YOUNG KINGFISHERS.

VII.—TWO AQUATIC MAMMALS

WATER VOLE—WATER SHREW

PLOP! That was all we heard, but it was sufficient to indicate that Tim, the Water Vole, had taken a plunge into the stream. He had just been feeding on the green grass which covers the bank, but as we approached he felt it would be more secure to dive into the water and swim to the other side.

If we wait long enough, we shall see him, for already bubbles are arising in mid-stream, showing that the Vole is near the surface so as to breathe better. Look! There he goes! Do you see him with his head above water, sniffing now and again? His little black eyes and whiskers are now quite plain. At last he has reached the opposite bank, and as he sits there in the sunshine nibbling at some more grass,

Fig. 17. Head of Water Vole.

he looks, does Tim, quite a little picture of his own. He is still very busy feeding, and must surely be rather hungry this morning. Clap your hands after watching him closely.

Plop! He has dived into the stream again, but this time he swims along the side, and at last clambers up the bank into his hole. What a clean, well-groomed little animal this is, so very different to the detestable Brown Rat, and in his greyish-brown fur, tinged with red, he is one of the nicest little creatures to be met with on the banks of our stream. He reminds one of a little Beaver, and it is distressing to hear people so frequently refer to him as a Water Rat!

That the Water Vole is a vegetarian we have long since

agreed; but most unfortunately the ravages of that harmful pest, the Brown Rat, are often in ignorance attributed to the Vole, whose entertaining habits we have been watching.

When he was sitting up on his haunches feeding off the opposite bank, did not Tim remind you of a Squirrel? Beaver-like, Squirrel-like, but certainly not Rat-like, what an interesting little animal that " plop " revealed to us! It does not always feed thus, but when it does, our interest cannot fail to be aroused.

During the early days of Summer, five or six little Voles

Fig. 18. Head of Water Shrew.

are born in a nest made up of dry Grass and other herbage. The morning and evening see this animal at its best, for then it is that food is mostly secured, and if one is fortunate enough to come across a number of Water Voles busily feeding and swimming—and some parts of the bank of our stream are quite riddled with their holes—it is one of the happiest sights to watch the active creatures at their work and play.

We may, after a careful search, find still another interesting mammal along our stream, and this is the Water Shrew, first cousin to the Common Shrew that we met with in the meadow.

It makes its home in a long, winding tunnel by the river, but also resorts to ponds, ditches, and similar places. It is a clever digger, and at the end of the lengthy burrow a nest is made of dry Grass and Moss. Here, during the merry month of May, when the Hawthorn is well in bloom, from five to eight young ones are born.

What kind of animal should you look for, do you think? It is subject to a good deal of variation, but is generally black and white. When in the .water, however, it appears grey, this effect being caused by small bubbles of air that cling to the fur; indeed, these often give the Shrew quite a silvery appearance. The length of the head and body is about three and a quarter inches, and the tail about two inches. The feet are white, and the tail has a stiff fringe of white hairs.

This Shrew is entirely aquatic in its habits, and is a superb diver and a splendid swimmer. It swims easily and silently, and if ever you are lucky enough to find it feeding at the bottom of a clear brook, you can promise yourself rich entertainment. Water insects of various kinds as well as Fresh-water Snails and Shrimps constitute its food, but the animal is accused, and probably with reason, of eating spawn and young fish. Dead animals are also, it is said, partaken of.

VIII.—FRESH-WATER FISHES

TROUT—DACE—MINNOW—GUDGEON—RIVER EEL—STICKLEBACKS

SOME kinds of fish are fonder of running water than that of a pond, and in the stream we shall find the beautiful Trout, whose greatest delight is a clear-running brook with a gravelly bed. The Trout is entitled to pride of place among the fishes in our stream, for it is a handsome species and belongs to the Salmon family.

Trout differ a good deal in colour and markings, and it is often difficult to tell exactly the correct name of a given species, there being so many of these fish reared artificially, the result of which is that many *varieties*, and not distinct *species*, are forthcoming. Some may be observed, for example, bronze-brown; some silvery-pink spotted with red; some very dark and almost black. The general colour is green or brown, spotted with red or black.

A quick swimmer, a magnificent sporting fish, a great feeder, these are the characteristics of a Trout; and if the reader happens to be by a river when the Mayflies are rising from their watery home, then is the time to search for a large Trout, and watch him greedily devouring the insects as they dance on unsteady wings down stream. Notice that the fish are invariably seen with their bodies facing up stream. There is reason for this, for not only is food more easily procured in this way, but water is thus carried through the gills. By means of the latter a fish breathes, it of course having no lungs like human beings and other animals.[1]

The life-history plate will give a good general idea of the wonderful story of a Fish as revealed to us by a study of the Rainbow Trout: firstly, the ovum or egg; then the young fish, or Alevin, as it is called; and lastly the perfect little fish. When it is twelve months old, or a yearling, it is about three inches in length, but long before that time it is a perfectly formed fish in every way.

When an Alevin, you will observe that the little stranger has a conical bag suspended under the belly. What purpose does this serve? It is a bag containing the red yolk of the egg, and during the first few weeks of the little one's life, this yolk forms the food upon which it feeds, for although the eyes are by then quite well developed, the mouth is only slightly so.

Being voracious in its habits, and obtaining an abundant food supply, the Trout soon makes up for lost time when it

[1] See *The Pond I Know*, p. 72.

does begin to increase in size. It often attains a weight of several pounds, and then affords rare sport to the angler, being a splendid game fish. It is said to live for over thirty years.

Do you not see a shoal of beautiful silvery fish disporting themselves near the surface of the water? Every now and then one of the little fellows darts clean out of the stream and shimmers in the sunshine like living silver. These are Dace, and may be easily distinguished from the Roach we found in the pond by their smaller size and absence of dark colour. They greatly prefer running water to the stagnant pond, and here they flourish abundantly, travelling about in shoals. Curiously enough they are not found either in Scotland or Ireland.

The general colour is almost silvery blue over the whole body, and the weight rarely exceeds more than one pound. Insects and various kinds of vegetable matter constitute the food; the spawning season is May or June.

Another small fish that inhabits our stream in large companies is the Minnow, one of the most beautiful little fish it is possible to imagine. It averages about four inches in length, and thrives splendidly in fast, clear-running waters. If a specimen be examined, it will be found to be dark green in colour with black along the back. It is silvery below, and the fins on the breast have a red tinge. Like some other animals which lead an aquatic life, the Minnow has the power of changing colour rapidly; the act is probably an unconscious one, but is made possible by there being more than one row of pigment cells just beneath the skin.

At the bed of the stream—and rarely elsewhere—one may find the Gudgeon, charming little fish that also live in companies. It is a lover of the river-bottom, and may at once be distinguished by having, like the Tench in the pond, two barbels upon the jaw. It is grey in colour, marked with dark brown.

The Gudgeon lives on insects, but has curious feeding habits, as those who have angled for it can amply testify. Numbers of these fish will permit a tasty bait to drag right over their bodies without making any effort to snatch at it, but when they come " on the feed," as anglers remark, they are very voracious, and it is possible to catch almost the whole shoal.

All the finny tribe so far referred to may be seen from

the bank of a stream when the water is clear, but one must in any case proceed very cautiously, for fish are easily frightened. The rambler is not likely, however, to see the River, or Fresh-water, Eel, for it is a

Fig. 19. Head of River Eel.

lover of the deep, muddy bottoms, and, except when it is thundery, rarely seems to come out into the open parts of the stream.

Could we see the Eel, we should find that it is somewhat Snake-like in appearance, and slippery to the touch, caused by very small scales with which its body is clothed. It is brown or green above with white or yellow below. The eyes and teeth are small, but the latter are very sharp. The head is long and pointed.

Young Eels, called Elvers, are like small pieces of dark thread, and it seems remarkable that these fragile little creatures eventually grow to be three feet long.

It is said that in the Autumn the female River Eel leaves our stream and makes her way to the sea for spawning purposes, even travelling overland if necessity demands it. Observers have recorded that, as Winter approaches, young Eels are seen ascending rivers from the sea. There is, however, a good deal still to be learned concerning these remarkable inhabitants of our fresh waters, and a careful study of their habits would probably reveal many interesting points at present unknown.

The fish we have so far mentioned deposit their spawn just where it best pleases them, but there are some others in the stream—known to every one as Sticklebacks—which do not resort to this method, but actually build a neat little nest that would do credit to a good many birds.

This barrel-shaped nest, which is the entire work of the male, consists of grass and stems cemented together by sticky threads obtained from the kidneys. Into this charming home the owner entices a female, who, having deposited her eggs, proceeds unconcernedly on her way. These eggs the male fish guards with jealous care, attacking every enemy that comes within reach.

Fig. 20. Three-spined Stickleback and Nest.

The three kinds of Sticklebacks figured in the illustrations are known as the Three-spined, Ten-spined, and Smooth-tailed species.

The reason for these names is obvious, for the first species has three, and sometimes four, spine-like projections on the back, the second has ten spines, and the third has a smooth tail.

Beloved by boys who go a-fishing with net and bottle, or string, bent pin, and a tasty worm, the Stickleback is a most interesting little fellow, and more worth watching than catching. The male—called a Soldier—is a gay creature in the breeding season, being adorned with red and green, and having bright eyes that glow with anger when his nest is approached too closely. He may be seen guarding the entrance to his home, and nobody is permitted to enter the portals except females who are willing to lay eggs therein. The nest is usually well hidden among water weeds. It is a small tangled ball of herbage, and it is pleasant to observe the pride taken by the male in his homestead and his exciting chase of would-be robbers.

The body of a Stickleback is clothed with bony plates in the place of scales, and these vary in number. Green, silver, and brown are the colouration, but the male, as mentioned, is adorned like a gay little red soldier during the breeding season. Various kinds of water insects, as also Fresh-water Shrimps, and many other minute animals, are fed upon by this inhabitant of our stream. There he passes the long Summer days, and if rather than catching him and transferring him to a stuffy bottle, it is decided to study his habits—even if at a disadvantage—much will be learned that would otherwise escape notice.

IX.—WATER INSECTS AND RIVER CRAYFISH

CADDIS FLY—MAYFLY—WATER MEASURER—GNATS—RIVER CRAYFISH

In the stream, as in the pond, there is a large variety of animal life hidden from view, and it is only as a result of exploring in the water, that any real idea can be obtained of the remarkable creatures which make the stream their home.

I

2

3

4

LIFE HISTORY OF RAINBOW TROUT.

1. EGG ENLARGED.   2. EGG HATCHING.
3. YOUNG TROUT WITH YOLK SAC.   4. PERFECT LITTLE TROUT A YEAR OLD.

WATER VOLE.

WATER SHREW.

Several of the little **pond** people will be here, too, for one is a copy of the other to a very great extent; we had better, therefore, make a selection from among these insect folk, and learn to know a few of them really well rather than a little about a good many.

If it be a nice day, and the water be clear and bright, peep into the stream where it is somewhat shallow, or fish out an old stick or stone. You may then make the acquaintance of the larva of the Caddis Fly.

Some of the curious little creatures may be seen crawling about the bed of the stream, but let us obtain a specimen and examine it. At length one is secured, but we find that the larva has retired inside the front door of its home, and refuses to come out again, no matter how pressing the invitation may be. See, the case in which

Fig. 21.
A. Caddis Fly.
B. Larva out of case.
C. Larvæ in cases.

the larva is so comfortably housed is made up of pieces of stick, leaves, and other materials, moulded together in a very ingenious way. If we secure another specimen or two, probably on an old stick or log that has been lying in the water for some time, we shall find that there are various kinds of houses built by these creatures.

Here is one, for example, composed of tiny portions of sand, and at one end there is a little shell as if placed there for ornamentation, much after the manner of the porch we build over our own front doors! Other specimens may be met with upon which small shellfish may be found sticking as firmly as glue; these and the owner of the house must needs travel about in company.

There are several species of Caddis Flies, and it would be an interesting operation for the student of aquatic life to pay special attention to the various kinds and the different homes they build.

But how come these remarkable little animals here, and what is their history? The female Caddis Fly lays her eggs either in the water or upon stones or plants hard by. They are not unprotected even then, being wrapped up in a sort of sticky envelope; a few days after being deposited they hatch.

The small babies stay in this environment some little time before daring to explore the mysteries of the stream, and it almost seems as if the tiny mites realised that, unless some sort of protection were adopted, they would stand very little chance of escaping from numerous enemies. Hence, in due time, the larvæ build the wonderful homes we have seen, and great skill is displayed in fashioning them; indeed, it has been found that no matter what material is used, the homes are usually of " the same specific gravity as the water, so that the worms have no difficulty in moving from place to place." The tiny fragments of sticks, leaves, moss, stones, seeds, rushes, sedges, shells of molluscs, etc., are fastened together by means of a sticky substance which, when exposed, hardens into a kind of silk.

If one tries to dislodge a larva from its home, it will be observed that the creature does not care to be so evicted. It clings tightly to its case, and is aided in this by means of little hooks situate at the end of the body, also by the help afforded by the third pair of legs, and in some species by three small humps.

It is interesting to see the little builder engaged constructing a home, and if one is taken from its shelter and placed in water with suitable building materials, it will construct a new homestead in less time than it takes a human being to make a rough and ready rabbit hutch!

In this home, then, the yellow fleshy larva resides, and when the time comes for it to change into a pupa, it closes the entrance to the front door, enters into the chrysalis state, and eventually comes out triumphant as the perfect Caddis Fly.

But see, the surface of the water is literally covered with the airy forms of a frail-looking insect, with wings like thin wire gauze, and three long processes like the tails of a kite upon the extremity of the body. You remember what was written of the Trout in an earlier chapter, how the fish loved to feed when the Mayfly was rising?

These, then, are Mayflies, just emerged from their watery home. One of the most remarkable points

Fig. 22. Mayfly and Larva.

concerning them is the short period the adult insects live after passing through their wonderful change. Sometimes they exist as perfect insects for a few hours only, " being born, so to speak, after sunset and dying before sunrise; while the longest livers, the patriarchs of the family, exist but for a day or two as a rule, though in captivity it is said that they have been kept alive for a week or even more."

The alternative name of Day Fly indicates that the life of the perfect insect is limited to a day; nevertheless the larvæ enjoy an existence of anything from one to three years.

If an adult specimen be examined, you will find that there may be one or two pairs of wings. The hinder pair, if present at all, will be observed to be much smaller than the front pair.

And yet, although the adult insects live for so short a time, the females manage, during their restricted sojourn on and around the bosom of the stream, to deposit small oval eggs in the water, and thus make sure that the species shall be continued. When the eggs hatch, the flat larvæ have three feathery appendages on the abdomen, long and bristle-like antennæ, and strong mouths. They do not build a tube like the Caddis Worm, but live unprotected in the open water or in U-shaped burrows along the bank. And why is the burrow so shaped, do you think? So that the larva can go in at one hole and out at the other without having to turn right-about-face!

As it grows, the larva changes its skin many times, and as the wonderful transformation proceeds, the pupa develops slowly but surely. Then, as a pupa, the creature leaves the water and at last turns into a Fly. It is not yet, how-ever, the perfect little gem we have been watching, for it has still to undergo another moult. It clumsily settles upon some inviting spot, and contrives to say good-bye to its old covering; then it is that the lovely little Mayfly emerges, and if a careful search be made on the herbage by the stream during the month of May, the empty skins, almost perfect in shape, may reward the searcher.

Curious to relate, the perfect Mayflies usually come out towards sunset and all about the same time. The male may be distinguished upon the wing by its noticeable up-and-down flight, and also by having larger eyes and longer tail-filaments than its mate.

As we stand on the old weather-worn bridge across the stream, we obtain a good view of a large number of long black insects, possessors of very long thin legs, and they are all skidding or skating on the surface in a most curious way. What, then, are these? They are called Water Measurers, and are near relatives of the Water Scorpion that we found in the pond.

With long black body and long limbs, does not this curious creature remind you somewhat of the structure of the Daddy Long-legs we found in the meadow? To catch the Water Measurer is more easily said than done, for it is very quick in its movements, and is a marvellous adept at clinging to a water weed. So little does it look like an insect when thus found, that it could be quite easily overlooked.

It is a splendid hunter, lying in wait for its prey, and then shooting out its two front legs and securing its victim in the folding joints, "which shut down just like the blades of a pocket-knife." Not only are insects captured in this way, but even our little friend the Stickleback is sometimes successfully attacked.

Fig. 23. Water Measurer.

A fierce, bold inhabitant of our stream, the Water Measurer possesses a " beak " which aids it considerably in sucking the blood of its victim. A close examination of a specimen will reveal a body covered with a velvety pile, which renders it incapable of being wetted. There are also a pair of long and narrow wing cases, under which the wings are situated; by means of these the insect can, if it chooses, fly from one part of the stream to another, or over the hills and far away to some sequestered pool.

There are at least nine different species of Gnats in England, and of these two or three are very fond of visiting our houses. The female of the Ring-footed Gnat is capable of inflicting a nasty " nip," but it should be noted that it is only the female which " bites."

D

Few people seem to regard Gnats as either useful or interesting insects, but let us search for a specimen by the stream and see what we can discover concerning them.

Keep a sharp look-out where the water is fairly still; among the rushes the force of the stream is checked, and it is there we may find the Gnat at home. The adult insects, it is true, come out into the open and dance merrily over the surface of the rippling stream, and a happy little company they are. The larva and pupa, however, must be sought for where the water is in no hurry to rush onwards towards the sea.

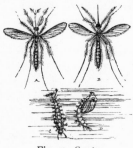

Fig. 24. Gnats.
A. Male   C. Larva.
B. Female.   D. Pupa.

The slim-bodied male may be distinguished from his mate by the plumed or feather-like antennæ, and whilst the female is also plumed her mate successfully out-rivals her in this respect.

It is curious to notice that, whereas Mr. Gnat largely lives on the nectar of flowers, Mrs. Gnat resorts to sucking the blood of animals, including man!

Could we discover a female egg-laying, we should witness a curious performance, for she deposits her eggs by settling on a piece of floating stick or herbage. Then she arranges herself in such a way that egg after egg is laid and collected whilst she is comfortably seated on her raft, until from 200 to 300 are all fastened together by a sticky substance. The eggs are so placed that the narrow ends are at the top, and the whole collection forms a sort of boat, which floats beautifully, being remarkably buoyant and self-righting. Even if pushed forcibly below the water the insect " lifeboat " will rise to the surface and float again!

After a few days in the water the eggs hatch, a kind of front door opening at the lower end and setting free the larvæ. Each larva has a somewhat large head, a large thorax, and a long body, and on the eighth segment there is a small tube which represents the breathing apparatus. This tube is thrust out of the water when the creature requires a fresh supply of air.

Where the water is stagnant these Gnat larvæ are of service, for they feed upon various decaying matter, and so help to cleanse the stream or pond in which they live.

The pupa is very different from the larva, having what on first sight appears as an enormous head, but which in reality is the head, thorax, wings, and legs of the future Gnat fastened up in a sort of envelope. The pupa, too, differs from the larva in floating head uppermost, as its two horn-like breathing organs are situated at the back of what we may call the head.

As time goes on, the little wanderer comes more frequently to the surface, exhibiting a desire to proceed upwards to the unknown world beyond, and when eventually the day of transformation arrives, it stays at the surface and remains motionless. Slowly but surely the body gets lighter in weight, until at last the skin splits and the perfect Gnat is revealed. Then the insect will rest for a while on the old pupa skin, using it as a raft on which to float until it is in a fit condition to join its brothers and sisters and dance merrily upon the wing.

Perhaps you can hardly imagine that our stream is inhabited by large numbers of a small Fresh-water Lobster! Yet such is the case, and sometimes baskets-full of this interesting little creature are captured and sold for the table. It is really called the River Crayfish, but it is certainly not out of place to refer to this inhabitant of our stream as a Fresh-water Lobster.

And how do you think this animal is enticed to enter nets sunk in the water? It is a great lover of raw meat, and if the net is thus baited, it proves too tempting, and lo! Master Crayfish finds himself a prisoner. It is green in colour, but, like the Lobster, turns to a brilliant red when boiled.

Where a stream is found with a good gravelly or rocky bed, there this creature may be sought for. The young are  produced from eggs laid in November and December, and they are very much like the adults, an important point worthy of notice, as this rule does not hold good with many of their

Fig. 25. Head of Crayfish.

relations. And where do you think the eggs are placed? They are actually fastened to the mother's hind legs with a kind of glue, and are there carried until they hatch the following May or June.

The River Crayfish, like its marine cousins, casts its shell, for, as the animal grows, it is necessary that the outer covering should also be enlarged. It has been observed that, when the old shell is about to be shed, the Crayfish loses its appetite, and this results in the body shrinking; thus the moulting process can be better performed.

Is it not remarkable to notice, when examining a cast-off shell, that the exact reproduction of the living creature is to be seen, even the eyes and antennæ being observable. After the old case has been thrown off the animal appears considerably exhausted; its body is then soft to the touch, and far different from the horny coat of mail that has been cast off. Soon, however, the outer covering hardens, the

DACE.

MINNOW.

GUDGEON.

THREE-SPINED STICKLEBACKS.

creature regains its appetite, and in a very short time it is again well protected by its armour.

The food of the Crayfish is made up of worms, insects, molluscs, and dead animals; it is usually during the night, when lying at the mouth of its hole or burrow, that prey is secured.

X.—NOT LOST BUT GONE BEFORE

A PARABLE OF THE DRAGON FLY

IT has already been mentioned, wherever there is water one may chance upon certain kinds of animal life; and whether it be pond or stream, there, sure enough, during the bright days of Summer one may espy the Dragon Fly.

In *The Pond I Know* attention has already been given to the life-history of this insect-dandy, but before we leave the stream, shall we endeavour to learn something further about this remarkable creature?

For this purpose, there is set out below a beautiful tale written by Mrs. Gatty, who died in 1873. This clever woman wrote many charming stories, but none perhaps that appeal more to readers of this book than her *Parables from Nature.*

No apology is needed, therefore, for introducing here one of the wonderful parables from Mrs. Gatty's book, which will, it is hoped, make a strong appeal to young people. It tells of a Dragon Fly nymph which, unlike his brethren, wondered what was beyond the watery element in which he lived; many were the hours spent in thinking and talking about this subject, until at last the spirit of inquiry spread among the others.

Then came the time when the nymph must leave his old playmates and climb up the weeds to the unknown land. Sorrowfully his friends gathered around him, and many were the promises begged and granted. Thus the story proceeds:—

" Promise! " uttered an entreating voice.

" I promise," was the earnest answer.

" Faithfully? " urged the first speaker.

" Solemnly," said the second.

But the voice was languid and weak, for the Dragon Fly Grub was sick and uneasy. His limbs had lost their old activity, and a strange oppression was upon him.

The creatures whom he had been accustomed to chase passed by him unharmed; the water-plants, over which he used to scramble with so much agility, were distasteful to his feet; nay, the very water itself into which he had been born, and through which he was wont to propel himself with so much ingenuity, felt suffocating in its weight.

Upwards he must go now, upwards, upwards! That was the strong sensation which mastered every other, and to it he felt he must submit, as to some inevitable law.

His friends and relations were gathered around him, some of his own age, some a generation younger, who had only that year entered upon existence. All of them were followers and adherents, whom he had inspired with his own enthusiastic hopes; and they would fain have helped him, if they could, in this hour of weakness. But there was no help for him now, but hope, and of that he possessed, perhaps, even more than they did.

Then came an earnest request, and then a solemn promise, that, as surely as the great hopes proved true, so surely would he return and tell them so.

" But, oh! if you should forget! " exclaimed one of the younger generation, timid and uneasy.

" Forget the old home, my friend? " ejaculated the sick Grub, " forget our life of enjoyment here, the ardour of the chase, the ingenious stratagems, the triumph of success? Forget the emotions of hope and fear we have shared together, and which I am bound, if I can, to relieve? Impossible! "

" But if you should not be able to come back to us," suggested another.

" More unlikely still," murmured the half exhausted Grub. " To a condition so exalted as the one in store for us, what can be impossible? Adieu, my friends, adieu! I can tarry here no longer. Ere long you may expect to see me again in a new and more glorious form. Till then, farewell! "

Languid, indeed, was the voice, and languid were the movements of the Grub, as he rose upwards through the water to the Reeds and Bulrushes that fringed its bank. Two favourite brothers, and a few of his friends, more adventurous than the rest, accompanied him in his ascent, in the hope of witnessing whatever might take place above; but in this they were, of course, disappointed.

From the moment, when, clinging with his feet to the stem of a Bulrush, he emerged from his native element into the air, his companions saw him no more.

Eyes fitted only for the watery fluid were incapable of the upward glance and power of vision, which would have enabled them to pierce beyond it; and the little coterie of discoverers descended, mortified and sorrowful, to the bed of the pond.

The sun was high in the heavens when the Dragon Fly Grub parted from his friends, and they waited through the long hours of the day for his return; at first, in joyful hope, then in tremulous anxiety, and, as the shades of evening began to deepen around, in a gloomy fear, that bordered at last on despair. " He has forgotten us," cried some. " A death from which he never can awake has overtaken him," said others. " He will return to us yet," maintained the few who clung to hope.

But in vain messenger after messenger shot upwards to the Bulrushes, and to various parts of the pond, hoping to discover some trace of the lost one. All who went out returned back dispirited from the vain and weary search, and even the most sanguine began to grow sick at heart.

Night closed at last upon them, bringing a temporary suspension of grief; but the beams of the next rising sun, while it filled all Nature beside with joy and hopefulness, awakened them, alas! to a sense of the bitterest disappointment, and a feeling of indignation at the deception which had been practised upon them.

" We did very well without thinking of such things," said they; " but to have hopes like those held out, and to be deceived after all—it is more than we can be expected to bear in patience."

And bear it in patience they did not. With a fierceness which nothing could restrain, they hurried about in the destructive pursuit of prey, carrying a terrible vengeance in all directions.

And thus passed on the hours of the second day, and before night a sort of grim and savage silence was agreed upon among them, and they ceased to bewail either the loss of him they had loved, or their own uncertain destiny.

But on the morning of the third day, one of the Grub's favourite brothers came sailing into the midst of a group who were just rousing up from rest, ready to commence the daily business of their life.

There was an unnatural brilliancy about his eyes, which shone as they had never done before, and startled all who looked at them, so that even the least observant had their attention arrested as he spoke.

" My friends," said he, " I was, as you know, one of our lost relative's favourite brothers. I trusted him, as if he had been a second self, and would have pledged myself a thousand times for his word. Judge, then, what I have suffered from his promise remaining still unfulfilled. Alas! that he has not yet returned to us! "

The favourite brother paused, and a little set in a corner by themselves murmured out, " How could he? The story about that other world is false."

" He has not returned to us," recommenced the favourite brother. " But, my friends, I feel that I am going to him, wherever that may be, either to that new life he spoke about, or to that death from which there is no return. Dear ones! I go, as he did, upwards, upwards, upwards! An irresistible desire compels me to it; but before I go, I renew to you—for myself and him—the solemn promise he once made to you. Should the great hopes be true, we will come back and tell you so. If I return not—but rely on me; my word is more to me than life. Adieu! "

The Grub rose upwards through the water followed by the last of the three brothers, and one or two of the younger ones; but on reaching the brink of the pond, he seized on a plant of the Forget-me-not, and clinging to its firm flower-stalk, clambered out of the water into the open air.

Those who accompanied him watched him as he left the water; but, after that, they saw no more. The blank of his departure alone remained to them, and they sank down, sad and uneasy, to their home below.

As before, the hours of the day passed on, and not a trace of the departed one was seen. In vain they dwelt upon the consoling words he had spoken. The hope he had for a time re-awakened died out with the declining sun, and many a voice was raised against his treachery and want of love. " He is faithless," said some. " He forgets us, like his brother, in his new fortune," cried others. " The story of that other world is false," muttered the little set in the corner by themselves. Only a very few murmured to each other, " We will not despair."

.   .   .   .

One thing alone was certain, he did not return; and the disappointed crowds took refuge from thought as before, in the fiercest rapine and excitement, scattering destruction around them wherever they moved.

Another day now elapsed, and then, in the early dawn following, the third and last brother crept slowly to a half-sleepy knot of his more particular friends, and roused them up.

" Look at my eyes," said he; " has not a sudden change come over them? They feel to me swelled and bursting, and yet I see with a clouded and imperfect vision. Doubt-less it is with me now as it was with our dear ones before they left us. I am oppressed, like them. Like them, an invisible power is driving me upwards, as they were driven. Listen, then; for on my parting words you may depend. Let the other world be what it will, gorgeous beyond all we can fancy of it, blissful beyond all we can hope of it, do not fear in me an altered or forgetful heart. I dare not promise more. Yet if it be possible, I will return. But, remember, there may well be that other world, and yet we, in ours, may misjudge its nature. Farewell, never part with hope. With your fears I know you never can part now. Farewell! "

And he too went upwards, through the cool water to the plants that bordered its side; and from the leaf of a golden King-cup he rose out of his native element into that aerial world, into which Water Grub's eye never yet could pierce.

His companions lingered awhile near the spot where he had disappeared, but neither sign nor sound came to them. Only the dreary sense of bereavement reminded them that he once had been.

Then followed the hours of vain expectation, the renewed disappointment, the cruel doubts, the hope that struggled with despair.

And after this, others went upwards in succession; for the time came to all when the lustrous eyes of the perfect creature shone through the masked face of the Grub, and he must needs pass forward to the fulfilment of his destiny.

But the result among those who were left was always the same. There were ever some that doubted and feared, ever some that disbelieved and ridiculed, ever some that hoped and looked forward.

Ah! if they could but have known, poor things! If those eyes, fitted for the narrow bounds of their water world, could have been endued with a power of vision into the purer element beyond, what a life-time of anxiety would they not have been spared! What ease, what rest would have been theirs!

But belief would, in that case, have been an irresistible necessity, and hope must have changed her name.

And the Dragon Fly, meanwhile, was he really faithless as they thought? When he burst his prison-house by the water side, and rose on glittering wings into the Summer air, had he indeed no memory for the dear ones he had so lately left? No tender concern for their griefs and fears? No recollection of the promise he had made?

Ah! so far from it, he thought of them amidst the transports of his wildest flights, and returned ever and ever to the precincts of that world which had once been the only world to him. But in that region also, a power was over him superior to his own, and to it his will must submit. To the world of waters he could never more return.

The least touch upon its surface, as he skimmed over it with the purpose of descent, brought on a deadly shock, like that which, as a Water Grub, he had experienced from emerging into air, and his wings involuntarily bore him instantly back from the unnatural contact.

"Alas! for the promise made in ignorance and presumption, miserable Grub that I was," was his bitter, constantly-repeated cry.

And thus, divided and yet near, parted yet united by love, he hovered about the barrier that lay between them, never quite, perhaps, without a hope that some accident might bring his dear ones into sight.

Nor was his constancy unrewarded, for as, after even his longest roamings, he never failed to return to the old spot, he was there to welcome the emancipated brother, who so soon followed him.

And often, after that, the breezy air by the forest pond would resound in the bright Summer afternoons, with the clashing of Dragon Flies' wings, as, now backwards, now forwards, now to one side, now to another, without turn or intermission, they darted over the crystal water in the rapture of the new life.

It might be, on those occasions, that some fresh arrival

RIVER CRAYFISH.

CADDIS FLY AND LARVÆ IN CASES.

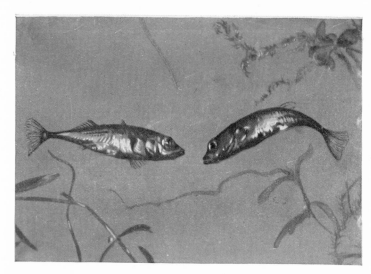

Smooth-Tailed Sticklebacks.

Ten-Spined Sticklebacks.

of kindred from below added a keener joy to their already joyous existence. Sweet assuredly it was to each new-comer, when the riddle of his fate was solved, to find in the new region, not a strange and friendless abode, but a home rich with the welcomes of those who had gone before.

Sweet also it was, and strange as sweet, to know that, even while they had been trembling and fearing in their ignorant life below, gleams from the wings of those they lamented were dropping like star-rays on their home, reflected hither and thither from the sun that shone above. Oh! if they could but have known!

Beautiful forest pond, crowded with mysterious life, of whose secrets we know so little, who would not willingly linger by your banks for study and for thought? There, where the Beech-tree throws out her graceful arms, glorying in the loveliness that is reflected beneath. There, where in the nominal silence the innocent birds pour out their music of joy. There, where the blue Forget-me-not tells its tale of old romance, and the long Grasses bend over their pictured shadows. There, where the Dragon Flies still hover on the surface of the water, longing to reassure the hearts of the trembling race, who are still hoping and fearing below.

Made At The Temple Press Letchworth in Great Britain

CALENDAR AND NOTES

OF

ANIMALS AND PLANTS

COMPILED BY C. S. COOPER, F.R.H.S.

I. BIRDS

CORNCRAKE or LANDRAIL.—A constant resident in England. *Male bird:* general colour of upper parts brown, mottled with black centres to the feathers; ashy-grey above eyes and on cheeks; breast and abdomen yellowish-grey; length 10 inches. *Female:* similar; length 9 inches. *Nest:* end of May or in June; on the ground; leaves and dry grass; *eggs* 7–10, stone-grey to greenish-white or buff, with spots and speckle of reddish-brown. *Food:* Earthworms, slugs, snails, seeds, and plants. *Call:* a grating and monotonous " crex, crex."

HOUSE MARTIN.—A Summer visitor, arriving towards middle or end of April, leaving for Africa in September. *Male bird:* purplish-blue black above, pure white below; a broad white band across the rump; feet and toes feathered; length 5½ inches. *Female:* similar; length 5 inches. *Nest:* May–August; under the eaves of houses, barns, etc., or under bridges; clay and mud, lined with hay, straw, and feathers; *eggs* 4–6, glossy white. *Food:* Gnats and small flies. *Song:* a delicate little warble.

JACKDAW.—A constant resident; many visitors from the Continent in Autumn. *Male bird:* black; crown glossy blue-black; sides of neck grey; bill and feet black; length 13 inches. *Female:* similar in size and colour. *Nest:* May and June; church towers, length 7 inches. *Nest :* April–June; usually near a stream, on banks or shelves of rock, in quarries, etc.; roots and moss, lined with hair; *eggs :* 5 or 6, pale French-grey, mottled with creamy-brown. *Food :* insects. *Call-note :* " chita-chita."

HERON.—A resident. *Male bird :* general colour above light ashy-grey; bluish-black crest, with two long drooping black plumes; face, neck, and under-surface of body white; fore-neck and chest with long white feathers; bill yellow; feet dull green; length 30 inches. *Female :* similar to male. *Nest :* March and onwards; usually on the topmost branches of high trees; sticks, with a lining of finer twigs; *eggs :* 3 or 4, greenish-blue. *Food :* fish, insects, snails, reptiles, Rats. *Call :* a harsh cry, something like that of Peacock.

KINGFISHER.—A resident. *Male bird :* general colour greenish-blue; back cobalt-blue; crown greenish-blue; sides of face orange-red; cheeks with stripe of bright blue; under-surface orange-red: bill black; feet coral-red; length 7½ inches. *Female :* similar, but less bright in colour; basal half of the under mandible red; length 7 inches. *Nest :* March–July; usually a hole in a river-bank; *eggs :* 6 or 7, pure glossy white, nearly spherical; laid on a heap of fish-bones. *Food :* fish and insects. *Call :* a kind of shrill " h'wee-h'wee," uttered very quickly when on the wing.

MUTE SWAN.—A resident, said to have been first brought to England by Richard I. from Cyprus. *Male bird :* body white all over; nostrils and lores black; bill reddish-orange; legs and feet dull black; length 5 feet; weight about 30 lbs. *Female :* similar, but a little smaller. *Nest :* April and May; generally near the edge of water; dead reeds and grass; *eggs :* 6 or 7, dull greenish-white. *Food :* aquatic plants, snails and insects. *Call :* a loud, trumpet-like note.

REED BUNTING.—A resident. *Male bird :* reddish above, streaked with black, with pale edgings to feathers; lower back ashy-grey; head and throat black; under-surface white, streaked with black on sides and flank; length 6 inches. *Female :* throat ashy fulvous, with a black streak on the sides; crown brown, streaked with black; under-surface white, streaked with dusky brown; length about 5 inches. *Nest :* March–July; generally low down in a marshy bank; dried grass, moss, reeds, with lining of fine grass and hair; *eggs :* 4-6, greenish or brownish-grey, scribbled and blotched with black. *Food :* insects, seeds, and grain. *Song :* a few short, shrill notes, succeeded by a long one; sounding like " sherrip " pronounced quickly.

SEDGE WARBLER.—A Summer visitor, arriving at end of April, leaving at beginning of October for South Africa. *Male bird :* russet-brown above, with dusky brown centres to feathers; yellowish-white streak over eye; throat and centre of breast and abdomen white; fore-neck, chest, and sides tawny-buff; bill brown; feet pale-brown; length 5 inches. *Female :* somewhat duller in colour; length 5 inches. *Nest :* May and June; among rushes, or in a bush beside a stream or ditch, or occasionally on the ground; stems of plants, coarse grass, and moss, with a lining of hair; *eggs :* 4-6, olive to brown or stone-grey, mottled with darker brown, often with a hair-like line of black. *Food :* insects, Earthworms, slugs and small caterpillars. *Song :* lively and modulated, very varied, uttered in a hurried manner; introduces the notes of other birds.

II. FISH

DACE.—*Body :* resembling Roach, but narrower and more tapering, silvery-blue, anal fin concave. *Weight :* rarely exceeding 1 lb. *Eggs :*

laid in May and June. *Food :* insects and vegetable matter. *Habits :* they prefer running water, and travel about in shoals.

GUDGEON.—*Body :* long and tapering; one barbel on each side of jaw; length rarely exceeding 7 inches. *Colour :* greyish, with dark blotches above, greatly resembling the surroundings. *Weight :* average 1–2 ozs. *Food :* water insects and worms. *Habits :* they prefer clear streams with gravelly bottoms, where they lie in shoals.

MINNOW.—*Body :* long and tapering. *Colour :* dark green, with patches of black along the back; silvery below; breast fins with tinge of red; in breeding season the males are bright with crimson and green; length about 3 inches. *Weight :* average ¼ oz. *Food :* water insects, flies, and midges. *Habits :* they live in shoals in the shallower parts of the river.

RIVER EEL.—*Body :* long and round, green above, white or yellowish below; head long and pointed or bloated. *Male :* greatest length about 1 foot 7 inches. *Female :* length nearly 4 feet. *Weight :* 3–6 lbs. *Eggs :* laid in the deep sea in Autumn. *Fry :* transparent, compressed from side to side, little thicker than a sheet of stout paper; head very small. *Young eels or " elvers " :* quite transparent; 2–5 inches long; enter the rivers February–May. *Food :* young fish. *Habits :* they hide in mud during day, and come out in search of food at night; will travel over land if the ground be wet.

THREE-SPINED STICKLEBACK.—*Body :* long and thin; three spines on the back, two at the sides. *Colour :* grey and golden; males in the breeding season very brilliant, upper parts bright blue, lower parts crimson, eye green. *Weight :* average ¼ oz. *Eggs :* laid during April in a barrel-shaped nest made of weeds by the male. *Food :* water insects, Fresh-water Shrimps, etc. *Habits :* the male guards the nest and will attack all comers; he is a bold fighter.

TROUT.—*Body:* thick. *Colour:* very variable; general colour yellowish; upper parts spotted with black and red, under surface silvery-white or yellow; fins light brown. *Weight:* up to 14 or 15 lbs.; average 2–5 lbs. *Eggs:* yellowish, with red yolk; laid in Autumn in a depression of the river bottom, and covered with gravel; hatch in following Spring. *Alevin:* eyes very prominent; yolk-bag beneath body; mouth not developed. *Yearling:* about 3 inches in length; sides of back spotted. *Food:* worms, snails, Fresh-water Shrimps, flies. *Habits:* very voracious; said to live over thirty years.

III. INSECTS

COMMON GNAT.—*Male:* antennæ very feathery. *Female:* antennæ plumed, but not so feathery; mouth provided with sharp lancets. *Eggs:* 200–300, laid in form of a raft in still water, plentiful in Summer. *Larva:* body slender and flexible; head and thorax large; breathes through special tube at hinder end of body. *Pupa:* "head" very large—consists of head, thorax, wings, and legs of future Gnat; breathes through a pair of stout tubes (respiratory trumpets) attached to the first thoracic segment; swims about, but takes no nourishment.

COMMON MAYFLY.—May and June. *Body:* long and slender; mouth rudimentary, not able to absorb food; wings gauzy, hind pair very small; three slender filaments at end of body. *Eggs:* laid in packets on the water; *Larva:* body ½ inch long; jaws strong; a row of thin, plate-like gills on each side of body; three feathery filaments at end; lives for about three years; burrows ⊂-shaped; feeds on vegetable matter. *Nymph:* resembles larva, but has rudimentary wings. *Pseud-imago or "Green Drake":* apparently a perfect insect, but covered with a skin. *Imago or "Grey Drake":* emerges from skin, and flies away; seldom lives for more than a few hours.

GREAT CADDIS FLY.—*Body :* $\frac{7}{8}$ inch long, stout, hairy; wings brown, very heavy, thickly covered with hair, expanding $1\frac{3}{4}$–$2\frac{1}{4}$ inches. *Eggs :* green; in a double cluster, held together by a gelatinous secretion; carried by female at extremity of body; mass affixed to stem of an aquatic plant, often a foot below surface of water. *Larva :* lives in a tube made of pieces of leaves and other vegetable matters arranged in a spiral manner; tube of large diameter, enabling larva to turn round inside, and appear at either end; head and thorax protected by horny covering. *Pupa :* passes stage in tube.

LESSER CADDIS FLY.—*Body :* yellowish-brown; head and thorax with yellowish down; upper wings pale brown, variegated with dark brown; expanding $\frac{7}{8}$ inch; lower wings shining and iridescent. *Eggs :* held together in a mass by a gelatinous secretion, and affixed to the stem of a water plant. *Larva :* head and thorax horny; rest of body soft; tail-segment with a pair of hooks; lives in a tube made of vegetable matter; feeds on water-plants and insects. *Pupa :* passes stage inside tube, with ends closed up. *Imago or Fly :* takes no food; dies in a few days.

WATER MEASURER.—*Body :* $\frac{1}{2}$ inch long; blackish-brown above, black beneath; covered with velvet-like pile; elytra blackish-brown; front pair of legs short, used for seizing prey; middle pair the longest. *Food :* aquatic insects, Water-fleas, etc.

IV. MAMMALS

WATER SHREW.—A native of Britain. *Body :* generally black above and white beneath; ears small; teeth 30, tips stained brownish-red; feet fringed with stiff white hairs; tail with similar hairs on lower surface. *Length* of head and body about $3\frac{1}{4}$ inches; tail about 2 inches. *Inhabits* winding burrows excavated in banks of rivulets, brooks, ditches, and ponds; swims well, and dives with ease to the bottom. *Food:* aquatic insects and larvæ, crustaceans and snails.

WATER VOLE.—A native of Britain. *Body:* covered with long and thick fur, usually greyish-brown with reddish tinge, but sometimes wholly black; head with a blunt, rounded muzzle; ears short, buried in fur; hind-feet long. *Length* of head and body 8¼ inches; tail 4½ inches. *Inhabits* banks of rivers, canals, brooks, and ponds, forming long burrows; swims and dives with ease. *Food:* vegetable substances, chiefly roots and grass.

V. MISCELLANEOUS

CRAYFISH.—*Body:* consists of twenty rings, forming the so-called " head " and " tail "; former, true head and thorax; latter, abdomen; hind pair of antennæ very long; five pairs of walking-legs, first pair bearing large " pincers." *Colour:* green. *Eggs:* laid in November and December; carried in masses called " berries," attached to female's legs; hatched in following May or June. *Food:* worms, insects, snails, and other animal matter. *Habits:* hides in a hole or burrow, catches prey chiefly at night.

VI. TREES AND FLOWERING PLANTS

NAME.	Time of Flowering.	Colour.	Height.
Aspen . . .	Mar. April	Reddish	Tree
Comfrey . . .	May June	Purple or Yellowish-White	1–3 ft.
Brooklime . . .	May—Sept.	Bright blue	1–2 ft.
Water-cress . .	May—Oct.	White	2–3 ft.
Greater Willow Herb .	July Sept.	Lilac-pink	4–5 ft.
Great Yellow Loose-strife	„ „	Yellow	2–3 ft.
Purple Loosestrife .	„ —Sept.	Purple, inclining	2–4 ft.
Hemp Agrimony .	„ —Oct.	Dull Pink	3–6 ft.

THE COWBOY I KNOW

THE
COMMON I KNOW

EDITED BY

W. PERCIVAL WESTELL, F.L.S., F.S.A. Scot.
& HENRY E. TURNER

*General Secretary of the School
Nature Study Union*

WITH

14 COLOURED

& MANY BLACK AND WHITE
ILLUSTRATIONS

LONDON
J. M. DENT & SONS LTD.

All rights reserved
Printed in Great Britain
by The Temple Press Letchworth
for
J. M. Dent & Sons Ltd.
Aldine House Bedford St. London
Toronto   .   Vancouver
Melbourne   .   Wellington

" Therefore am I still a lover of the meadows, and the woods, and mountains, and of all that we behold from this green earth; of all the mighty world of eye and ear, both what they half create, and what perceive; well pleased to recognise, in Nature, and the language of the sense, the anchor of my purest thoughts;—the nurse, the guide, the guardian of my heart,—and soul of all my moral being."—WILLIAM WORDSWORTH.

CONTENTS

LIST OF ILLUSTRATIONS

COLOURED PLATES AND HALF-TONES

ILLUSTRATIONS IN THE TEXT

THE COMMON I KNOW

I.—INTRODUCTION

How many of you really enjoy a history lesson? Maybe
you do not think it worth your while to concern yourself
with people who lived, and events which happened, ages
ago. But when you are older, no doubt you will appreciate their value more, for then you will realise that it is
only by a knowledge of the past that you can obtain a
thorough understanding of many of the things which form
part of your daily life.

Our Commons, for instance—those broad, breezy places
over which we love to ramble at our own sweet will—what
does history tell us about them? Their origin remains
somewhat obscure, although clever men have spent much
of their time in examining old books and manuscripts dealing with this subject.

It is generally agreed, however, that Commons are part
of what remains of the ancient Folklands. Do you know
what these were? They were the public lands in the old
English times, those lands which belonged to the nation,
and which were not in the possession of any individual or
family or town.

When England became one kingdom, the Folklands
were very extensive, and were under the control of the
King and the Witan. Evidence of this still exists in what
are now known as the Crown Lands.

In ancient days there was no standing army, and the King, in the event of war, had to rely upon his barons and knights to provide him with the necessary soldiers. How could he repay these nobles for their services, and keep them faithful to his cause? Generally they were rewarded with fine estates taken from the Folklands, and thus the latter decreased in size.

Nor was this the only way in which the Folklands suffered; large tracts were also handed over to the Church, and considerably added to her power and source of income.

At a later date, when might was stronger than right, hundreds of acres, which formerly had been cultivated in common by a community or village, were enclosed by powerful barons for their own profit or pleasure. Against these barons the poor commoner might appeal, but it was always in vain; compensation was sometimes allowed, but it was out of all proportion to the great loss sustained.

Thus, by one means or another, the common lands of England practically disappeared, with the exception of those parts which could not be cultivated with advantage, usually owing to the poverty of the soil.

But if the ploughman has ignored and despised these " sandy wastes," Nature has dealt very graciously and often very liberally with most of them, as you will be forced to admit when you go in search of their countless treasures.

In England, the common lands now belong to the Lord of the Manor, although certain people, called commoners, have special rights there. Blackstone, the eminent legal authority of former times, describes a common as being " a profit which a man hath in *the land of another*, as to feed his beasts, to catch fish, to dig turf, to cut wood, and the like."

Matters in Scotland are not quite the same. There a

Common is "the right of property existing in several individuals—frequently the inhabitants of a whole village—
in a piece of ground; but there is no over-lord."

Those of us who love the Common, find it difficult to
regard it as a waste place, as a spot not worth stealing. To
us it is the home of many a dainty flower, the haunt of
feathered songsters, and the happy hunting ground of
things that creep and things that fly.

Modern law has fortunately come to its aid, and has for-
bidden further encroachments. Let us, therefore, be grateful, for in these days of an ever-increasing population and
overcrowded towns, who can estimate the enormous value
of these free and open spaces? They are, indeed, the lungs
of the city, where one can breathe the pure air, and, for
the moment, forget the busy street and its smoke-laden
surroundings.

II.—TREES AND BUSHES

BLACKTHORN—HAWTHORN—GUELDER ROSE—FURZE—
ELDER—SILVER BIRCH

IT may be as well to remind you once again that few of our
trees and plants remain faithful to one special locality, or
refuse to adorn any but that particular haunt. For instance, dearly as they may love the shelter and the shade of
a densely inhabited hedge, nevertheless they will not
hesitate to take up their residence on the sunlit and less
congested Common.

Among these impartial children of Nature we may
reckon the Blackthorn, a typical tenant of the hedge, but
growing in great profusion on the Common.

What country rambler is not familiar with its white

starry blossoms, which show up so well in the early days of Spring against its black tangled thorny boughs? These dense clusters of blossoms appear before the leaves, and when they fall, they clothe the ground as with a carpet of snow.

Should you have the opportunity of examining a blossom, the five petals and bunch of stamens will probably remind you of the rose. Beware, however, of the spikes, those sharply pointed thorns at the ends of the twigs; they are not pleasant to the touch, as cattle have discovered to their cost when foolishly seeking a meal off the smooth, narrow leaves.

Fig. 1. Fruit of Blackthorn.

The Blackthorn belongs to the Plum family; the fruit, known to us as the Sloe, ripens in Autumn and is far from being a luxury. It is round and has a purple tinge; but although in appearance it is inviting, yet usually one bite is enough for an average person—the taste being harsh in the extreme.

Perhaps some of you are familiar with these lines:—

> The ripening sloe, yet blue
> Takes the bright varnish of the morning dew.

What is this bright varnish? It is a wax probably secreted to protect the undeveloped fruit from the attacks of insects or from the harmful effects of damp.

Man, however, has no scruple with regard to handling Sloes. He gathers them in large quantities, and with them makes preserves and wines; indeed, it is said that much of the so-called port wine owes its origin to the fruit of the Blackthorn.

As with the Blackthorn, so with the Hawthorn; both are familiar objects of the hedge, and both are equally at home on the Common. Judging from appearance, the Hawthorn should prefer the Common, for there it is allowed to grow in perfect freedom (save when the cattle browse upon its leaves), and is not subject to the constant pruning which falls to the lot of its brethren in the hedge. Indeed, when left alone, it becomes a gnarled and bushy tree, a wonderful contrast to the victim of the clipping shears.

Fig. 2. Hawthorn.

Can you guess the reason why it is such a favourite with those who desire to enclose their lands? Go to yonder hedge, and see if you can suggest a worse foe to the would-be trespasser than the Hawthorn. Its numerous twisting branches, the dense network of twigs, the sharply pointed thorns, all these combine to make a perfect fence; and woe betide the unfortunate wight who tries to force a passage between them.

When the leaves first appear they are of a pale green, but time and the weather soon deepen their shade, and detract from their early freshness. They are best described as wedge-shaped, although they vary considerably; sometimes they are divided into three lobes, but at other times into five.

The blossoms appear in May, and this explains the other name—probably the most familiar one—by which the tree is known, the May Tree. These blossoms are grouped in flattened clusters, and are well worth close examination. Once again we have the five dainty petals fitting into the green calyx cup, and once again we have a group of stamens in the centre; these, however, have bright pink heads, and give a splash of colour to the scene.

Generally speaking the petals are white, but as you all are aware, we have pink May and red May, and very charming these beautifully tinted flowers are; indeed, many a rustic garden owes part of its Spring glory to their presence.

Autumn's gifts to the tree are the glorious clusters of berries, the Haws, so well known as to need but little description here. First green and then red, they attract the hungry birds, which flock to the feast so temptingly placed before them, and thereby assist in dispersing the seed.

Do you know the name of yonder bush, down there by the edge of the Common? Let us get a nearer view of it, and make a sketch of its leaves. Note that these are thin and tender and of a vivid green; the three lobes into which each leaf is divided are coarsely toothed, and almost, if not entirely, free from hairs.

What should you say was the height of this bush, or are you no good at measurements of this sort? Cannot we say that it is a little taller than a very tall man? That will fit the case this time, although its brothers have been known to reach twelve feet in height.

Pass your hands along the stems and branches. These you will find as smooth as the leaves. Now who can guess the name? Yes, it is the Guelder Rose, and had we found it in bloom, there would have been no difficulty in deciding what it was.

Look at these small swellings on the leaf stalks. They are called honey-glands and are said to attract Ants and Wasps, which in turn protect the plant by keeping off caterpillars and other harmful insects.

We must pay the Guelder Rose another visit later on, when its masses of creamy-white blooms make it a con-

BLACKTHORN.

FLOWERS OF GUELDER ROSE.

FRUIT OF GUELDER ROSE.

spicuous figure of this spot. Each flower taken separately might fail to be seen, but when grouped together, as they are, in dense clusters, they command attention from man and insect alike. Those in the outer row are considerably larger than their partners of the inner rings, but they are without stamens and pistils. All their strength has been expended in increasing their petals—a form of advertisement for attracting insects.

Autumn deals very lovingly with this new friend of ours. The leaves assume a rich purple ere they fade and fall, whilst the green oval berries

Fig. 3. Fruit of Elder.

"redden to a pure and limpid crimson, like drops of transparent blood or rubies from the trees in the garden of Aladdin."

The Guelder Rose is sometimes spoken of as the Water or Marsh Elder, from the resemblance of its blossoms to those of the Elder. Indeed, these bushes are relatives, and may often be found in one another's company.

Few plants have legends associated with them to such an extent as the Elder. Some declare that Judas chose this tree on which to hang himself; others regard it as the emblem of woe; another section assert that it possesses the power of driving away evil spirits.

Be that as it may, nobody will deny that the Elder can be of great service to man. Its easily hollowed stems may be fashioned into musical instruments or—and this will please you children better—a pop-gun or a pea-shooter. Elderflower water and Elderberry wine at once suggest further uses, and their names are sufficient to denote their origin.

Talking of names may remind us that Elder is said to

have been derived from a word meaning "kindler"—"a name which we may suppose it acquired from its hollow branches being used, like the Bamboo in the tropics, to blow up a fire."

So much, then, for Tradition! Now let us look at the tree itself. The younger shoots have a bright green appearance, but if you examine the older branches, the green has given place to a dark grey, and the smooth surface to one that is rough and corky. The wood is remarkable for its elasticity, and for the large amount of pith which it contains.

The leaves consist of five, seven, or even nine oval leaflets with toothed edges, and these give a feathery appearance to the bush. As in the case of the Guelder Rose, so here the creamy white blossoms are arranged in flattened clusters; but the berries are rounder in shape, and assume a purple black hue when ripe.

Let us leave the borders of our Common for a time, and wander across its wide expanse. On all sides we meet with the golden Furze, "whose wealth of golden blossoms stretching over many acres of ground, the sweet fragrance of its flowers, and the long duration of its flowering season, are points that arrest the attention even of the most indifferent."

It is described by the Rev. C. A. Johns as "a much-branched, spreading shrub, almost leafless, except in its seedling state, when the leaves are composed of three narrow, soft leaflets. It attains maturity in about four years, but in sheltered places continues to grow until it reaches a height of from twelve to eighteen feet."

"Its natural habit is, however, to grow on dry, exposed Commons, which, in its flowering season, it covers with a gorgeous sheet of golden blossoms, entirely concealing its somewhat unsightly branches. Perhaps no plant is so broadly characteristic of English scenery and the English climate as Yellow Whin—another name for Furze. It does not thrive in hot countries, and if removed to a much colder climate pines and dies; it is rare even in the Highlands of Scotland."

As the plant grows in age, the soft, hairy leaves of its babyhood cease to appear, and in their stead we get the familiar spines.

Furze—or to give it a still further title, Gorse—belongs to the great Pea and Bean tribe, and you should endeavour to prove the truth of this by examining first the blossom and afterwards the seed case.

The petals are five in number, and when in bud, the upper one, called the standard, protects the other four; the two side petals are termed wings and enclose the two lowest of all; these are joined along the

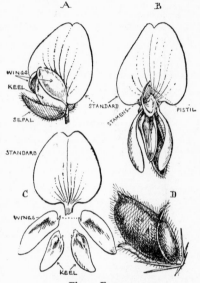

Fig. 4. Furze.

A. Flower before fertilisation.
B. Flower after fertilisation by Bee.
C. Petals of Flower.
D. Fruit (pod).

lower margin to form the keel, and here it is we must look for the stamens and pistil.

The whole blossom is partly surrounded by a comparatively large yellow calyx, which is divided into two lobes and covered with dark hairs.

" Another point of interest will be found in the little

black hairy pods which succeed the flowers and contain
the hard, shiny seeds.   When they are perfectly ripe and
the pods quite dry, the two valves separate with a snap,
and each curls up so quickly that the seeds are flung away
with force." [1]

Before we leave the trees and bushes of our Common, we
must pay our respects to the Lady of the Woods, as the Silver
Birch is poetically named.   It might also be christened the

STAMINATE
CATKIN

PISTLLATE CATKINS

Fig. 5. Catkins and Leaves of Silver Birch.

Lady of the Common,
so often is it to be
found there — a veri-
table Queen of Beauty.
Who can fail to ad-
mire its flaky silver-grey
bark, and its graceful,
loosely-hung leaves
dancing at the whim of
every passing breeze?
Can you see those
dark horizontal lines on the trunk?   They are lenticels or
breathing holes, and correspond to the stomata of the leaves.
You can find them on all kinds of trees, but they are specially
noticeable on the Silver Birch.

The pollen-bearing catkins first appear in the Autumn,
but do not reach maturity until the following Spring.
Those that bear the seed, however, are not in evidence
until a later date; at first they are erect, but towards the
Autumn, being heavy with seed, they also droop, and thus
remain until their contents are scattered by the wind.

[1] *The Romance of Wild Flowers*, by Edward Step.

III.—PLANTS OF THE COMMON

WILD THYME—SMALL KNAPWEED—YARROW—SPEAR PLUME
THISTLE—EYEBRIGHT—LING—CROSS-LEAVED HEATH

THE Common is usually a very dry place, so that one will
not be surprised to find growing there the Wild Thyme, a
plant which loves a light and well-drained soil; it is, therefore, equally at home on mountain slopes and dry pastures.

Whenever it fixes its abode on an exposed spot, its many
branched stems creep along the ground, as if anxious to
seek protection from the wind.

The rosy purple flowers are borne at the end of a short
stem, and are usually so crowded together as to suggest a
spike. Though small in size, these blossoms have a delightful and refreshing fragrance, which doubtless assists in
attracting the Bees to the scented honey.

The leaves, which grow in pairs, are very small and egg-
shaped. They are dark green in colour, and sometimes the
smooth edges are rolled back until they almost meet behind.

But if the Wild Thyme be modest and retiring, the
same cannot be said of the Small Knapweed, a soldier-like
plant, whose tough stems often reach a height of two feet.
The upper leaves are usually lance-shaped, with edges that
are smooth or only slightly toothed; those nearer the root,
however, may be broader and deeply lobed.

The chief point of interest lies in its thistle-like flower
head, which consists of a hard green ball surmounted by a
densely packed group of crimson florets; the latter are
tiny tubes—so characteristic of the composite flowers—
and are kept in position by a circular row of dark brown

scales. It is the dark colour and the ball-like appearance of the flower head that give to the plant its various names, including that of Hard-head.

Should you wish to discover in what ways the Knap-weed differs from a Thistle, compare it with that Spear-plume Thistle which is growing close by. This aggressive plant may be seen decorating the hedge-bank or any waste place where it has been allowed to obtain a footing.

The first sign of its presence, before the stem has been developed, is a beautiful rosette of dagger-like leaves arranged in a circle on the surface of the ground. What a dangerous rival such a warlike plant must be to the less aggressive plants of the neighbourhood!

Here again the leaves are lance-shaped, but they are deeply cut into strong, toothed lobes, each of which is sub-divided; these various divisions end in long, sharp spines, and when we remember that the leaves themselves are continued some distance down the stem to form spiny wings, we must agree that the plant is of a most militant nature.

The case, which holds the flower head, is shaped like an egg, and consists of a series of narrow bracts terminating in long spines. The long corolla tubes, dull purple in hue, remind one of a soft plume, quite a contrast to the spiky leaves and stem. The blossoms are succeeded by the feathery, shiny seeds, so characteristic of the Thistle family, and the silky down buoys them up when the time of the Autumnal dispersal is at hand.

Another composite flower that we may meet with on our Common is the Yarrow, which flowers from late June to the end of October. Its leaves are narrow and very long, and consist of numerous leaflets; the latter are cut into hair-like segments, thus giving the whole leaf a feathery

Furze.

ELDER.

appearance. So many sections are there to each leaf that the plant is often spoken of as Milfoil, which is the Latin way of saying Thousand-leaf.

At first sight the blossoms might be mistaken for a bunch of tiny Daisies, or even for a group of simple blossoms; closer observation is necessary to prove that we are examining one of the composite family, for " in the Yarrow the florets of the disc are small and might easily pass on a cursory view for a group of stamens; while the florets of

Fig. 6. Small Knapweed.   Fig. 7. Yarrow.

the ray, the exterior and ray-bearing blossoms, are so few in number—ordinarily five or six—that these rays in like manner might to the novice appear but the petals of some simple flower, like the five of the Buttercup." [1]

One need not wait long by the side of Yarrow in bloom to learn how attractive it is to the many insects which come in search of its rich store of honey.

But in our quest for the larger plants, we must not overlook our little friends that seem to cuddle close down to Mother Earth. Look at the quaint flower, for instance, that seems to be peeping at us from the close-cropped turf.

[1] *Familiar Wild Flowers*, by F. E. Hulme.

Is it not an easy matter to understand why the ancients named it Eyebright?

Here it is but a dwarf, measuring only a few inches, but in some places there are specimens which appear to make a special effort, and more than treble their usual height.

Kneel down for a few minutes, so that you may get a good view of the leaves. Can you describe them? Yes, they are oval and of a dark green colour; they are without stalks and the edges are sharply toothed.

So much for the leaves, but what about the blossom? Notice the tube-like calyx with its four sharp teeth. See how beautifully the corolla fits into it; this corolla has two lips, the upper one being cut into two lobes, and the lower one into three.

Fig. 8. Eyebright.

Perhaps the most interesting features to you are the streaks of purple and the blotches of yellow which decorate the white surface of the petals. These are said to be the honey guides, and assist the insect visitors in finding their way to the nectar.

It must be confessed that Eyebright has been accused and found guilty of stealing; it has the bad habit of preying upon the roots of other plants, and thus robbing them of their food. Hence it is sometimes spoken of as a parasite.

But at last we have found something with which we are all familiar—the Common Ling or Heather. This, perhaps, is the most widely distributed of our wild plants, and must not be confused with the Heaths. Its very small leaves are densely packed, being arranged in four rows on opposite sides of the stem.

Strange to say, the very small and bell-shaped corolla is concealed by the rose-coloured calyx, at the base of which, as if to add to the deception, there are four small green bracts having the appearance of a second calyx.

The Heaths require a peaty soil, and flourish best amidst moist surroundings. The Cross-leaved species suggests its own special feature, for here the leaves are placed cross-wise in whorls of four. The plant is crowned by heads of drooping flowers of a rose-coloured hue.

The Purple or Fine-leaved Heath has exceedingly narrow-pointed leaves arranged in threes, with numerous purple flowers that suggest fairy bells. It is among the Heaths and Heather that the Bee loves to ply her trade, for there she may be sure of a rich and plentiful supply of honey.

IV.—MORE PLANTS OF THE COMMON

BIRD'S-FOOT TREFOIL—COMMON FLEABANE—COMMON RAGWORT—TORMENTIL—MILKWORT—SUNDEW

IF we visit our Common during " the leafy month of June," in all probability we shall chance upon the golden blossoms of the Bird's-foot Trefoil.

This charming plant sends up from its roots several trailing branches, which are arrayed in dainty leaves; each of the latter consists of five leaflets, although at first sight we might be inclined to say that only three were present, as the other two are situated at the base of the stalk. Accord-ingly it is scarcely correct to describe Bird's-foot as a Trefoil.

As we examine the bright yellow blossoms, let us re-member that the plant is another member of the Pea and Bean family; we may, therefore, expect the petals to be arranged in a manner similar to those of the Furze already described. Compare the two flowers for yourselves, and endeavour to find the points of resemblance.

The thin cylindrical seed-pods are usually an inch in length, and when they are arranged in a cluster of three or four, they present the appearance of a bird's foot.

Yellow is certainly one of the most conspicuous colours of the Common, and if we were to confine ourselves only to

Fig. 9. Bird's-foot Trefoil.   Fig. 10. Fleabane.

the blossoms of that particular hue, we should have sufficient material to occupy our attention for some time.

Among these would be the Common Fleabane, which favours a moist soil, and dearly loves to take up its abode by the side of a ditch or stream, and thus become the companion of the Forget-me-not and the King-cup. Its presence is often a hint to the farmer that his land is not properly drained.

The round solid stem sends out numerous branches, and is well supplied with oblong leaves, which clasp the stem at their base; these are covered with hairs; in fact the whole plant is of a woolly nature.

A single glance at the brilliant golden blossoms will convince you that you are looking at a composite flower; the ray florets have grown into long slender straps, and doubtless are useful in advertising the plant.

As to whether Fleabane is obnoxious to, and destructive of, a particular kind of insect as suggested by its name, is a matter of doubt; tradition says that this particular pest was sure of an untimely death though it " only sniffed the smoke from the Fleabane's burning leaves and stems."

Ragwort is another plant that frequents the ditch bordering our Common, but its yellow star-like blossoms may also be seen lighting up the unploughed soil of many a neglected piece of waste ground.

How it came by its name is more or less vague, but the majority seem to agree that it owes its title to its deeply cleft and feather-shaped leaves; these are lobed and toothed it is true, but it is rather a stretch of the imagination to call them ragged. Others ascribe the name to the thin and straggling ray florets, which are thought to give an untidy appearance to the flower head.

Ragwort is the cousin of Groundsel; unlike that plant, it does not bloom all the year round, but only from June to October. The stem is stout and well-branched, sometimes rising to a height of three or four feet.

In the arrangement of their florets, the blossoms of Common Ragwort resemble those of the Daisy, for here, again, we are dealing with a composite flower.

Quite a different type of plant is the Tormentil, which throughout the Summer months may be had for the seeking on banks, on heaths, and in woods. Look! There are numerous specimens growing almost beneath our feet. Let us gather some, and see what we can discover about these modest flowers.

The four pale yellow petals do not overlap, but permit of the green bracts—or at least part of them—showing up between their golden surfaces. The bracts are four in number, and longer than the four sepals. Each blossom has a separate stalk, which always springs from the axil of the leaf, that is to say, from that point where the leaf joins the stem.

Notice the difference between the leaves that grow direct from the root and those which belong to the stem;

Fig. 11. Ragwort.   Fig. 12. Tormentil.

the former have stalks and are deeply cut into five fingers, whereas the latter are sessile and are only cut into three. Does the word " sessile " puzzle you? It means " seated " —seated upon the stem—or, in other words, without a stalk.

The root is said to contain a quantity of tannin, and to be of great use in the preparation of leather.

When we were hunting for the Tormentil, did you notice a humble little blue flower nestling among the grass? See, here is one, and there is another! Indeed, the supply is most plentiful, for the plant is far from being rare. Years ago it was christened Milkwort, from the belief that if cows partook freely of it, their milk would increase in quantity and improve in quality. Like most of our ancient legends, this must not be taken too seriously.

The leaves, as you have doubtless observed, are arranged singly along the stem, and, though small, may be described as lance-shaped.

The grouping of the blossoms may possibly remind you of that of the Hyacinth, for these dainty flowers are suspended from a spike, hanging each from its own tiny stalk. Although the corolla is usually blue, yet quite frequently it is red or pure white.

Probably the calyx is the most interesting feature of the Milkwort; this consists of five sepals, two of which are comparatively large, and, being purple, have the appearance of petals. When the seeds are ripe, strange to say, this purple tinge disappears, and all five are then of the same colour, namely, green. There are those who declare that this is a sign to would-be insect visitors that their services are no longer necessary for the purpose of fertilisation.

Fig. 13. Round-leaved Sundew.

No plant is more capable of arousing our curiosity than the Sundew. A few minutes' walk will bring us to a well-known bog, and there this marvellous plant grows in plenty. The roots are very small, and have but a slight hold of the moist ground, as though they were not needed except to obtain the necessary supply of moisture. From what source, then, is the nitrogenous food derived?

Look closely at the leaves, for therein lies the answer to that question. They are nearly circular in shape, and radiate from the root somewhat like the spokes of a wheel resting almost flat on the ground. Each leaf has several rows of crimson hair-like tentacles capped with tiny rounded heads; these are glands which excrete a sticky fluid resembling liquid gum.

" The leaves are no doubt mistaken for dewy flowers by small insects, which alight upon them in the hope of finding honey or to sip the supposed dew. . . . The Fly touches the tentacle-glands with its limbs, and is held by the gummy liquid. . . . Now there is poured out a digestive fluid, which actually dissolves the soft parts of the Fly, and when the process is complete, the leaf absorbs this extract of Fly to the manifest advantage of the plant." [1] Thus the Sundew, in common with such plants as Venus' Flytrap, obtains the necessary nitrogen, and all is well—at least for the plant.

V.—THREE MAMMALS OF THE COMMON

RABBIT—STOAT—PIPISTRELLE BAT

IF there is one spot the Rabbit loves it is an open, breezy Common, where the soil and the soft, springy turf enable it to burrow underground to its heart's content.

Early morning, and then again towards dusk, are the best times to see the Rabbit above ground. Long before the work-a-day world wakes from its slumber, Brer Rabbit has come from his home below, and started nibbling at some succulent plant. Later in the day it is, of course, possible to observe this happy-go-lucky little mammal, but if you would see it at its best, be up with the Lark, or before it, and observe Bunny enjoying an early breakfast.

Can it be that the Rabbit's love for partaking of its

[1] *The Romance of Wild Flowers*, by Edward Step.

Spear-Plume Thistle.

CROSS-LEAVED HEATH.

meals at early morn and dewy eve is due to the moisture
then found upon the herbage? When the heat of the day
advances, and the dew upon the ground disappears, then
the plants become drier, and probably not nearly so tasty
as when the sweet breath of morn or eve is upon them.

Come to the Common and see the frolicsome creatures,
but do not make a noise, for these are timorous beasties.
Look up the hillside yonder. There are quite a number of
the brown and grey coloured Rabbits all busily feeding.
But see, some of the more wary are already pricking up
their ears, for they scent danger ahead! Clap your hands
and watch the artful rascals skip along.
There they go, the little white bob-tails
showing up prominently as a sort of danger
signals, and acting as a warning to their
fellows that something is amiss.

Fig. 14. Skull of
Rabbit.

One or two of the least timorous stay
behind to have a last hasty nibble. Now
and again they glance towards us as much as to say: " Go
away. What right have you to disturb us here? " At last
all are safely housed in their underground home, and when
we walk to the hillside, nought remains but the entrances
to the warren, as it is called, and all is peace and quietness.

You remember the Hare we saw in the meadow? That
was a larger and more ungainly animal than the Rabbit,
who is a gay little chap; he loves to hop, skip, and jump,
and cut all manner of curious capers, which, to those who
watch him, afford as much enjoyment as going to a
pantomime!

Near by there is a thick bush. Peep into it carefully.
Do you see anything? Fortune does not favour us perhaps, but very often one of the laggards skulks in some
undergrowth, having been unable to reach the entrance to

the home before the intruder approached. The animal will remain perfectly still, until almost trodden upon, and its resemblance to its surroundings is often very remarkable indeed.

" And does the Rabbit build its nest in these burrows? ' you may ask. Sometimes it does, and at others it does not, for the nest may be found in a field, or a green lane, at a few feet below ground. Grasses are largely used for a homestead, and in this snug dwelling from five to eight young ones find a safe harbour. But is it a safe harbour? At times it is not, for the Stoat—we met his cousin the Weasel in the Hedge—preys upon both old and young Rabbits, and finds this Common a happy and fruitful hunting ground.

Larger than the Weasel, the Stoat is a really beautiful animal, and were it not for its abominable smell, it would probably be more highly regarded. The gamekeeper, however, would hardly be more kindly disposed towards it smell or no smell, for the Stoat is one of his worst four footed enemies. It loves the eggs of both the Partridge and the Pheasant, and has a clever knack of taking an egg out of the nest, and carrying it homewards. As many as seventy eggs have been found, all neatly packed away for a rainy day.

" And how does the Stoat manage to get the eggs to its own homestead without breaking them? " you may inquire. The more usual method seems to be for the animal to push the egg along the ground by means of its snout. The common Brown Rat has also been credited with a similar habit.

In colour the Stoat is warm brown above and yellow below. The long tail is tipped with black, the teeth are sharp, and the muzzle is prominently ornamented with a fine moustache. Sometimes this animal turns white in Winter, and it is then known as the Ermine.

In its movements this is a wonderful mammal, for it can dart, creep, leap, and run with amazing dexterity and cunning. It will stalk a Rabbit with ease, and the poor Bunny often becomes very terrified at its approach. So much so, indeed, that it is on occasions impossible for the Rabbit to move any further; its eyes close; its little heart palpitates; it seems to lose all power over its limbs, and it takes some time for it to revive if it happens to escape the clutches of the Stoat.

In addition to Eggs and Rabbits, this animal preys upon Birds, Rats, Voles, and other wild creatures. It is a good swimmer, and most solicitous for the well-being of its family. The five to eight young ones are born blind during the early days of Summer, and these do not attain the adult state until the first year's birthday has been celebrated.

When you go to the Common towards the gloaming hour, to watch the Rabbits have their evening meal, then will be a good time to see the Pipistrelle Bat upon the wing. This curious little creature is very common in the country, yet there are many people who express surprise when told that it does not lay eggs like a bird, but produces its young alive!

The roof of a barn or a house, a hollow tree, quarries, pits, and caves, such are a few of the places chosen by Bats wherein to rear their young and spend the hours when they are not upon the wing. The Pipistrelle is reddish-brown in colour, but the fur is relieved towards the eye with black hair, and the face is naked.

Insects, as well as flesh, constitute the food of this small winged mammal of our Common. Its endurance upon the wing is remarkable; its keen powers of touch and smell are very acute, but the little black eyes do not appear to be of very great assistance to it. It has been seen on the wing at mid-day, caring nought for the brilliant sunshine, but looking strangely out of place. It is at night, when the Chafers, Moths, and other creatures come from their hiding-places, that the Bat is seen at its best, for it is almost inseparably associated with the hours of darkness.

The flight is jerky, but the animal can remain upon the wing for hours at a stretch, insect-hunting the whole time. Although not generally liked, this is a really useful inhabitant of our country, the abundance of insect life that is destroyed being incalculable.

Usually only a single young one is born, but Bats are largely gregarious, or social, in habits, numbers often being found together. And how do you imagine they sleep and rest? When thus found, they will be seen to be hanging head downwards, clinging to one another. The first one to anchor must surely be possessed of considerable power to carry a whole regiment, as it were, and these curious Flitter Mice, as some country people call them, are evidently firm believers in the motto that " Union is strength."

VI.—BIRDS OF THE COMMON

STONECHAT—LINNET—WHINCHAT—MEADOW PIPIT— RED-BACKED SHRIKE—COMMON BUNTING

WHEREVER there is a Furze common, there, sure enough, one may find the gay little Stonechat, a very typical bird, resorting to solitary places, but one that manages to pass the time actively and pleasantly. Be on the look-out for a small bird with a jet black head and throat, and bright chestnut-red breast. You cannot fail to notice him if you are at all observant, for time and time again he will perch at the summit of a bush, and utter a complaining note that eventually drives one away.

He is a very persistent singer, and his monotonous note may be heard the whole day long. The bird seems to hate being watched, especially when nesting.

Active in habits, handsomely attired, quite a little soldier in his bright chestnut and black livery, the Stone-chat is fully entitled to a prominent place among the feathered friends to be found upon the Common. He may pair for life, as his less gay consort nearly always seems in his company, and the two appear very much attached.

In the Spring it is a pretty sight to watch this Furze-loving bird courting. He then sings a low, sweet love song, and when also he hovers in the air, and gracefully alights on a pliant twig at the top of a bush, it is delightful to watch the airy little creature. If thus seen, a search should be made for the nest, and this will probably be found at the base of a Furze bush and close to the ground. It is a neat homestead, and is built of dry grass and moss, with a hair and feather lining. If you peep inside, you will probably find from four to seven pale blue eggs, and these may be unspotted, or have a faint red circle of spots at the larger end.

When the young birds have left the family nursery, it is an engaging sight to see them flitting from bush to bush accompanied by their parents, and is one of the most entertaining of the many interesting ways of baby birdland.

On the Furze bushes, and flying overhead, singing as it goes, you cannot fail to notice the Linnet. Country people call this the Brown Linnet, to distinguish it from the Greenfinch, which they name the Green Linnet.

The male is an inconspicuous brown bird, except when in his courting attire, for then he puts on his best Sunday waistcoat, and is a handsome fellow indeed, the vest being rich red in colour. This is one of our commonest Finches, and as it is in the habit of flocking to a great extent, it becomes very noticeable to those who have an inclination to observe the ways of birds. Even in the midst of the nesting season, Linnets will gather together in a small company and repair to some favourite feeding ground. They will visit the meadow, for example, when the Dandelions are in seed; in the Autumn and Winter, when the Thistles have seeded, then is a good time to observe this bird to advantage. Various other kinds of seeds are eaten, and during the Winter young buds are also partaken of.

As a song bird the Linnet varies, for whilst some specimens are really fine musicians, there are others whose powers of song are not very noticeable. Nevertheless, the Linnet is highly esteemed as a cage bird, but it is the bird of the open Common we are considering, and not a mite in feathers imprisoned in a wretched little cage.

If the neat nest be sought for, search should be made in a Furze, Blackthorn, or Hawthorn bush. It is made of grass and has a lining of hair. The five bluish-white eggs are spotted with light brown and purplish-red.

The two birds last met with are residents upon our Common, but there is another bird we shall meet with, which is only found there during the Summer. When seen it will remind you by its actions of the Stonechat; indeed it is in reality a near relative of that bird.

The Whinchat—for such is its name—spends the English Winter in far-away Northern Africa, but towards the end of April it manages in some mysterious manner to find its way back, not only to England, but to the same Common, and even to the same bush, that it tenanted the year previously! We have already referred to the wonderful subject of the migration of birds, for it is one that is always attracting the attention of the keen student, who is desirous of getting behind the veil in birdland.

Well, here is the Whinchat arrived back safely upon our Common once more, and we will watch the bird, and leave for another occasion a discussion as to how and when the feathered traveller arrived. And when it has come, it seems to love solitude, for we find it upon the loneliest part of the Common, or upon the bleak moor, or heath, or some uncultivated place far from the madding crowd.

Fig. 15. Whinchat.

Where Furze abounds, there this species is known to the country people as the Furzechat, Furze being only another name for the Whin, which we have already seen in a blaze of splendour.

A detailed description of the species is unnecessary; it is a larger bird than the Stonechat, but not so big as its handsome cousin, the Wheatear. The male is dusky brown and white, with a bright yellowish-red neck and breast. Look out for a prominent white streak over the eye, and if you see it you may be fairly certain of the identity of the bird under observation.

The nest, like that of the Stonechat, requires a good deal of finding, for it is built upon the ground and is usually well hidden. If you are successful in coming across it— and you will have to exercise much patience if your efforts are to be rewarded—you will not fail to notice the coarse grass outside the structure, as well as the straw and moss. There may also be some fibrous roots and horsehair. The four to six eggs are pale blue.

In its vocal efforts the Whinchat resembles the Stone-chat in the persistency with which the notes are uttered, but the song of the former is well worth listening to, and its notes do not possess that monotonous character which one associates with the Stonechat.

Fig. 16. Meadow Pipit.

When you are on the Common, listen intently for every sound; indeed, wher-ever you are in the country, use your ears as well as your eyes. Birds are such shy, timid creatures that they very often escape detection unless they give voice. Therefore, keep your ears well open. If you do, then you will surely hear the tinkling song of the Meadow Pipit.

We met with the Tree Pipit in the meadow, and you may think, perhaps, that the Meadow Pipit should also be found there. This is not so, however, for a Common or Moor is a typical habitat for this bird to choose.

Away over the Scottish hills, where there is scarcely a human being to be seen, the Meadow Pipit holds undis-puted sway, and the whole day long the hills and valleys echo with its tinkling song. So, too, on our Common. There, the livelong day, the Meadow Pipit soars and sings his tinkle, tinkle, tinkle.

You may mistake him for a Skylark when he is soaring, but you will notice, on closer acquaintance, that he is a darker and smaller bird altogether; that he ascends into

RABBIT AND YOUNG.

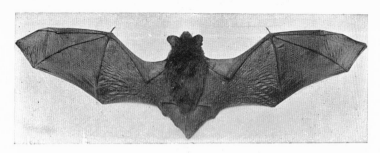

PIPISTRELLE BAT.

COMMON LIZARD.

HONEY BEES.

A. DRONE.   B. QUEEN.   C. WORKER.

the air in circles is true, that he will fly into a tree or bush is also certain, but the song, whilst pleasing and in thorough keeping with the surroundings the bird frequents, cannot be compared with the soul-inspiring melody of the better known bird.

Although a lover of the air, the Meadow Pipit builds its neat little nest upon the ground, the materials used consisting of wool, grasses, roots, and moss, with a lining of fine grass and a sprinkling of hair. Inside this cosy home five or six dark coloured eggs lie snugly hidden; soon after the baby chicks are hatched, they are clothed in black down, which makes them look like little black niggers.

If at any time you are fortunate enough to discover a bird of this species off its nest, you may then notice its curious antics over the top of the herbage surrounding the home; the parent will not fly away helter-skelter, squealing loudly, like a Thrush for example, but she will rather flutter over the grasses, and sometimes pretend, or feign as we say, to have a broken wing. This is a ruse whereby you may be directed away from the nest, and as the Pipit resents interference with its home affairs, it is as well to have a peep inside the nest, and then hie away as quickly as possible.

In the Winter this bird is a constant visitor to sheepfolds and other places in the South of England, where it is not found in the Summer. It may then be met with in little parties searching for insect food, and the two shrill alarm notes are sure to arrest attention if you possess a quick ear.

Steady! Use these field glasses and look at yonder bush! Near its summit there is a brown, grey, and yellow bird which has a prominent dark eye stripe, long tail, and large beak. Do you see it plainly now? Very well, let us proceed cautiously towards the bush and get a closer view.

The bird still sits there, making no attempt to move. What is it?

It is a Red-backed Shrike, or Butcher Bird as it is more commonly called, and is another Summer visitor to our Common. Why is it called Butcher Bird? It is so named because it has the habit of catching for its food such small creatures as birds, frogs, lizards, and large insects and then placing them on thorns in the vicinity of the nest. This is the Shrike's larder, and if you happen to find one, you will

probably wonder how the creatures became impaled in such a curious way. The Shrike resembles the Owl in casting up the indigestible portions of its food in the form of pellets.

Now you can see the bird to better advantage. Notice the hooked beak, and how like the creature is to a small bird of prey. It seems to be a very silent species, rarely giving voice, and is at all times of a solitary disposition.

Fig. 17. Head and Foot of Red-backed Shrike.

Where there is a thick bush or tall hedge, there one may search for the nest. It may be high up or low down, being found in both positions, but the bird appears to prefer placing its homestead out of reach. It is built of grass, moss, and roots, lined with down or wool.

The full clutch of eggs consists of from four to seven, and there are two distinct types. One is bluish or greyish-white, spotted at the larger end with ash, and the other is pinkish-white, spotted with light brown and grey.

It seems strange that this bird, which is so silent when in a wild state, should be able to attain considerable power as a musician when kept in captivity. Beyond a harsh scolding note of defiance when the nest is approached, little vocal effort is made, but it is said to be able to learn tunes and airs with much exactness when kept as a pet.

Every now and again, have you not heard a short, rusty little song which reminded you of a part of the song of the Yellow Bunting — that bird we met with in the hedge? It is difficult to get a glimpse of the songster, for he manages to keep well out of sight. Patience, however, will bring its own reward, and by keeping quiet, the Corn, or Common Bunting may be observed.

It is our largest British Bunting, and being clothed in a sombre brown dress is far different to the gay-clad Yellow Bunting and the Reed Bunting that we met at the stream. Here, again, is a bird of lonely places. You may find it high up on the downs, upon a Common, in a large open field, and elsewhere. It may be observed,

Fig. 18. Larder of Red-backed Shrike.

too, among the quietude of a country lane, and where there are telegraph wires it is very fond of perching upon them.

Sometimes the Common Bunting takes up its position on a clod of earth, or the topmost twig of a bush, and sings with immense seriousness the rusty notes for which it has become famous. A careful watch may reveal the nest among tangled grasses, or low down in a hedge. Straw, dry grass, roots, and sometimes hair are used, and the four large eggs are dull white, streaked and blotched with liver colour, inclining to black.

Probably you have not failed to observe that upon the Common we have made the acquaintance of feathered people characterised by their solitary dispositions, thus showing how in different environments various creatures are found admirably adapted tc the surroundings they frequent, and the life they lead.

VII.—REPTILES

COMMON LIZARD—GRASS SNAKE—ADDER

You will remember that, when we paid our visit to the pond, we made the acquaintance of the Newt, and it was shown in what way the Lizard is sometimes mistaken for the Newt, and the chief distinguishing features were set out.

We shall certainly not find the Newt upon the Common, but on the sandy track of country on the hillside yonder, we may search with hope of success for the little Lizard, whose scuttling into the herbage often causes the wayfarer to remark, " What was that? I thought I heard something move! " The " something " was probably a Lizard, for, when disturbed while sunning its body on some warm patch of earth, the active creature makes haste to hide, as it scents danger ahead!

A good deal of difficulty will probably be experienced in finding a Lizard on the Common, or perhaps we should say that it will not be an easy task to see it properly. If you are fortunate enough to come across one enjoying a sun-bath, and you remain very quiet, then success may be achieved, but if the little wanderer is disturbed, it will prove a difficult task to find it again amongst the herbage, as it contrives to keep close to the ground to hide its body securely from view.

Lizards are very quick-moving animals, and even if you do, by some clever strategy, manage to secure one, do not hold it by the tail, as these creatures have the curious habit of breaking off a portion or the whole of the tail, thus making good their escape!

We have already met a relative of the Common Lizard in the meadow, stupidly called the Slow, or Blind Worm, but we shall find in the case of the little fellow we are now stalking, that it is red or brown above, spotted with both darker and lighter colours. If you get a glimpse of the under parts, you will find that the male is orange to red, with bold spots of black; his mate is pale orange or yellow, and may be unspotted.

When first born, the six to twelve young ones are black in colour and measure about an inch in length. If you are fortunate enough to see some baby Lizards you will observe one of the prettiest sights in Reptile-land, the wee mites running about nimbly, playing hide-and-seek in a most delightful way.

Fig. 19. Head of Common Lizard.

It should be remembered that Lizards—at any rate the small species that we have in this country—are harmless; indeed, they are very useful creatures, feeding upon insects of various kinds.

There is a much larger reptile than the Lizard on our Common, and although at first sight it may appear formidable, the Grass Snake—for such is its name—is, like the Lizard, perfectly innocent as regards any harm done to human beings. Yet this handsome Snake is frequently killed because of the poison fangs of which it is supposed to be possessed; but, as a matter of fact, the only venomous, or poisonous, Snake we have among us is known as the Adder or Viper.

It is as well to be able to distinguish one from the other, although, unless you live in a good Snake district such as the New Forest in Hampshire, it is not likely that you will come into contact with the Adder. It is well to notice here what few people seem to recognise, that Snakes, and other similar creatures, rarely attack a person unless " cornered " and unable to escape, or when the instinct of mother or father is such that the young must be protected at all costs.

So it comes about that these creatures scuttle away at one's approach, and are probably more frightened at the sight of a human being than the latter is of the reptile.

The Grass Snake you may see upon the Common, for it appears to come out into the open more, and will sometimes make its appearance from a hedge-bank and cross a road. What would your first impulse be on seeing it? To get a

GRASS SNAKE   ADDER

Fig. 20. Heads of Grass Snake and Adder.

stick and kill it? Surely not, more especially if you knew the creature's habits and that it intended no harm.

This harmless reptile is very common in some parts of England, and if during the Summer you happen to see a long green and yellow Snake measuring from twenty-four to thirty-six inches in length, then you can congratulate yourself that you have had a peep at the Grass, or Ringed Snake.

Sometimes when you are passing over the Common you may find the slough of this species, for it casts its skin with great regularity, and a similar remark applies to the Adder.

An interesting point of comparison between the Grass Snake and the Adder, besides the smaller size, different colour and markings, and poisonous nature of the latter, is in regard to the eggs and young.

Perhaps you did not know that a Snake laid eggs? Such, however, is the case so far as concerns the Grass Snake, for the leathery-shelled eggs are deposited in a manure heap, the warmth from the latter greatly assisting in hatching them. If you happen to see some eggs of this Snake when they are almost hatched, you must remember that they are then much larger than when first laid, for they absorb moisture and attain twice their original size.

The Adder, on the other hand, does not lay eggs, but produces its young alive, and these number from fourteen to forty. It should be stated, however, that before the young Adders are born they are enclosed in thin-shelled eggs, but these hatch out in the body of the mother, and when the time comes for the little ones to make their appearance, they are out of the shells and delight in accompanying their parents for some time.

The Adder only measures about eighteen inches in length; it is dark brown in colour, has a V-shape mark on the blunt head, and a dark zig-zag line runs down the back, which makes identification very easy.

If you go to the London Zoo, you will probably notice some of the Snakes rapidly moving their forked tongue in and out of the mouth, and although the thick glass is ample protection against danger, you may feel an inclination to move still farther away! But do you know that the tongue is quite an innocent organ, and that the Adder, for example, does not poison a person by means of its tongue?

" How then is the deed accomplished? " you may ask. There are two sharp fangs in the upper jaw, and these are set back in the Snake's mouth. By means of these the Adder bites, and having done this, a green-coloured poison travels down the fangs and into the wound. After that the fangs are withdrawn, but, if occasion demands it, they are re-inserted with great swiftness.

And what do Snakes live on? The two British species we have made the acquaintance of prey upon Birds and their Eggs, Mice, Lizards, Insects, Frogs, Toads, and other creatures.

Although many persons seem to have a distinct hatred of reptiles and similar forms of wild life, the young naturalist desirous of knowing something of the wild life of the country, should not utter exclamations of fright at the sight of a harmless animal.

It is really surprising how few kinds of British animals are to be dreaded because of any harm that they are capable of doing to human beings. True enough, there are some which, like the Adder, are not at all desirable companions when they find themselves in a tight corner, but it is as well to remember that the lower animals, like ourselves, are possessed of remarkable powers when they find that they have to make a bold bid for liberty.

Many a brave deed is accomplished on the spur of the moment, as it were, and when the man, woman, or child who has performed some extraordinary action reflects upon what happened and the risk that was undergone, wonder is often expressed as to how courage and pluck enabled the deed to be carried out.

Strictly speaking, then, there are few wild animals of which the young naturalist need be afraid, for experience has shown that, so long as they are not molested or interfered with, they mind their own business and attend to their own affairs.

It is to be hoped that a more intimate knowledge of many of our wild creatures will result in a better understanding concerning them, for it is only as a result of know-

NEST OF MEADOW PIPIT CONTAINING EGGS OF CUCKOO.

MEADOW PIPIT FEEDING YOUNG CUCKOO.

STONECHAT.

NEST AND EGGS OF STONECHAT.

ing something of their home life that an accurate opinion
may be formed as to whether they are, or are not, likely to
cause any bodily harm to the person who comes into contact
with them.

VIII.—BUTTERFLIES OF THE COMMON

LARGE WHITE BUTTERFLY—SMALL HEATH—GRAYLING—
WALL BUTTERFLY—DINGY SKIPPER—SILVER-STUDDED BLUE

WHEN the Common is garlanded with wild flowers, and
wears its best and prettiest dress, then is a good time to
take a quiet saunter and observe the Butterflies flitting
from flower to flower in the attractive manner we are so
familiar with. Quite a number of different kinds may thus
be met with, and of these we shall hope to see some worthy
examples during our little tour.

Do you remember how we made the acquaintance of
the Small White Butterfly in the meadow? We are sure
to meet with its larger cousin on the Common, and a very
fine creature it is. The Large White is not so abundant as
its smaller relative, and may at once be distinguished by the
larger size.

In colour it is white above and yellow underneath,
and care should be taken to notice the difference between
the male and his mate. Both sexes have the fore wings
tipped with black, but the female may be known by the
two spots and a dash of black present upon the upper surface
of the fore wings. The yellow under-surface is relieved in
both sexes by two black spots on the front pair of wings,
and in some specimens the sulphur yellow has a very
pleasant effect. Yet, whilst such a gay tenant upon the

Common, the Large White has a nasty habit of visiting gardens, and depositing its eggs upon the owner's choice cabbage plants.

This act often has dire results, as the larvæ, when hatched, are ravenous babies, and soon make sad havoc among the cabbages. The Ichneumon Fly then performs useful work, as described in *The Meadow I Know;* in some seasons it is safe to assert that, were it not for the efforts of the Ichneumon in thus keeping in check one of the gardener's worst enemies, the cabbages would present a sorry appearance indeed.

You may see the Large White upon the wing in early Spring, for it is one of the first to appear from its Winter quarters; as the Summer approaches, the numbers increase, until it is possible to keep one or more of them in view during the whole time a country walk is undertaken.

When the warm days arrive, the Small Heath makes its appearance too, and at almost every step one takes among the grasses and the flowers a Butterfly of this species is disturbed. It is an obliging insect, for it does not fly very far away; but you must exercise keen vigilance in watching it, for when it settles and closes the wings, the dull colour of the under parts ably protects their owner from view.

Here flies a Small Heath among the Grasses. Notice her colour, which is pale tawny, bordered with grey or brown. Now she has settled, and is spreading out her wings in the Summer sunlight. You can see that at the tip of the fore wings there is a black spot.

What is she doing here? Probably searching for a convenient spot in which to lay her eggs, these being deposited on a blade of grass. Later on a search may be made for the green larva, which will be found to be striped with a darker shade of the same colour, and pink towards the end of the body.

Another fine Butterfly that haunts our Common, as well as open spaces where the soil is chalky, is the Grayling, and this may be noticed when the sun is pouring down its scorching rays, and the countryside bears a parched look as if rain were sorely needed. The heat seems to affect the Grayling Butterflies, for they may be seen to flicker over the tops of the flowers as if movement were quite an unpleasant labour to them. Numbers may thus be observed, and a pleasant time may be spent watching the insects toying upon the wing.

So beautifully fashioned is the " plumage " of the Grayling, a combination of brown, tawny green, and red, that it is often difficult to see one even although it has settled just in front of the wayfarer. And when the wings are closed it is a greater puzzle still, until, on stooping down, one finds the insect quietly resting upon some wayside flower.

You will not fail to notice the two black spots on the fore wings, and the additional one on the hind wings. Two spots of black are also present on the under side of the fore wings, which are ochre in colour tinged with orange. Like the Small Heath, the Grayling is attracted to the Common by the Grasses which flourish there. Among these the dull creamy eggs are laid, and if examined through a glass they will be found to be ribbed and to have a slight depression at the top.

But stay, just look on that bare cart track across the Common, for a fine Butterfly of some kind has settled there. Proceed cautiously and let us have a peep at the beautiful creature. There, he has flown ahead and stopped again! Be not discouraged, for the Wall Butterfly—as he is called

—has the habit of thus trying one's patience. At last we get fairly close to the pretty insect and can plainly see him spreading out his wings to the fullest extent, as if in rich enjoyment of the merry life he leads.

What was his colour? Shall we say bright tawny, strongly veined with black and brown, and with transverse markings which make the pattern work very pretty? Did you observe the prominent black spot in the top corner of each fore wing and the row of similar spots on the outside of the hind wings? Could we have seen the under markings, we should have found that the colour was not nearly so bright as that above, grey, brown, and yellow being mingled together.

You may see the Wall Butterfly upon the wing in May and June, and again in July and August, for it has two broods, and wherever there is an open sunny spot, you should keep your eyes open for a sight of this handsome species.

If you visit the Common in May, especially the higher part on the summit of the hillside, when the shades of evening steal on apace, look closely at the tall Grasses, and you may espy some Skipper Butterflies settling down for their night's repose. The wings are closed down over the back and serve the purpose of a nightgown.

You may thus see the Dingy species, or perchance the Grizzled, and the herbage on closer examination proves to be populated by quite a large number of these little Butterflies. The Dingy Skipper may be easily distinguished from his Grizzled relative by his more sober attire, the latter being a really beautiful kind when looked at carefully, the grizzled patterns upon the wings affording much food for thought to the young entomologist.

The upper surface of the Dingy species is, as its name

implies, dingy in colour, being a mixture of red, brown, and grey, and the under wings are so coloured that, when at rest upon a dead seed-head, the insect is most difficult to detect. You have already seen the fine patches of Bird's - foot Trefoil growing upon the Common, and it is there a search should be made for the eggs and larvæ.

There is one more Butterfly tenant of the Common we should hunt for ere we leave, and that is the Silver-studded Blue, a near relation of the Common Blue. On the heathery part of the district and where it is sandy, there this species of Blue Butterfly should be located during July and August. The male is purplish-blue on the upper wings, but underneath it has far different markings, these being very light blue spotted with black and orange.

How very different the female is, for she will be found to be sooty-brown in colour, with a tinge of blue; she also possesses a band of orange markings on the outside of the hind wings, and these are present at times on the fore wings also. She, too, is darker coloured underneath than her handsome little mate, and to see the two courting and caressing is a pretty and engaging sight.

To achieve success in the study of Butterflies and Moths it is a capital idea to make up one's mind to become acquainted with the favourite district in which certain species are found, and why; to ascertain the situation in which the eggs are laid, and when; to get to know the favourite food plant whereon the larva may be found, and the colour and form of the larva; to find out the colour and form of the pupa and where it may be sought for; and the time of year that the perfect insects are to be observed upon the wing.

In course of time, a good idea will, as a consequence, be obtained of the different species of Butterflies and Moths

D

in certain localities, and the amount of information that will be forthcoming in carrying out these operations will be of an interesting nature, and many points will occur which would otherwise be overlooked.

The same rule holds good with a large number of other insects, such as, for instance, the Beetles, and after a while the young observer should be able to compile lists and notes which may prove of great value, and at the same time have acquired on his own account valuable information that can really only be ascertained as a result of careful observation whenever opportunity offers.

Reliable lists of local animals and plants have not by any means been compiled to the extent that they might have been, and a good work is waiting to be accomplished by all those who are interested in Nature.

What may appear at the time as a note of little interest should be recorded, for in after years it may prove to be of value in determining some Nature secret to which that apparently trivial record may be the key.

IX.—BEES AND BEETLES

HONEY BEE — TIGER BEETLE — DEVIL'S COACH HORSE
    BEETLE — GRASS BEETLE — SEVEN-SPOT LADYBIRD —
    DOR BEETLE

To the young naturalist who is desirous of becoming acquainted with the Honey Bee and quite a number of interesting Beetles, the Common is a happy hunting ground, and will amply repay attention.

Although the spot we are visiting is some distance away

from the nearest Beehives—there are a few Hives in the old orchard attached to the farmstead yonder—it is remarkable to notice the miles these industrious and persevering Bees travel in search of pollen and nectar.

Where wild flowers flourish eager search should be made for the Hive, or Honey Bee; as soon as the first floral treasures commence to peep out of their leaf-strewn bed in early Spring, the Bees come forth from their citadel and commence pillaging. Theirs is a wonderful mission, for not only do they display untiring energy in collecting the necessaries of life which the plants so obligingly afford

FEMALE   MALE   WORKER
OR QUEEN   OR DRONE   OR NEUTER

Fig. 21. Honey Bees.

them, but all unconsciously they perform useful service in carrying pollen from flower to flower, and thus largely aid in the important work of the fertilisation of plants.

If only a Bee could speak, what a wealth of interesting information it could give us! Perched on the tip of a dainty flower, resting for awhile in the heat of a Summer's day, would it not proudly explain to us the uses of the various parts of its most wonderful body?

" Look at my eyes! " it might cry, " you have only two, but I am the owner of five." And then, maybe, it would let you count them, two large ones covering the sides of its head for observing distant objects, and three smaller ones in the front for seeing things near at hand, such as those in the Hive, for example. One day you may have the opportunity of examining one of these large eyes under the microscope, and you will be startled to find that it consists of about six thousand facets.

If the Bee should remain friendly, perhaps you would be able to persuade it to show you its long shining brown tongue—as slender as a thread—with which it is able to lap up the nectar. Doubtless you will be surprised at its length, almost as long as the Bee's body; but it folds it up very nicely in the mouth, and fits it into a little groove under the head.

" And what becomes of all the nectar? Does it eat the whole lot? " These are questions which you are anxious to ask our little friend. No, it does not eat all, but some is stored up in its honey sac adjoining the stomach; by the aid of tiny muscles the contents are squeezed into the mouth again, and placed in the honeycomb. While in the Bee's body the nectar undergoes a slight change, and becomes what we call honey

Even the six legs deserve mention; they are furnished with claws, which may be described as the Bee's box of tools. On the hind pair are those wonderful baskets for carrying pollen—the special food of baby Bees—formed of a tiny groove and stiff hairs which bend over and complete the circle.

By this time the Bee may wish to explain the import-ance of its feelers, for by means of them it is said to hear and smell. These antennæ—to give them their correct name—are very sensitive, and help the Bee to find its way in the dark recesses of the Hive, and to exchange news with its friends.

Now the Bee has flown away, and we are left to wonder about the Drones which live in luxury and idleness, and about the Queen and her hundred thousand eggs. We should dearly love to see our friend again, and watch it

GRASS SNAKE.

ADDER.

BUTTERFLIES OF THE COMMON.

1 and 2. SMALL HEATH, Male on left and Female on right.
3 and 4. GRAYLING, Female above, Male below.
NOTE.—The Upper and Undersides are shown of both species.

scrape the " varnish " off the sticky buds of the Cherry or Poplar tree for its propolis, with which it is wont to fortify its home. But time is short, and these and other points must be discussed on some future occasion.

But see, there is a bright coloured insect sunning its body on a bare patch of earth!

Be quick, or it will be gone ere we see it properly. Our little friend is a Green Tiger Beetle. Notice the bright green wing-cases and the white spots on the outer surface of the fore wings. Now the insect has shifted its position, and the beautiful blue of the hind part of the body can be seen to advantage.

How well the Tiger Beetle runs. True, but observe his long, slender legs, which serve it well when upon the ground. Although it possesses wings, it flies in a jerky, hesitating way, for running nimbly along is the more usual method of locomotion.

Fig. 22 Green Tiger Beetle.

You should search for this Beetle when the hot days arrive, and, if you are successful in finding the larva, you may have a chance of seeing it burrow in a sandy place, where it lies in hiding until some unwary insect visitor comes along. It then secures its prey.

We are fortunate in our Beetle-hunting to-day, for here is a long-bodied black specimen running across the pathway, stopping ever and anon to turn up the end of its " tail " in a most curious way. That act at once identifies the creature as the Cock-tail, or Devil's Coach Horse Beetle. It hates to be placed on its back, and will make effort after effort to right itself. Yet, it will, *of its own accord*, sometimes remain on its back and feign death in a most realistic manner!

Although so formidable-looking, this is not a harmful

creature, except, perhaps, that its strong jaws may inflict a nasty " nip." But why does the Coach Horse turn up its " tail " so abruptly and on the least interference? Some say it is for the purpose of protecting itself by warning people not to tamper with it, but, strictly speaking, it resorts to this curious habit so that it can be assisted in folding up the very long wings which are to be found underneath the very short wing-cases.

And what does this Beetle live on? It feeds upon carrion, refuse, and decaying matter of all kinds, and is thus a useful insect scavenger which should be encouraged. If you desire to find the larva of this species, search should be made under stones, or it may also be turned up when digging in the garden.

After a shower of rain, how refreshed and beautiful our Common looks! The dust has been washed from the leaves and flowers, and when the sun shines again, the rain drops still left upon the foliage glitter like so many liquid diamonds.

Fig. 23. Devil's Coach Horse Beetle.

Then is a good time to scan the grasses in search of the Grass Beetle. This is a dark blue-black Beetle with a plump little body, and may be found busily feeding upon grass after rain. Several will probably be seen close together; indeed, one may chance upon quite a large number on neighbouring grass stems where, previous to the shower, few, if any, had been seen.

It does not often happen that a Beetle can be discovered enjoying its meal, as these creatures contrive to keep out of sight as much as possible. A few moments may, therefore, be spent in watching the Grass Beetle having its vegetarian dinner, a remark which applies equally well to many other kinds of wild creatures.

This Beetle does not possess any wings, and has the habit, when it is handled, of exuding a red liquid from its joints.

As we wander across the Common various small insects alight upon our bodies, and some of these—being so very tiny—are well worth examination under a glass. Others can be studied with the naked eye, and if it be evening time, when the large Beetles are upon the wing, it is possible

Fig. 24.
Grass Beetle
(reduced).

Fig. 25. Seven-spot
Lady-bird.

Fig. 26.
Dor Beetle.
(reduced).

that one will fly against our face and give, as a result, quite a sudden shock.

Thus we may perhaps make acquaintance with two more Beetles before our journey comes to an end. First, there is the Lady-bird, which has a habit of seeking assistance on her journey by alighting on one's hand or clothing. Should you thus find one, count the spots upon her body. Perhaps there may be seven; if so, then it is the Seven-spot Lady-bird that has honoured you with a visit.

Everyone seems to have a warm place in their affection for these useful little Beetles—for such they are. Do not you young folks, when you catch one, recite the following lines and then toss the creature into the air:—

Ladybird, ladybird, fly away home,
Your house is on fire and your children are gone!

And in what way is this gay little creature of service to mankind? It feeds very largely upon the Green Fly, which is such a pest in gardens, hop fields, and orchards, and should be encouraged whenever seen. Care should be taken not to destroy the larva of the Lady-bird. It is a curious little creature, smoky black or grey in colour, marked with yellow and white. This larva is of an active disposition, and has six jointed legs in front and a slightly hairy and rough body.

The black and creamy white pupa is short and stumpy, whilst the eggs are white and are laid in clusters on various kinds of plants during the Spring.

When you are watching this insect, notice how beautifully the wings are tucked away into the red or yellow " wardrobes," and how careful the creature is not to spoil its wings.

Our second Beetle, that is so fond of alighting on one's person, is the Dor Beetle, a bright black insect with violet margins. Probably the Beetle will find its nightly wanderings temporarily checked as a result of contact with your own face, and you may then discover it in a state of excitement upon the ground. Pick it up and look at the steel-blue colour on the under sides and legs, and notice also the gloss of purple or green.

After examination, release the captive, for this is another " Sanitary Inspector," the insect inspecting and clearing away various kinds of refuse, and does not disdain to lay its eggs in a manure heap!

There are several different kinds of animals which are of service in clearing away refuse and decaying matter, and their usefulness in this respect should not be overlooked.

X.—WONDERFUL SPIDERS

GOSSAMER SPIDERS—GROUND SPIDERS—FAIRY
LAMP-MAKING SPIDER

EVEN when Summer's lease has run out and the new tenant Autumn has entered into possession of the country-side, much is to be seen and heard upon the Common. When the chill October air is upon us, have you not noticed the shining threads spun by the Gossamer Spiders, and how wonderfully linked together they are, like a huge number of minute wires? As you walk along you come into contact with the floating threads and must continually brush them from the face.

It does not require close scrutiny to reveal the Gossamer threads, which when—

Stretched from blade to blade,
The wavy network whitens all the field.

When there has been a heavy dew overnight, then is a good time to see these webs and strands of silk to advantage, the dew showing up prominently the Virgin's Thread, as the flossy silk is called in some parts of France.

Various small kinds of Gossamer Spiders are responsible for this curious decoration of our Common, and if one be watched it will be seen to climb a grass stem, and cast into the air thin strands of silk. The current of air then acts upon them, for the thin threads will be observed to mount upwards, and after a succession of " lines of communication " have been thrown out, the strands loop and become attached one to another in a wonderful network, reminding

us of the overhead wires to be seen at some large Telephone
Exchange in London!

Attached to these floating threads the Gossamer Spider
takes a journey into the air, and when watching it thus
engaged, one can easily realise how well the term aeronaut
may be applied to these interesting creatures.

Spiders are, of course, not insects, for they do not
undergo the same change as an insect, but lay eggs from
which young Spiders are born. In structure, too, there is

Fig. 27.
A. Gossamer Spider and Web.
B. Spider greatly enlarged.

no distinct head, thorax, and abdomen, the two former
being joined together. That they are useful creatures is
undoubted, feeding as they do upon insects, which, if not
thus preyed upon, would multiply and make this earth a
far less desirable place on which to live.

The traps that are set for the capture of their prey are
very ingenious arrangements, and the handsome Garden
Spider, or the Common House Spider, will serve equally
well for observation in this respect. The maze at Hampton
Court is quite easy to get out of as compared with some of
the webs of the Garden Spider!

There are many different kinds of Spiders, and similar
creatures, too, called Harvest Men, which are not true

Spiders, although closely related to them. If, by chance, you should pay attention to the ground, you will probably notice some of the Ground Spiders running nimbly over the surface. Perchance you may discover one of them carrying a little white bag beneath its body. This will be a female with her cocoon containing eggs, some species carrying the egg bag about with them until the young are hatched.

Have you ever seen a Spider's foot under a high power microscope? If not, you have a treat in store, for this is a remarkable sight and will enable you to understand better how the Spider is able to make such good use of its limbs. To the naked eye the wonderful structure of the foot is invisible, but the microscope reveals three curved claws which bear upon them little teeth or pegs. The claw may be compared to a sort of bent comb, and the foot is well clothed with hairs.

This remarkable appendage helps the Spider to traverse, Blondin-like, along its thin " tight-ropes," to control and adjust its well-known threads and webs, and doubtless affords it support in various other ways. There are eighteen pegs or teeth on the largest claw of the three; on the second largest there are fifteen teeth, and on the smallest there are three or four teeth.

As the filaments of silk issue from the spinnerets the Spider is able to regulate the rate of issue by the comb-like claws, which also help it to clean its body. Thus you will observe how very useful and essential it is that the Spider should be the possessor of a foot so fashioned.

When you are tramping among the herbage on the Common, look closely for the pretty cocoon of the Fairy Lamp-making Spider, for the dainty little fairy lamp is well worth examination. This cocoon is composed of silken threads, which are pure white when first constructed;

the lamp is suspended with the larger end at the bottom, and is shaped something like a fancy Chinese lantern. Later on the lamps become coated with mud, and after this takes place they so nearly resemble a blob of dirt that the casual observer would never imagine that a little silken palace is enclosed within such a curious exterior.

This mud plaster is apparently put on for the purpose of protecting and preserving the wondrous lamp-cocoon, for although the rain may descend and the wind blow, the little home remains intact and takes no harm.

Within the silken lamp the eggs are secreted, and when these hatch, the Spiderlings, as we may call them, cling to the empty mud-cases. Each one then throws out a gossamer thread, which is borne away by the wind until it becomes anchored to herbage of some kind. " Upon alarm or disturbance, the tiny creatures scatter each along its line, and the dispersion is like a little puff of smoke. After a little time they return to the case. Finally the case is deserted, each Spiderling ' making tracks ' of its own, and settling down to life, perhaps very far from the old home." [1]

We have thus seen how it is possible by intelligent observation to find quite a representative collection of animals and plants upon our Common, and what an enjoyable time may be spent watching their interesting habits and winning ways.

It is a good plan to keep a record of the different kinds of animals and plants that are found, for in this way it is surprising to notice how many species are to be observed even in a restricted district.

Stalking and observing wild creatures, making notes concerning them, and profitably employing one's time in pursuit of a delightful hobby, cannot fail to stimulate

[1] *Gleanings from the Fields of Nature*, by E. T. Connold.

1

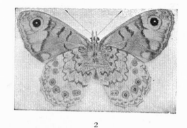

2

3

5

6

4

MORE BUTTERFLIES OF THE COMMON.

1, 2, and 3. WALL BUTTERFLY, Female on left, Male below.
4. DINGY SKIPPER, Female above, Male below.
5 and 6. SILVER STUDDED BLUE, Male on left, Female on right.
NOTE.—The Upper and Undersides are shown of each species.

LIFE HISTORY OF LARGE WHITE BUTTERFLY.

1. EGGS GREATLY ENLARGED.   2. LARVÆ.   3 and 4. PUPÆ.   5. MALE (above) AND FEMALE (below)

interest in the tenants of the countryside, and whether it be Hedge, Pond, or Wood; Meadow, Stream, or Common, something worth looking at or listening to, will be found at all seasons of the year.

Each walk that is undertaken will not fail to supply some interesting note that has previously escaped attention, and one of the greatest charms of studying Nature and her wonderful children is the varying aspect under which one may observe them, and the wealth of facts concerning them which are continually accumulating and affording such a fund of interest and pleasure.

MADE AT THE TEMPLE PRESS LETCHWORTH IN GREAT BRITAIN

CALENDAR AND NOTES

OF

ANIMALS AND PLANTS

COMPILED BY C. S. COOPER, F.R.H.S.

I. BIRDS

COMMON BUNTING.—A resident. *Male bird:* upper parts brown, with black centres to feathers; cheeks and throat dull white; under surface dull white; fore-neck and breast tinged with rufous-buff; sides of body browner and streaked with black; length $7\frac{1}{2}$ inches. *Female:* similar; length $6\frac{1}{2}$ inches. *Nest:* May and June; low in a hedge, or among coarse grass, or on the ground; dried grass and straw, lined with fine grass, roots, and hair; *eggs* 3–6, generally 4; dull white, blotched, streaked and speckled with purplish-brown, inclining to black. *Food:* seeds, grain, and insects. *Song:* wheezy and unmusical. *Call-note:* like " chuck " or " chit."

LINNET.—A resident. *Male bird:* reddish-brown above; fore-head and breast crimson; abdomen dull buffy-white; bill bluish-grey; feet dull brown; crimson of head and breast is replaced by dark brown in Autumn; length $5\frac{1}{2}$ inches. *Female:* browner than male; no crimson on head or breast; length $5\frac{1}{3}$ inches. *Nest:* April, onwards; in a Furze, Blackthorn, or Whitethorn bush; cup-shaped, of moss, twigs, and grass, lined with hair, wool, and feathers; *eggs* 4–6, usually 5; ground-colour bluish, spotted with purplish-grey and reddish-brown. *Food:* soft seeds, especially Flax and Hemp; berries and buds in Winter. *Song:* flute-like, soft, mellow, sweet, and varied.

MEADOW PIPIT.—A resident. *Male bird :* olive-brown above, with blackish centres to feathers; throat and breast tawny-buff, spotted with dull brown; abdomen white; length 5¾ inches. *Female :* similar, but less spotted below; length 6 inches. *Nest :* May and June; on the ground; dry grass and moss, lined with finer grass or hair; *eggs* 4–6, reddish-brown, mottled with darker brown. *Food :* insects, with seeds and grain when hard pressed. *Song :* a series of slightly metallic notes, with little variation.

RED-BACKED SHRIKE.—A Summer visitor, arriving at end of April or beginning of May, wintering in S. Africa. *Male bird :* general colour above vinous-chestnut; head and hind neck blue-grey; cheeks and under surface vinous-pink; bill and feet black; length 7 inches. *Female :* general colour above reddish-brown; head duller grey, washed with brown; cheeks, fore-neck, and breast yellowish-buff, with bars of brown; length 7 inches. *Nest :* May onwards; trees and hedgerows; grass-stalks, roots, and moss, lined with dry grass, wool, and hair; *eggs* 4–7, varying considerably; pale bluish-white, with rufous spots and underlying spots of violet-grey; or greenish-white, with brown spots, and underlying spots of violet-grey. *Food :* large insects, Mice, small birds, etc. *Call-note :* a kind of " chuck," generally uttered when on a perch.

STONECHAT.—A resident. *Male bird :* general colour above black; head, sides of face, and throat black, with white patch on sides of neck; fore-neck and breast orange-chestnut, inclining to cinnamon on sides of body; bill and feet black; length 5⅓ inches. *Female :* upper parts dark sandy-brown, with black centres to feathers; head like the back; throat ashy-white, with black patch on lower part; under parts orange-chestnut; length 5 inches. *Nest :* end of April or beginning of May; generally well hidden on the ground; dry grass, rootlets, and moss; lined with rootlets, hair, and feathers; *eggs* 4–6, pale bluish-green, with light reddish-brown spots. *Food :* insects, Earthworms, and grubs. *Song :* a short, sweet warble, uttered when perched or hovering; April to middle of June; other notes persistent but unvaried.

WHINCHAT.—A Summer visitor, arriving about middle of April, leaving for Northern Africa about the middle of October. *Male bird :* dusky brown above, with blackish-brown centres to feathers; crown darker than back; broad white streak over the eye; cheeks white; throat, breast, and sides cinnamon; breast and abdomen sandy-buff; bill and feet black; length 5⅛ inches. *Female :* browner than male; throat and sides of body more orange; cheeks brown; length 5 inches. *Nest :* May and June; well hidden on or close to the ground; dry grass, moss, and straws; lined with fine grass and horsehair; *eggs* 4–6, greenish-blue, faintly speckled with reddish-brown. *Food :* insects, Earthworms, and grubs. *Song :* a low, sweet warbling. *Call-note :* " u-tack, u-tack," uttered in a short and sharp manner.

II. INSECTS

DEVIL'S COACH HORSE BEETLE.—Mostly seen in Autumn. *Body :* 1⅛ inch long; dull dead black; elytra small; wings long; jaws strong; tail often raised. *Eggs :* one-tenth inch long, one-twelfth broad. *Larvæ :* hatch in Spring, very predacious, living on insects and carrion. *Pupa :* in the ground; wings extended beyond elytra and folded over body.

DINGY SKIPPER BUTTERFLY.—May and August. *Wings* expanding 1–1¼ inch; dull brown, with a marginal row of pale dots; fore wings with two rather indistinct darker bands; under sides paler. *Eggs :* April; on Bird's-foot Trefoil. *Larva :* June, and September–April; pale green, with two yellow lines on each side, and a row of black spots above each; feeds on Bird's-foot Trefoil. *Pupa :* April and July.

DOR BEETLE.—Found in Summer, common in dung. *Body :* 1⅛ inch long, oval and convex; black, green, or steel-blue; violet-blue beneath; elytra with 14 fine lines on each. *Eggs :* laid in manure heaps in Autumn. *Larvæ :* pass Winter in manure heap.

GRASS BEETLE.—Found on commons, hedgebanks, and heaths. *Body :* ½ inch long; rounded, very convex; wingless; elytra shining black; antennæ and legs reddish-brown. *Habits :* lives in, and feeds on, grass; exudes a red liquid from the joints if touched.

GRAYLING BUTTERFLY.—July and August. *Wings* expanding 2–2¾ inches; dull brown; fore wings have two black spots with indistinct white centres in paler band; hind wings with one white-centred black spot in a paler band. *Eggs :* July; laid on grasses. *Larva :* August–June; upper part brownish, with three dull greyish-green stripes; under surface dull greenish; feeds on various grasses. *Pupa :* June.

GREEN TIGER BEETLE.—Summer. *Body :* ½ inch long; head broad, with prominent eyes and long antennæ; legs long and slender; elytra golden-green, with yellowish spots; under surface shining copper. *Larva :* whitish; jaws strong; eighth segment furnished with hooks by means of which the larva holds on to side of burrow; feeds on insects. *Habits :* the perfect Beetle is carnivorous.

HONEY BEE.—*Queen :* body tapering. *Male or drone :* body broad and thick; abdomen blunt, with tufts of hair; eyes very large. *Worker :* body stout, armed with a sting; basal joint of the tarsi of hind legs concave; tibia of hind legs with cavity and fringe of stiff hairs=the pollen basket. *Eggs :* one in each cell; hatch in three days. *Larva :* fed by nurse-bees for five days; cell then sealed; cocoon spun; changes to pupa in three days. *Pupa :* changes to perfect Bee on twentieth day from laying of egg.

LARGE WHITE BUTTERFLY.—End of April–June, and end of July–August. *Wings* expanding 2⅛–2⅔ inches; white; fore wings with tip black; hind wings with a black spot. *Male :* fore wings spotless. *Female :* two black spots and a black dash on the margin of fore wings. *Eggs :* May and June, and August; on Cabbage, Garden Nasturtium, and Cruciferous plants. *Larva :* June and July, and September; yellowish spotted with black; a row of raised black spots on each side of the back; feeds on Cabbage, etc. *Pupa:* July, and September–June; common on walls and palings.

SEVEN-SPOT LADYBIRD.—Summer and Autumn. Feeds on Green Fly. *Body:* ¼ inch long; hemispherical; elytra red, with a little white; each wing-case has three black spots, and one common to both; sometimes one or two spots absent. *Eggs:* laid in packets among the aphides. *Larva:* black or grey, marked with yellow and white, body hairy and rough; very active; feeds on aphides. *Pupa:* short and stumpy; black and creamy white.

SILVER-STUDDED BLUE BUTTERFLY.—July and August. *Wings* expanding 1–1⅛ inch. *Male:* purplish-blue, hind margins brown; under side bluish-grey; under side of hind wings with a row of orange spots. *Female:* brown, sometimes with a purplish blush; fore wings spotless; marginal red spots on hind wings. *Eggs:* July–February. *Larva:* May and June; brown or green; a white line on each side; reddish-brown line on back; feeds on Bird's-foot Trefoil, Clover, and Vetches. *Pupa:* June.

SMALL HEATH BUTTERFLY.—June–September. *Wings:* expanding 1–1¼ inch; tawny, shading into brown at margins; under side of fore wings with a black eye in a buff ring; hind wings greenish-grey beneath, with 3–6 white dots in a brown band. *Eggs:* May; laid on grasses. *Larva:* July, and August–May; apple-green, with three deep green stripes bordered with whitish; head and under side yellowish-green; feeds on grasses. *Pupa:* April and September.

III. MAMMALS

PIPISTRELLE BAT.—A native of Britain; March–November. *Body:* covered with rufous-brown fur, becoming paler on under parts, lower part of each hair black; muzzle blunt, large glandular swellings at sides; ears sub-triangular, tips rounded, lobed; feet small; wing membrane beginning at base of toes. *Length* of head and body 1⅔ inch; tail 1⅓ inch. *Inhabits* old buildings, towers, and steeples; usually reposes during the day; flies in the twilight; hibernates during Winter. *Food :* insects, especially Moths.

RABBIT.—A native of Britain. *Body :* round and plump; covered with fur, brownish-grey mingled with tawny; under parts white; tail blackish above, white beneath; legs long and thick; ears long, scarcely tipped with black. *Length* of head and body 16½ inches; tail 3⅔ inches; ears 3⅛ inches. *Weight* 2½–3 lbs. *Inhabits* burrows excavated in sandy soil. *Food :* grass, Corn, Carrots, and other vegetables. *Natural enemies :* Fox, Polecat, Stoat, Weasel, and birds of prey.

STOAT.—A native of Britain. *Body :* much elongated, of nearly equal thickness throughout; covered with short fur, reddish-brown above; yellowish-white on chin, under parts and inner surfaces of legs and feet; head oblong, flattened above; muzzle obtuse; ears large, broad, rounded; tail black at tip. *Length* of head and body of male 10¾ inches; tail 6½ inches; female smaller. *Inhabits* stony places and thickets, sometimes a Rabbit's burrow. *Food :* Rabbits, birds, eggs, etc.

IV. REPTILES

ADDER or VIPER.—A native of Britain. *Body :* 18–20 inches long; head flat, triangular; scales on head numerous and small; jaws can be moved up and down; teeth in jaws, and two rows in palate, those in upper jaw not conical; two curved teeth or poison fangs, one on each side of mouth; tongue long, grey, and forked. *Colour :* variable; brownish, olive, or nearly black, or warm red-brown; dark mark between the eyes; an obscure V on crown; a broad zigzag line of dark lozenge-shaped spots along the back of body and tail. *Inhabits* dry woods, heaths, commons, and sandy banks; will lie basking in the sunshine; hibernates through Winter. *Food :* Mice, Lizards, small birds, eggs, and insects.

COMMON LIZARD.—A native of Britain. *Body:* $5\frac{1}{2}$–6 inches long; head depressed, nose sharp; palate without teeth. *Colour:* upper parts brown, olive, or reddish, with a black band on each side from the head to the tail; a second dark band along the side, edged with white; under parts spotted with black on a whitish ground, generally tinged with blue or green. *Inhabits* sunny banks, thickets, and copses; movements very rapid and sudden; sight and hearing acute. *Food:* insects.

GRASS SNAKE or RINGED SNAKE.—A native of Britain. *Body:* average length about 36 inches; head slender, tapering; scales on head few and large; upper jaw immovable; both jaws and palate with conical teeth, two rows in both upper and lower jaws; no poison fangs; tongue forked to $\frac{1}{3}$ of its length. *Colour:* variable; upper surface generally brownish-grey with a greenish tinge; two parallel rows of small black spots along the back; larger blotches of black along each side; under surface dull lead-colour, sometimes mottled. *Inhabits* copses, hedgerows, and moist situations; is a good swimmer and will dive under water; hibernates in Winter. *Food:* Frogs, Toads, Newts, Mice, young birds, and eggs.

V. TREES AND FLOWERING PLANTS

Name.	Time of Flowering.	Colour.	Height.
Furze	Feb.—July	Yellow	2–5 ft.
Blackthorn	Mar., April	White	Tree
Silver Birch	April, May	Whitish	,,
Hawthorn	May, June	White or pink	,,
Milkwort	,, —Sept.	Blue, purple, pink, or white	2–6 ins.
Elder	June	Creamy white	Tree
Guelder Rose	,, July	,, ,,	
Tormentil	,, —Aug.	Yellow	6–10 ins.
Wild Thyme	,, ,,	Rose-Purple	6 ins.
Small Knapweed	,, —Sept.	Purple, inclining to red	1–3 ft.
Yarrow	,, ,,	Outer florets white or pink; central yellow, often rose	6–18 ins.
Common Ragwort	,, ,,	Golden Yellow	1–4 ft.
Sundew	July, Aug.	White	2–6 ins.
Spear Plume Thistle	,, —Sept.	Purple	4–5 ft.
Eyebright	,, ,,	White or lilac	1–8 ins.
Ling	,, ,,	Purple, inclining to red or white	12–18 ins.
Cross-leaved Heath	,, ,,	Rose Pink	12–18 ins.
Fine-leaved Heath	,, ,,	Crimson, sometimes white	12–18 ins.
Bird's-foot Trefoil	,, ,,	Yellow, tinted with red	4–18 ins.
Common Fleabane	,, ,,	Yellow	6–12 ins.

NATURE AND
OUTDOOR BOOKS

DENT'S
"OPEN-AIR" NATURE BOOKS
EDITED BY
W. PERCIVAL WESTELL, F.L.S.
AND
HENRY E. TURNER
General Secretary of the School Nature Study Union.

Cloth, Extra, Calendar and Notes, 1s. 6d. net.
Three Books in One Volume, 4s. 6d. net; Six Books in One
Volume, 7s. 6d. net; Cloth, Extra, etc.

1.—THE HEDGE I KNOW	4.—THE MEADOW I KNOW
2.—THE POND I KNOW	5.—THE STREAM I KNOW
3.—THE WOOD I KNOW	6.—THE COMMON I KNOW

7.—THE SEA SHORE I KNOW

Each book sets out the salient features of the environment; its Geology and its animal and vegetable inhabitants. The text is written in a simple, bright, interesting, and informative manner, so as to appeal to children of the middle standards.

The illustrations are a special feature and are so produced as to give the child a thoroughly accurate impression of the objects depicted in their natural surroundings.

There are 8 coloured plates in each book made direct from photographs of the natural objects, besides a number of half-tone photographic illustrations of the living animal or plant, the importance of which need hardly be emphasised.

PRESS OPINIONS

"Without rivals in their particular sphere."—*The Guardian.*

"The information is reliable throughout, and the pictures are quite beyond praise."—*School Nature Study.*

"A series which no teacher of Nature Study can afford to overlook."—*Irish School Weekly.*

"A true conception of Nature Study is presented, and the facts are all scientifically correct. The illustrations are specially beautiful."—*Educational News.*

J. M. DENT & SONS LTD., 10-13 BEDFORD ST., STRAND, LONDON, W.C.

PLANTS AND THEIR WAYS

An Introduction to the Study of Botany and Agricultural Science By ERNEST EVANS, Head of the Natural Science Department, Technical School, Burnley.

Small Crown 8vo, pp. 8+171. Price **2s.**

CONTENTS

INTRODUCTION—THE STRUCTURE OF FLOWERS— THE FUNCTIONS OF FLOWERS—FRUITS AND SEEDS —GERMINATING SEEDS AND SEEDLINGS—GROW- ING-POINTS — STEMS AND THEIR FUNCTIONS— ROOTS AND THEIR FUNCTIONS—LEAVES—THE FUNCTIONS OF LEAVES—PLANTS AND THEIR FOOD —WHAT PLANTS DO WITH THEIR FOOD—PLANTS REQUIRE OXYGEN—TRANSPIRATION—THE COLOUR OF PLANTS—THE FLOWERING PLANT—THE FERN PLANT—CULTIVATED PLANTS AND TREES—PLANT SOCIETIES—THE STUDY OF PLANTS IN THE FIELD —A GENERAL REVIEW OF PLANT LIFE—QUESTIONS —INDEX

PRESS OPINIONS

" Mr. Evans has laid teachers under a debt of gratitude by his *Plants and their Ways.*"—*Schoolmaster.*

" A really excellent course of work which will prove of distinct value to teachers and students of the subject."—*Teachers' Times.*

" This manual can be cordially recommended to teachers who have to deal with plant life as part of the school curriculum in town or country."—*Aberdeen Journal.*

ANIMALS AND THEIR WAYS

An Introduction to Zoology and Agricultural Science. By ERNEST EVANS.

Small Crown 8vo, pp. 8+184. Price **2s.**

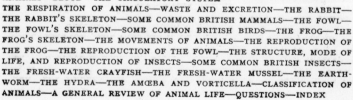

CONTENTS

INTRODUCTION TO THE STUDY OF ANIMALS — THE FOOD OF ANIMALS—DIGESTION OF FOOD BY ANIMALS—BLOOD—THE CIRCULATORY SYSTEM— THE RESPIRATION OF ANIMALS—WASTE AND EXCRETION—THE RABBIT— THE RABBIT'S SKELETON—SOME COMMON BRITISH MAMMALS—THE FOWL— THE FOWL'S SKELETON—SOME COMMON BRITISH BIRDS—THE FROG—THE FROG'S SKELETON—THE MOVEMENTS OF ANIMALS—THE REPRODUCTION OF THE FROG—THE REPRODUCTION OF THE FOWL—THE STRUCTURE, MODE OF LIFE, AND REPRODUCTION OF INSECTS—SOME COMMON BRITISH INSECTS— THE FRESH-WATER CRAYFISH—THE FRESH-WATER MUSSEL—THE EARTH- WORM—THE HYDRA—THE AMŒBA AND VORTICELLA—CLASSIFICATION OF ANIMALS—A GENERAL REVIEW OF ANIMAL LIFE—QUESTIONS—INDEX

DENT'S SCIENTIFIC PRIMERS

EDITED BY

J. REYNOLDS GREEN, Sc.D., F.R.S.

Fellow of Downing College, Cambridge

WITH NUMEROUS ILLUSTRATIONS

2s. net each volume

ASTRONOMY

Sir F. W. Dyson, Astronomer Royal.

BIOLOGY

Prof. Harvey Gibson, Professor of Botany in the University of Liverpool.

BOTANY

Dr. J. Reynolds Green, F.R.S., Fellow of Downing College, Cambridge.

CHEMISTRY

Prof. Sir W. A. Tilden, F.R.S., Professor of Chemistry in the Royal College of Science, S. Kensington.

GEOLOGY

Prof. J. W. Gregory, F.R.S., Professor of Geology in the University of Glasgow.

PHYSIOLOGY

Prof. W. D. Halliburton, F.R.S., Professor of Physiology, King's College, London.

ZOOLOGY

Prof. J. Graham Kerr, F.R.S., Professor of Zoology in the University of Glasgow.

PRESS OPINIONS

"We congratulate the publishers of this series of really excellent 'Scientific Primers.'"—*Education.*

"Written with sureness of expression and accuracy of statement to be expected from the leading authorities by whom they are written . . . they form an ideal avenue to the wonders of science."—*Nottingham Guardian.*

ANIMALS IN BLACK AND WHITE

By ERIC FITCH DAGLISH

Six Books, each containing Woodcuts of 20 Animals.

Crown. 4to. 2s. 6d. net each.

I. LARGER BEASTS.   II. SMALLER BEASTS.
III. LARGER BIRDS.   IV. SMALLER BIRDS.
V. REPTILES.   VI. FISHES AND SEA ANIMALS.

These volumes are something quite new in nature books. Both the woodcuts and the text are the work of Mr. Daglish, "first of all a naturalist . . . but also a considerable artist" (*Times*.) The text, though written in simple language and in a way which should be easily understood by a child, is of definite informative value, conveying actual facts as to the appearance, character, habits, food, and distribution of each animal. The woodcuts present their subjects in simple yet eloquent terms, showing the shape, the markings (where necessary), a typical attitude, and general characteristics. "Mr. Daglish's work," says the *Observer*, "is an example of specific knowledge filtered, as it were, through an artisitc sensibility, and the result is an unqualified success." The *Daily News* calls Mr. Daglish "the Bewick of our times."

PRACTICAL NATURE STUDY FOR SCHOOLS

By OSWALD H. LATTER, M.A., Senior Science Master at Charterhouse, formerly Tutor at Keeble College, Oxford.

3s. 6d.

PRESS OPINIONS

"We heartily commend this book to all teachers who include Nature Study in their time-tables."—*The School Guardian*.

"It is impossible to speak too highly of the skill with which the questions have been framed."—*The School World*.

THE TEMPLE NATURE READERS

Book II. . . 1s. 9d.   Book III. . . 2s. 3d.

Edited by M. T. YATES, LL.D.

Carefully graduated to meet the requirements of Classes corresponding to Standards II and III in Public Elementary Schools.

NAME THIS FLOWER

A SIMPLE WAY OF FINDING OUT THE
NAMES OF COMMON PLANTS WITHOUT
ANY PREVIOUS KNOWLEDGE OF BOTANY
WITH 372 COLOURED PLATES REPRE-
SENTING PLANTS TO A UNIFORM SCALE
OF ONE-THIRD THEIR NATURAL SIZE
AND 2715 OTHER FIGURES

BY

GASTON BONNIER
Professor of Botany at the Sorbonne ; Member of the Institute

Fcap. 8vo, 7s. 6d. net

BRITISH FLORA

A MEANS OF FINDING QUICKLY AND
ACCURATELY THE NAMES OF A PLANT
AND ITS PLACE IN THE VEGETABLE
KINGDOM, WITH OVER 2000 FIGURES IN
THE TEXT, DICHOTOMOUS KEYS BASED
ON BRACKETS AND A GLOSSARY ILLUS-
TRATED BY FIGURES

BY

GASTON BONNIER
Professor of Botany at the Sorbonne; Member of the Institute
Author of " NAME THIS FLOWER "

Fcap. 8vo, 7s. 6d. net

DENT'S
NATURE PICTURES
FOR SCHOOL WALLS

Reproduced in Full Colour from Drawings by

E. J. DETMOLD

ONE SET OF EIGHT IN STOUT PORTFOLIO . .	£1 7s. 6d.
THE COMPLETE SERIES OF 24	£3 10s.
SINGLE PLATES	3s. 6d. each.

LIST OF SUBJECTS

1 HERON	13 NIGHTINGALE
2 WOODPECKER	14 GOLDFINCH & BLUE TIT
3 BLACK LEGHORN CHICK	15 GOLDEN PLOVER
4 DORMICE	16 SKYLARK
5 WREN	17 SEAGULL
6 CHAFFINCH	18 BULLFINCH
7 JAY	19 CRAB AND SMELTS
8 BARN OWL	20 LOBSTER
9 HEDGEHOGS	21 SONG THRUSH AND TIT
10 SQUIRREL	22 WOOD-PIGEON
11 YOUNG LAPWINGS	23 MOORHEN
12 HARE AND RABBIT	24 YELLOW-HAMMER

BIRDS AND GREEN PLACES

A Book of Australian Nature Gossip.   By ALEC H. CHISHOLM.

With 2 Colour Plates and 70 in Half-tone.   Royal 8vo.   **15s.** net.

This book contains a most comprehensive collection of ornithological photographs, as well as first-hand information on certain birds that has not hitherto been given in the textbooks.   Some of the subjects are: mystery birds of the jungle, the wonderful lyre-bird, birds of the great plains, the almost extinct paradise parrot, Prince Edward's lyre-bird, bird life on Dunk and Fraser Islands, the varied mocking-birds of Australia, and the extraordinary bower-birds.   A list of scientific names of birds is given, as well as a full Index.   *Prospectus post free.*

OTHER NATURE BOOKS

EVERYMAN'S LIBRARY

Cloth.   2s. od. net each

Darwin's Voyage of the Beagle.

    „   Origin of Species.

Huxley's Essays: Man's Place in Nature.   With Introduction by Sir OLIVER LODGE.

Tyndall's Glaciers of the Alps and Mountaineering in 1861. Introduction by Lord AVEBURY.

Walton's Compleat Angler.

White's Natural History of Selborne.

Miller's Old Red Sandstone.

Belt's The Naturalist in Nicaragua.

Bates' Naturalist on the Amazon.

Hazlitt's Essays.

Waterton's Wanderings in South America.

Peaks, Passes and Glaciers, by Members of the Alpine Club.

Cobbett's Rural Rides (2 vols.)

Wright's Encyclopaedia of Gardening (2s. 6d. net).

WAYFARERS' LIBRARY

Cloth.   1s. 6d. net

Afoot in England.   By W. H. HUDSON.